Texas Heroes
A Dynasty of Courage

Mona D. Sizer

Illustrated by Janie Petty

Republic of Texas Press
Plano, Texas

Library of Congress Cataloging-in-Publication Data

Sizer, Mona D.
  Texas heroes : a dynasty of courage / Mona D. Sizer.
     p. cm.
  Includes bibliographical references (p.) and index.
  ISBN 1-55622-775-2
  1. Texas—Biography. 2. Texas—History. 3. Heroes—Texas—
Biography. I. Title.

  F385 .S58 2000
  920.0764—dc21   00-024677
                                          CIP

Printed in the United States of America

ISBN 1-55622-775-2
10 9 8 7 6 5 4 3 2 1
2001

All inquiries for volume purchases of this book should be addressed to
Wordware Publishing, Inc., at 2320 Los Rios Boulevard, Plano, Texas 75074.
Telephone inquiries may be made by calling:

(972) 423-0090

Acknowledgments

As always I would like to thank my editors Ginnie Siena Bivona and Dianne Stultz for their unfailing enthusiasm and support throughout the project.

I would like to acknowledge James Sizer, my husband, friend, and dictionary, research source, and thesaurus for little known facts about many of the various wars, battles, arms, strategies, and so on and so forth. Without you, big guy, I'd have been at a loss to know what I was reading as well as writing.

I would like to acknowledge Allen Damron, my cousin and weapons authority, who allowed me to read large portions of the manuscript aloud to him and gave me important corrections that only someone with his expertise would know. As always, Allen, you were there for me.

I would like to thank librarians at the Lon C. Hill Memorial Library in Harlingen and at the Richardson Public Library in Richardson, in particular the inter-library loan departments, for their help in locating materials.

I would like to acknowledge Janie Petty's fine drawings of the heroes. Using likenesses from busts, paintings, drawings, and photographs all copied from books on library copy machines, she drew accurate and stylish likenesses for the reader's pleasure.

Finally, I would like to acknowledge Mary L. Steele, my teacher for three years in Raymondville High School. I've never forgotten the thrill of horror when she told us about the Alamo. Besides teaching accurate history, she taught respect for the importance of history.

Contents

Canadian River

Llano Estacado
Quanah Parker

Colorad

El Paso
Del Norte

Pecos River

Rio Grande

John Co

Chester

S
Ba

**Louis Juchereadu de
St. Denis**

José de lo
Santos Benav

Red River

Farmersville
● *Audie Murphy*

Carthage

Milton M. Holland

Trinity River

Angelina River

Sabine River

Brazos River

ock

rg

Austin

Sabine Pass

Guadalupe

Houston

Dick Dowling

an ntonio

The Alamo

River

Galveston

Nueces River

do

† The Alamo
James Bowie
David Crockett
William Barret Travis

Palo Alto

Brownsville
John S. Ford

vii

The Nature of Courage

Courage is the ability to conquer fear and perform acts that place the body in harm's way. Careful note should be taken of the definition because it describes the very essence of heroism and likewise the nature of some of mankind's rarer members. Cowardice, its antithesis, is the weakness that quails at the first sign of a threat and runs away from the face of danger.

Unfortunately, this definition describes a much larger number of men to a lesser degree. Fortunately for our own images of self, most of us are seldom tested. Good and evil, virtue and vice, courage and cowardice are called upon in extreme situations, which civilization seeks to eliminate from our daily lives. The Greeks, whose philosophy influenced all Western civilization, believed that the good life for man was lived well between those extremes. Nothing in excess was their motto. Their ideal state was the Golden Mean.

They also believed that men who lived at the edge of the extremes are always present. Their qualities are enhanced beyond or degraded beneath those of the mass of people who live their lives in an ordinary and civilized manner. Ironically, they are necessary to the advancement of civilization.

The Greeks believed these men, these philosopher kings, these monsters, these heroes, these cowards were fated to be so. All lives were controlled eternally by Three Fates who spun thousands of ordinary threads. From time to time they would spin a thread of gold. The man whose life was golden was the hero. They did not care to name the opposite thread that produced the coward.

We no longer believe in the thread of gold, but we do believe in the pressures of society. Stresses and strains are exerted on all people by those around them. The majority of us are shaped by the pressures from both sides—that is, from good and evil. An excess of evil creates a deserter. An excess of good is awarded the Congressional Medal of Honor.

The very name of Texas exerts such pressure by tradition and example of unusual courage. From the time the state became a recognizable area of land, differentiated from the Spanish colony of Mexico, its people raised higher and higher the bar over which courage vaults.

Adventurers performed with such dazzling bravery that their deeds became the stuff of legends. The ordinary people who saw these men in action told and retold their tales of defiance and derring-do: of a line in the sand, of sacrifice, of superhuman victories against impossible odds.

Texas's young men and women of each successive generation felt the pressure those tales exerted. The expectation of bravery entered the collective consciousness—the very culture—until courage was the proper behavior.

Their voices speak to us from their letters, their memoirs, the bases of their statues:

"I shall never surrender nor retreat. Victory or death."

"You can retreat and go to hell if you wish! These are my men, and I am going to fight."

"Set my new house on fire, so that nothing of mine shall pass to the enemy."

Their voices ring through history and breed the kind of courage that makes us willing to fight and die under the Lone Star, the kind of courage that makes us Texans.

Read hereafter a few of their accounts.

If a novelist were to write them, her words would be judged too exaggerated, well-nigh impossible. Such men could never have done these deeds.

Yet they did!

They were Texans and every word is true!

The Diplomat

Louis Juchereau de St. Denis

So intrepid was Louis Juchereau de St. Denis that when the Conde de Fuenclara, Viceroy of New Spain, heard that the redoubtable Frenchman had died of old age, he crossed himself piously and cried out, "Gracias a Dios!"

Who was St. Denis that a viceroy thanked God for his death? Why was his death such a blessing to the king's representative, the man who above all others in the New World spoke for the King of Spain?

From his first appearance in the land of the Tejas or Texas Indians, the government of New Spain reacted with consternation and disbelief. The officials had no idea what to do with him or about him. They regarded him as a danger, yet they couldn't name the danger he posed.

They knew with terrible certainty that he undermined their influence with the Indians, who had come to regard the Spaniards as interlopers. Indeed, St. Denis was welcomed and loved by the Indians Spain sought to convert and exploit. His popularity threatened their unquestioned possession of what they had claimed for their own by the grace of God and the Holy Roman Catholic Church. Ironically, without his influence the missions and presidios that were the bastions of European civilization in the New Philippines—as they called Texas—would never have been built.

For almost thirty years, slyly but mercilessly, he harassed the government while he supported the churchmen, using one against the other for his own ends. His efforts forced them to pay attention to Texas. Faced with losing the great territory, they redoubled their efforts to colonize and control it—efforts that led to the loss of it entirely.

Few people who read about Texas heroes can read about him without smiling. His deeds—both true and flagrantly embroidered—constitute a paradox unique in Texas history.

To this very day, a unique hero is hard to find.

Therefore, he fittingly takes his place in Texas history as a man who by his daring, his diplomacy, and his keen intelligence contributed to the creation of the state.

Louis St. Denis is, therefore, the first Texan in a dynasty of courage that began in 1713. Pragmatic yet romantic, daring yet sly, hard-headed yet utterly charming, he stepped onto the earliest pages of Texas history where the Caddo Indians, surely original Texans, welcomed him.

The state of Texas was still unformed, its boundaries fluid. The name itself was mispronunciation of a word variously spelled *Texia*, *Texa*, *Tejia*, and *Teja*. With it the Caddos greeted the first Spanish explorers. Teja or Texa meant "friend." Many friendly people were Tejas or Texas. For those like Fray Agustin Morfi, who wrote about it, "Texas" became the preferred spelling. The Anglo-American settlers saw the "x" and gave it the English pronunciation.

Texas—the beautiful and rich land—stretched before the Spaniards who made their way three hundred and sixty leagues (over a thousand miles) north from Mexico City sometime around 1688. At first, they looked at it with avaricious eyes.

Surely gold lay just beneath the green grass and in the beds of the clear-flowing rivers and streams. The friendly people they met surely mined the precious metal as did the Aztecs around Mexico City and the Incas in Peru. Where were they hiding it?

With the gold-hungry came the soul-hungry. The priests of the Roman Catholic Church came seeking heathen tribes to convert to Christianity. They found a happy childlike people to civilize and bring to serve God and His Church. "Serve" was the operant word. Quickly, they erected the mission San Francisco de los Tejas to be the center for that service.

Neither group considered the Indians to be intelligent, clever equals capable of choosing whom and what they would become. Neither the native languages with their pictographic writing nor their complex cultures impressed the Spanish. For both *conquistadors* and churchmen, the Indians were savages to be exploited to an end.

When the *conquistadors* found no gold, and the churchmen met with resistance to their kind of civilizing, both groups withdrew, leaving their first rude buildings to the elements. Only when the French became interested in the land did the government in Mexico City see a reason to return.

Only one man did not forget the friendly Indians. A truly remarkable priest, Father Francisco Hidalgo, despaired of ever convincing any officials to send an escort of soldiers to reclaim the souls of the Texas Indians. His requests for an *entrada* of churchmen and soldiers to carry the cross back into the heathen lands had been met with indifference by Viceroy Fernando de Alencastre, Noroña y Silva, Duke of Linares. Made shrewd by desperation, on January 17, 1711, Father Hidalgo wrote a letter to the governor of New France. He made three copies, which he sent by different routes, to be certain it would reach its goal. At that, the letter languished until May 13, 1713, when it came into the hands of that shrewd old politician Antoine de La Mothe, Sieur de Cadillac.

Governor Cadillac had been placed in his position by a private monopolist Antoine Crozat, Marquis de Chatel, whose stated purpose was to make another fortune to go with the one he already possessed. Trade with Spain was the answer. Spain was mining silver and gold from the mountains of the Sierra Madre Orientals and coining their own money in the mint in Mexico City. Indeed, between 1560 and 1821 Mexico's only industry was mining gold and silver. Importing a small portion from Peru, the country minted two billion dollars in silver (in an age when a penny bought what a dollar buys today) and sent another two billion to Spain in ingots.

Two-thirds of all the silver in the world passed through the port of Veracruz. Of course, robbery and graft were rampant. From the time the silver left the mines, bandits robbed the trains. In the docks, receivers skimmed off what they considered their share. On the high seas, the buccaneers and sea dogs patrolled the Spanish Main.

During the seventeenth and eighteenth centuries, Spain, France, and England all sought to strengthen their claims to the rich new world. Ostensibly at peace in their European diplo-matic relationships, they carried on covert rivalries all along the coastlines of North and South America, which their intrepid explorers had claimed so high-handedly.

In early 1713 Cadillac first sent a ship loaded with trade goods under the command of a man named Jonquiere to Veracruz. De Linares, the Spanish viceroy, would not let the vessel unload its cargo.

The Spaniards were determined that the French should have no success along the Gulf Coast. Although they had made little resistance when Bienville and Iberville had landed their settlers at Biloxi and Mobile, they had strict orders to allow the French-men no more than a foothold. Spain's plan was to boycott and blockade the tiny settlements at the mouth of the Mississippi. If the French traders and colonists could be kept in rags with no money to buy supplies, eventually they would fall prey to hostile Indians or mutiny among themselves, abandon their positions, and return home.

As well as any, Cadillac understood their strategy. Disap-pointed, but not surprised by Jonquiere's rebuff, the governor decided that trade with the Indians might be just as profitable. But how to reach them? And how to tell which were friendly and which murderous?

Cadillac's eyes must have lit up when he saw Father Hidalgo's letter. The governor had been stationed for twenty years at Detroit without achieving financial or political success. The French mission in the New World was primarily trade. They wanted trade with the Indians, trade with the Spaniards, trade that would secure exotic goods to return to the lucrative markets of Paris. An invitation to a land with new sources of commerce was almost too good to be true. It would give the French a diplo-matic entry that would smooth their way. A clever official could make his fortune.

Furthermore, Cadillac had just the man in mind to make this passage. A gentlemen of inestimable qualities who had come down the Mississippi to make his fortune for the mutual benefit of all.

Louis Juchereau de St. Denis was born September 17, 1674, in Canada, in the province of Quebec. His father was for a time Lieutenant General of Montreal. Returning to Paris in 1700, the elder St. Denis pleaded with Louis XIV for permission to set up trading posts throughout the Mississippi River Valley—the extent of which was only just beginning to be realized. The French king was glad to grant the charter because Spain also had claimed this land through the efforts of Hernando de Soto.

The eastern seaboard from Massachusetts to Georgia belonged to England. The French contested English rights to Canada in Quebec. Florida, Texas, and the whole of Mexico were Spanish first through the efforts of Ponce de Leon, Cabeza de Vaca, and Hernan Cortes. In contest was Texas, claimed by the French through the efforts of Rene Robert Cavalier, Sieur de la Salle, who had built a fort at Espiritu Santo Bay near the present town of Navasota.

The Spaniards had searched out the French fort. The expedition commander reported that La Salle's colony had been destroyed by Indian attacks, and the *sieur* had been murdered by his own men. The commander reported further that he had hanged the murderers and burned the remains. France had suspicions, but she could not prove anything—not even their claim since the site had been burned.

More successful were Jean-Baptiste, Sieur de Bienville's settlements along the northern edge of the Gulf Coast at Biloxi and Mobile. Still his colonies were in danger of running out of supplies and starving because of the Spanish blockade.

So the rivalries raged.

In 1701 Juchereau de St. Denis, the elder, began to operate a trading post and tannery on the Mississippi. His position was that of middleman between trappers in the wilds and the salons and courts of France where the fashions dictated furs. The rivers and forests of America had them in abundance. Their other riches must be waiting for the clever trader.

When the father obtained the charter, his son sailed down the Mississippi to Louisiana to make his fortune. Everyone who knew St. Denis described him then and for the rest of his life as "gay, brilliant, and utterly charming." The *beau ideal* for a cavalier, he was the kind of man who would rise wherever he was placed.

From the first he saw his real calling as an intermediary between widely differing peoples. His plan for all was that if money could be made, then all would be happy. At twenty-five he had begun to learn the languages of the Caddos and Karankawas, so he could trade with them and not be cheated. The Spaniards were already in the area. The War of the Spanish Succession was flaming in Europe. He learned that language too, perhaps hoping that he would never have to use it. Still, if he came into contact, if a skirmish ensued, perhaps it would save his life—perhaps not.

Comme ci, comme ca!

In 1713 he stepped onto the pages of history as commander of the French fort at Biloxi. He had rapidly risen to that position in part through his relationship by marriage to Pierre Le Moyne, Sieur d'Iberville, who founded the town. Mainly he had earned the post through his own merits.

With the arrival of Father Hidalgo's letter, Cadillac thought of St. Denis as the ideal gentleman for the job. His commander at Fort Biloxi possessed the unique skills to head such a trade mission. The man was well acquainted with the Indians in the area, as well as respected. He spoke their language. Moreover, since many of the Indians with whom they wished to trade were in the territory claimed by Spain, St. Denis's fluent Spanish made him the ideal choice in that respect. It is interesting to note how many times the word "ideal" is associated with this amazing man.

In September 1713 Cadillac sent St. Denis on a trade mission with goods valued at ten thousand francs—a fabulous sum in those days. How easy to write about the undertaking! How difficult to carry it out!

When the Frenchman started out, he could well have been going to his death. Although the nature of these Indians was believed to be understood, less friendly tribes such as the proud Natchez could easily attack the expedition. Only a man with a deft diplomatic touch stood much chance. Indeed the entire French enterprise rested on St. Denis's shoulders. All Crozat's talk of rich mines and fabulous furs for the markets of Paris faded in the light of Indian tribes at war. Not uncommonly, an Indian would bring pelts that included scalps to trade for corn. Sometimes, the entire bundle including the hair had belonged to a French fur trapper.

As St. Denis and his men moved farther into territory claimed by Spain, the fate of La Salle's colony was ever in their minds. Although Spain had couched the report in sympathetic terms, were they telling the truth? Finally, the goods were being transported up the Father of Waters, the mighty Mississippi River where disaster waited for all. A swift-moving, half-submerged log. A sudden storm raising the waves to oceanic heights. A treacherous whirlpool in the shifting, wallowing currents.

Some men will dare almost any danger, especially when duty and the hopes of profits are combined. Does the hope of profit make him any less a hero? Perhaps.

Perhaps it makes him less a fool.

Up the Mississippi they paddled, then into its first main tributary heading west. Another fork—one ran south back to the Gulf, the Atchafalaya. The main course ran northwest. Steadily, imperturbably, St. Denis commanded his men to keep to the main. At last he and his goods arrived at the main village of the Natchitoches Indians situated on an island in Upper Cane River about one hundred twenty miles northwest of its jointure with the Mississippi.

St. Denis immediately saw the advantages of the location. Besides providing water and food, the river was a natural barrier against invaders of any other tribe or nationality. Rather than drive the Indians from their homes as the Spanish perhaps would have done, he persuaded the Natchitoches to let him and his men build houses among them. In exchange for the right to live with them, the Frenchmen would offer the constant protection that St. Denis's weapons and skills of generalship offered.

So that the Indians would recognize other advantages, St. Denis set up a system of barter whereby tools and seeds were traded for their services as guides, hunters, and fishers.

The advantages of civilization with its accompanying peace and prosperity offered too many opportunities for the Natchitoches to reject. With no protest, they allowed the French houses to be built among their own structures. Eventually, the entire compound was surrounded with a fort. Everyone could live together under St. Denis's protection. By 1714 Natchitoches was as permanent a settlement as any place could be in the American wilderness.

How different from the Spaniards, who built presidios and churches apart from the villages and expected the Indians to work for them.

With a thriving community as a base to fall back to, the cavalier returned to Mobile to obtain more trade goods and then set off on the march west. Twelve of his most daring companions and several Indians accompanied him. A twenty-day march brought him to the land of the Texas Indians on either side of the Sabine River. Somewhere along the way, St. Denis joined the trace of El Camino Real, the royal road the Spanish had followed all across the southern part of the United States. His destination then became Mission San Juan Bautista and the Presidio del Rio Grande where the town of Piedras Negras stands today. It was the gateway to Spanish Texas.

What a land it must have been!

The climate was excellent, neither too cold nor too warm. As St. Denis and his men walked among the poplars, willows, elms, black pines, and white walnuts, they were never far from the sight of buffalo, deer, bear, and wild boar.

The streams they crossed seemed alive with trout, carp, catfish, turtles, and alligators. Otter played in the shallows and beavers built huge dams that created small, clear lakes. Ducks and wild geese floated on them, cranes stalked their shallows or spread their wings and flew away overhead.

The fields were green with plants—some recognizable, some strange. They saw thyme, lavender, and sage such as grew in the

South of France. Blackberries and strawberries were there to be picked and eaten as they walked. Indigo, wild sweet potatoes, sassafras, wild onion, and a plant that resembled lettuce brushed against their boots and leggings.

Beside St. Denis walked an Indian woman whom he had named Angelique. She had been baptized by Spanish priests and spoke the languages of the Texas tribes. According to the legend, in gratitude for her bravery and assistance as his translator, St. Denis named the Angelina River for her.

Probably he needed only minimal help from her. Perhaps in the manner of many leaders before and since, he pretended that he did not speak the language. By listening to what was being said among the people who thought him ignorant, he learned much more than he would have by questioning.

On the western side of the Angelina, St. Denis's first Indian encounter was with the Texas Confederacy. It consisted of the Hasinai, the Nacogdoches, and the Nabedache. Their land lay between two rivers with a small mound on the upper banks of the one called the Neches. The Indians said the mound had been raised by their forefathers. A great temple was supposed to be built on it, but it was never begun. The Spaniards had come and converted the tribes to Christianity. The mission Nuestra Señora de Guadalupe was built instead and abandoned as Father Hidalgo had said. They were industrious and very friendly, probably because they were so glad to see the powerful weapons the Europeans carried.

Wherever St. Denis went, he was always well received. He quickly made friends, explained his mission, and persuaded some of them to join him. He assured them that he would protect them against any danger they might encounter. Very soon, he won their confidence and inspired their loyalty.

He was a very different sort of hero indeed. With smiles and handshakes and reason, he marched through lands where others had lost their lives in the time an arrow could be nocked to a bowstring or an axe could fall.

From the goods provided him by Cadillac, he quickly distributed tools and seeds to plant. Again the nature of the goods he distributed testifies to the fact that his mission was strictly for trade. St. Denis never came to make war or to take territory.

He could and would fight only if he had to. No one knew how well. Perhaps he did not know himself. Marching westward, he came to the banks of the San Marcos River, a tributary of the Guadalupe. There he had an opportunity to find out.

His party, whose numbers had been reduced to four Frenchmen and about two dozen Indians, was suddenly attacked by a large band of perhaps two hundred Lipan Apaches. They were the most feared of tribes in central and west Texas because they had captured the wild horses lost or strayed from the Spanish expeditions and presidios. Mounted, they hunted the buffalo and staged raids on their neighbors. Shrieking and whooping, they rode down on the little party following El Camino Real.

To turn tail and run would have brought almost certain death. To stay and fight offered just as little hope. St. Denis rallied his men. While the Texas fitted arrows into their bows, the Frenchmen loaded their weapons.

On the Apaches came. At St. Denis's command, he and his men fired at will. While the Texas's arrows did some damage, the four rifles did much more. Acrid black smoke rose from the barrels. Four charging men among the leaders were thrown backward off their horses, struck like magic by missiles that could not be seen and killed more surely than if they had arrows in their hearts.

The fearsome noise set the horses to bucking. Likewise, some of the warriors had never heard the thunder before.

Cool in the face of danger, St. Denis stood his ground, reloading and firing, reloading and firing—setting an example that encouraged his companions, while it threw the Apaches into consternation.

Despite their overpowering numbers, the attackers were cowed. They called for a truce. St. Denis, as he never failed to do, proceeded to negotiate with them. So sensible and so charming was he that he earned their respect and secured unimpeded passage the rest of the way to the mission of San Juan Bautista on the Rio Grande.

The twenty-one Texas Indians who had accompanied him thus far decided to return home. With them they carried the story of the Apache attack and St. Denis's heroic defense. St. Denis's legend grew among the tribes of the entire eastern Confederacy. The Apaches carried the same story to the western Indians.

Within days the Spaniards began to hear rumors of him. Their concern and consternation grew. This Louis St. Denis was clearly a man capable of taking Texas away from them, not by the power of arms, not by the fear of God, but by the power of his words spoken sincerely man to man.

In August 1714, with four Indians and three Frenchman, St. Denis crossed the Big River where the Texas town of Eagle Pass stands today. They arrived at the Presidio del Rio Grande, the fort guarding the mission of San Juan Bautista from which Father Hidalgo had written the letter.

What St. Denis's thoughts were as he walked into the lion's den, we will never know. A half dozen terrible fates awaited him. He could be shot. He could be hanged. He could be imprisoned and left to rot. He could be stripped and set out on the desert to die.

With a flourish and an elegant bow, he presented himself to the presidio commander.

Captain Diego Ramon was flabbergasted. Frenchmen did not stroll into his headquarters after crossing hundreds of miles into Spanish territory. The man was trespassing. He was illegal. He was a—a—

While Ramon was sputtering, St. Denis asked to see Father Hidalgo. He produced the letter of invitation along with his French passport, signed by no less than Governor Cadillac of Mobile. Although the papers were in order and the signatures on them and the invitation *bona fide*, the captain was unmollified. The padre had no business to write such a letter. The Frenchman had no business at all being in Spanish territory.

Au contraire.

St. Denis explained that he had come for the express purpose of establishing commercial relations between Coahuila and

Louisiana. He had brought goods to trade for grain and cattle which were greatly needed in Mobile.

Ramon countered by demanding to know why he had come so far for such small stuff. Furthermore, Father Hidalgo was not at San Juan Bautista. St. Denis replied truthfully that the religious missions in Texas where he had hoped to trade had been found abandoned, but tribes of friendly Indians had directed him here.

Again St. Denis spoke in the voice of sweet reason with a knowing look and an inclining of the head. Since he was under orders, he could do no less than to accomplish his mission.

To accomplish a mission was something Ramon could understand and respect. Ramon looked him up and down. The man was handsome and well spoken—a thoroughly pleasant fellow. Moreover, he was obviously of good blood—something aristocrats of the eighteenth century believed they shared in common across national boundaries. St. Denis was probably up to no good, but the captain could not be sure. He confiscated the upstart's goods and placed him under house arrest.

In 1714 the Texas frontier was a new world indeed. Civilized and well-educated men recognized each other almost immediately. The old world antipathies were far, far away. Even Mexico City was over three hundred leagues. Undoubtedly, Ramon longed for polite society. He would enjoy the Frenchman's company. He could hang him later.

Ramon sent St. Denis's goods and papers to the Duke de Linares in Mexico City along with a request for orders. When he did so, he knew an answer would be a long time coming. In the meanwhile he would allow St. Denis to mingle with his family, give them a touch of home and culture they had only rare chances to enjoy. Rather than languish in a Spanish *carcel*, St. Denis was entertained in the captain's own house as an honored guest. The Frenchman's considerable charm had carried the day for him.

Ramon also sent word to Don Martin Alarcon, a Knight of Santiago, the governor of Monclova, Coahuila. He requested that St. Denis be allowed to remain a prisoner in the presidio. Alarcon had no quarrel with the arrangement.

The summer passed quite pleasantly as St. Denis's life turned into a work of romantic fiction. To this day no one knows exactly what his true feelings were. Certainly, he seized opportunities whenever they presented themselves. Whether he did so because he was sincere, or whether he calculated his moves and the effect they would have on the Spanish government is a question that can never be answered.

Nevertheless, while playing the gallant, polished gentleman in the captain's house, St. Denis courted and won the hand of the captain's beautiful granddaughter, Manuela Sanchez Navarro y Gomes Mascorro. She was seventeen. He was forty.

The nature of their attachment is forever open to speculation. St. Denis was an adventurer and a hard-headed businessman. In terms of sophistication and life experiences, he was worlds beyond the gently reared girl. On the other hand, she was beautiful, she was young, she was of the nobility, however provincial. Such young women had been in short supply since he left Quebec at age twenty-five.

What she thought of him can only be imagined. Despite his culture, charm, and reputed good looks, he was still a man of her father's age. Given her youth and lack of experience, a flirtation seems unlikely. She would have been reared to obey her father and her grandfather. On this provincial outpost, leagues from any civilization, she had few young eligible men to choose from. She was probably more than willing to accept the handsome Frenchman. Forever the puzzle will remain. Did she succumb to romance or practicality?

Undoubtedly her father made no objection to the idea of a French son-in-law since he approved the engagement. Although St. Denis was a prisoner of the state with charges of an unspecified nature brought against him, the fact remained that he had come at the invitation of a well-known priest with a passport from Governor Cadillac of New France as well as impeccable references and considerable wealth in trade goods. To the captain's way of thinking, the match was well made. If the viceroy sent for

St. Denis, tried him, found him guilty of spying, and executed him, Manuela as his widow would still have the trade goods. She could not lose, whatever was decided in Mexico City.

Likewise, St. Denis must have seen the opportunity such a match offered him. His own thoughts probably ran somewhere along these lines. He had always planned to marry sometime. He had lived a dangerous life and had seen many men die—men younger than he. His father had been dead a dozen years. He had not had time or opportunity to meet many young ladies of good family since leaving Quebec for the southern Mississippi.

The opportunity to ingratiate himself with the captain and to align himself with a Spanish family of good repute would undoubtedly stand him in good stead in his trade negotiations. He would have a foot in both camps. As a show of his good intentions, he even offered to become a Spanish citizen if he could marry Manuela.

Historians have long debated his next act. On February 15, 1715, St. Denis managed to send a secret letter to Cadillac. Some think it confirms that he was in fact a spy for France. Was he marrying the ingenuous Manuela as a means to stay in Mexico and work from within? Some maintain that he was playing both sets of authorities against each other, willing to jump whichever way seemed most profitable to him. Those who want to give him the benefit of the doubt believe he was merely reassuring Cadillac that he was tending to business. Then why was he being secretive? No one will ever know, but here is what he wrote.

First, he talked about the good fortune about to happen to him. He did not mention his marriage to Manuela. Further on he wrote about the silver mines at Boca de Leonez sixty-one leagues from the presidio. The miners and merchants had silver with which to purchase his goods. He seemed to mention the mines only in passing. If the letter were intercepted, it would read like another observation of his travels. He ended the letter by reminding Cadillac of the risks involved and asking that Cadillac serve as his patron upon his return to Mobile, indicating that at that time he intended to return and resume his life there. Many questions about St. Denis will never be answered.

While he waited for a reply and before the marriage could take place, twenty-five soldiers came from Monclova, Coahuila, to take St. Denis to Don Martin Alarcon. They did not take him gently, nor without a formal protest from Captain Ramon.

The soldiers put chains on St. Denis's wrists, tied him on a horse, and took him away forthwith. His three companions followed after protesting rigorously and declaring their loyalty. When the soldiers brought their prisoner before the governor, Alarcon ordered him thrown into prison as if he were a common criminal.

Sacre Bleu!

When St. Denis protested, the governor promised him the freedom of the presidio in Monclova if the Frenchman would renounce Manuela. The romantic story is that the governor of Coahuila considered Manuela to be his intended bride although no formal agreement had been drawn up. When rumor reached him of the engagement, he became enraged.

Freedom or a Spanish *carcel*?

For whatever reason St. Denis became engaged to the young lady, he refused to be blackmailed into giving her up.

While Alarcon was threatening St. Denis, he threatened Manuela also. He dispatched a message to her saying that if she did not consent to marry him, he would take matters in his own hands and put St. Denis to death. He had the right to do so, for the Frenchman entered Spanish territory without authorization undoubtedly for the purpose of spying.

Rather than replying with pleas and promises, Manuela wrote directly to the viceroy in Mexico City. The contents of her letter are amazing, revealing her to be a very clever young lady. In her letter she too suggested that St. Denis might be a spy, but one with vital information. The governor of Coahuila was holding him unjustly and cruelly. If he were to die, that information would be lost. The viceroy would be better served to order him to Mexico City.

Fortunately for St. Denis, Manuela's influence exceeded Alarcon's. A little more than six weeks after Captain Ramon had sent St. Denis's goods to Viceroy Linares, the escort arrived in Monclova to take the prisoner to Mexico City. The quick action saved St. Denis much suffering and probably his life.

St. Denis made a great protest that he first wanted to return to the presidio on the Rio Grande. Not knowing of Manuela's letter, he must have thought he was going to his death. For all he knew, he "would be shot or meet with an accident trying to escape" on the journey to Mexico City. If he survived the trip, he would be nearly five hundred leagues from New France. He could see his plans failing with each league that brought him deeper into Spanish territory. Alarcon had imprisoned him. What would Linares do?

He arrived in Mexico City in June 1715. Almost a year had passed since his sudden appearance at the presidio. By that time he had made friends with all the men in his escort. They admired him and treated him as a guest rather than what he really was, a prisoner possibly on his way to his execution.

Again his phenomenal luck did not desert him. Or perhaps his bravado along with Manuela's suggestions impressed Linares.

In the capital the viceroy received his strange prisoner with some sardonic show of cordiality. Obviously, he believed St. Denis to be a spy. He kept him under close guard and brought the Frenchman before him again and again. Over and over he demanded the story, listening to every word, analyzing every detail, for some contradiction, some betrayal. Despite the strain of these meetings, St. Denis never faltered in his story. He had come from New France to see missions built among the Texas Confederacy to protect the peaceful Indians from the Karankawas and allow them to prosper.

"So that France may trade with them and win their loyalties," Linares undoubtedly pointed out.

St. Denis declared that France did not want to undermine the love the Texas had for Spain. Wisely, he never said that there was no love to undermine. He maintained that the boundary between the two nations should be the Mississippi River. Since he knew that France had no intention of establishing such a boundary, he must have been trading for his life at this point.

Over and over again the viceroy compelled St. Denis to write a detailed proposal for the missions—where they were to be built, which tribes they were to minister to, and in particular what route he had taken to bring him from the Mississippi to the Rio Grande without meeting a single Spanish soldier or priest. St. Denis might have been flattered that Linares was making use of his information. And why not? The viceroy was greatly disturbed by the great emptiness of the land claimed by Spain. He realized that France could have colonized the whole of Texas without Spain even knowing they were anywhere about.

On August 22, 1715, Linares called a *junta* of war. His co-operative prisoner St. Denis was called upon as an advisor and expert to detail why such a council was necessary. A Frenchman to explain why the "French menace" must be curtailed. The danger was real as Linares saw it. If the French opened an illicit trading route using the same road as St. Denis, they would be dangerously close to the silver and copper mines in Durango as well as suborning the natives whose friendship was valuable to Spain.

Obviously, hostile natives would do everything they could to keep Spain from utilizing her lands. If they were friendly with the French—

The situation was unthinkable.

Boldly, St. Denis insisted that the Indians of the Texas Confederacy wanted missions. To a man, the council agreed. They must have missions. An *entrada* must be organized, a march of missionaries and soldiers such as had not been seen in that century. It would be in the nature of a holy crusade. Linares's council became excited at the very thought of instigating such a holy spectacle. The truly faithful among them must have prayed joyfully for weeks.

How St. Denis must have struggled to conceal his smile as, humbly, he volunteered to lead it.

Swept up in the thoughts of glory to God and King, Linares's council accepted his offer. A historian of the latter half of the eighteenth century, Fray Juan Agustin Morfi, records that all thought it was "...compatible with [St. Denis's] honor to enjoy the confidence of the viceroy."

Later he wrote that "...during the time [St. Denis] was among us...the most scrupulous investigation failed to reveal ...the least reprehensible act on his part."

Perhaps as a final assurance that all would be well, Linares allowed St. Denis to become a Spanish citizen and to return to San Juan Bautista to marry Manuela. No one will ever know whether St. Denis was delighted or confounded. His little bride-to-be. Did he even remember her? Nearly half a year had passed since he'd seen her.

On his way back north, St. Denis managed to send a letter to Cadillac advising that the Spanish were coming to establish the missions. The French governor was further advised to send a brigantine to Espiritu Santo Bay, where La Salle's ill-fated expedition had built Fort St. Louis in 1687. He also suggested that the King of France demand that the boundary of Louisiana be fixed at the Rio Grande.

Whatever St. Denis was, he was not a friend of Spain. He was playing a dangerous game. If an inkling of his true feelings had been perceived, if he had in any way betrayed himself, he would have been summarily executed. As it was, he fooled them all completely.

Meanwhile, with visions of a place assured for them in Heaven, the council decided to send twenty-five soldiers and a number of missionaries to East Texas for the purpose of establishing four missions among the Texas Confederacy. Each mission was to be guarded by family men who would take their wives with them. The Spanish wanted no trouble with the Indians over depredations against their women.

(The reason for the failure of the earliest mission, San Francisco de los Tejas, established in 1690, was the licentious behavior of the soldiers with the Indian women. Considered a failure, it was abandoned in 1692.)

While St. Denis was to head the expedition, the man in charge of the soldiers was Captain Domingo Ramon, the son of the captain at the Presidio del Rio Grande and Manuela's uncle. Each of the twenty-five soldiers was to receive four hundred pesos. The salaries testify to the seriousness with which Linares and his council regarded this expedition. They wanted good men who would do a good job. Ramon and St. Denis were both given salaries of five hundred pesos a year, a princely sum in those days. Not only had St. Denis gotten exactly what he wanted from Spain, he was being paid by both the Spanish viceroy and the French governor. The Ramon family as well had profited from their alliance with him. They must have been congratulating themselves and Manuela on her good fortune.

Five missionaries from the college of the Holy Cross of Queretaro, four from Our Lady of Guadalupe of Zacatecas, and three lay brothers represented the Catholic Church on this expedition. At their head marched Father Hidalgo. Twenty-three years had passed since he had seen his beloved Texas Indians. His hair had turned white, but his energy and his faith had not aged. Morfi reports that he walked with a straight back. His countenance fairly glowed.

St. Denis was allowed to gallop on ahead of the slow-moving expedition to be reunited with Manuela. He certainly knew that in all probability he owed his life to her. She knew what honor he had brought to her family. They wanted to be married immediately.

Before the wedding could be arranged, St. Denis was called upon to perform something like a minor miracle. The Frenchmen who had accompanied him on his original trek across Texas had boasted of his power over the Indians. Diego Ramon, the presidio's commandant and Manuela's grandfather, needed St. Denis to prove himself.

The Indians who had lived for generations around the San Juan Bautista mission—the presidio and mission's entire reason for being—had long been regarded by the Spaniards as somehow a little less than human. In exchange for protection from the Apaches, they had been exploited and in some cases abused. Finally, the tribe had decided to tolerate the treatment no longer. They had deserted to the last man.

Their leaving meant the mission and the presidio no longer had a function. Unless the Indians could be persuaded to return, the command, including the commandant and his family, would be recalled. How Ramon's pride must have suffered as he asked his future grandson-in-law, a man he had objected to at the outset of the relationship, to exert his influence over the Indians.

St. Denis, of course, complied. Accompanied by only one of his men, he rode out after the Indians. Since they traveled in a caravan with women, children, and all they possessed, they traveled slowly and made no effort to hide their trail.

Still, St. Denis risked his life to ride up to them. The bitterness that had marked their leaving could have turned to violence if a pair of unarmed white men tried to stop them. Furthermore, St. Denis did not speak their language. The common language between them was Spanish, which they had cause to hate.

When he rode into their midst, they formed a tight circle around him. At that point he could not have escaped if he had tried. His speech is recorded by Charles Gayarre in his *History of Louisiana*, published in 1903. Although the original source is doubtful, the words ring true. St. Denis was always reasonable. Briefly, he apologized for past wrongs and promised that things would change at the mission. His most telling arguments, however, came when he spoke of the fate of the tribe as it moved into unknown territory. They had heard of his encounter with the Apaches on the way to the presidio. They knew his guns had made the difference. He reminded them that the soldiers' guns offered their best protection.

When they regarded him stolidly, he reminded them they had no idea where they were going or what dangers they might encounter. "You do not know what bitter weeds grow in the path of the stranger!"

He advised them to return and see if their circumstance did change. If it didn't, then they could leave for a second time forever. The fact that he had come to beg them to return should give them hope.

After a brief powwow, they agreed to follow him back. When St. Denis arrived at the gates of the presidio with the entire caravan stretched out behind him, Manuela and her father were overwhelmed with joy.

The other Spaniards were somewhat less enthusiastic. This was no ordinary man. From their mouths his story spread across all Mexico and even back to Spain. What would happen to them if he proved treacherous? What if he incited the Indians to rise against them?

Manuela and Louis were married in the most elaborate wedding the frontier had yet to see. The ritual was conducted by seven priests. The streets were lined with Indians and Spaniards all cheering—the Indians because the reforms were actually occurring, the Spaniards because St. Denis had given each soldier a lagniappe and a cockade of yellow ribbon for his hat. The fiesta lasted three days.

On February 17, 1716, perhaps four months after the elaborate wedding, the *entrada* set out for eastern Texas. Manuela did not accompany her husband. The journey was, after all, business, and she had every reason to believe she was pregnant. She accepted every woman's lot on the frontier—to bid her man good-bye knowing perfectly well that she might never see him again.

What St. Denis thought is unknown. Did he regret leaving her? Or was his whole being intent upon the impending success of his mission? Two years had passed since he had set out to walk across Texas. Two years fraught with danger, intrigue, and imprisonment had passed since he had set out from Natchitoches. Everything he had worked for was about to come to fruition.

With his mind dazzled by hopes, doubts must have plagued him too. Had Cadillac received his letters? Would his marriage be seen as traitorous? What about the Spanish citizenship? It might be construed as currying favor with the enemies of France. Would Ramon somehow discover his duplicity and regard him as an enemy of Spain? Would he be arrested and returned to prison in chains? Would he be tried and executed as a spy?

Though faced with fearsome prospects, he carried everything off with great insouciance. The other members of the *entrada* followed him as if he were a true Crusader, which in a way he was.

By June 20 they arrived at the site of San Francisco de los Tejas. Here St. Denis left the expedition and rode ahead by himself. Ramon tried to stop him, reminding him of the possibility of meeting Karankawas, but St. Denis assured the captain that he would be in no danger.

On June 26 he returned with five chiefs and twenty-nine Indians all riding on horseback and following St. Denis single file—an impressive repetition of the caravan returning to San Juan Bautista. While the priests rejoiced at the sight of so many souls eager to return to Christ's Church, Captain Ramon noted unhappily that the Indians were wearing garments trimmed with or variously tailored out of bright blue cloth, decorated with glass beads, and—most important—armed with French guns.

While the Indians greeted the Spaniards in a friendly manner, Ramon further noted that they deferred to St. Denis in all things. Furthermore, they thanked him effusively for returning the missions to them. Ramon and the others took unpleasant note that the Indians were more enthusiastic about the return of St. Denis than they were about the return of Jesus Christ to their lives.

A ceremony followed in which a peace pipe was smoked and the chiefs delivered speeches of welcome to the Spaniards. Ramon answered their speeches. All the communication was translated by St. Denis, even to the oath of allegiance to the Catholic Church. Ramon quickly realized that the entire Spanish contingent was at a distinct disadvantage. Nephew by marriage or not, St. Denis wielded too much power for Spain's good.

Four missions were built within a twenty-five-mile area of each other. The first was Nuestra Padre San Francisco de los Tejas. Father Hidalgo, the priest who had written to the French in the first place, was given it as his church. The three others were Nuestra Señora de la Purisima Concepcion, Nuestra Señora de Guadalupe de los Nacogdoches, and San Jose de los Nazonis.

As soon as the padres and soldiers were settled in their missions, St. Denis took Ramon and a contingent of soldiers on to visit the French settlement at Natchitoches, where St. Denis was again hailed as a returning hero.

As they continued to Mobile, Ramon became increasingly alarmed. When the river down which they were traveling joined the mighty Mississippi, he realized that the settlement was west of what St. Denis had said should be the boundary line. Nevertheless, while among the French, Ramon traded for horses, flagrantly disregarding the laws of the Spanish government. In so doing, he set the stage for the profitable black market that Cadillac and St. Denis hoped to run.

As if Ramon had given permission, St. Denis began organizing another trade mission. Even though he had never been repaid for the goods confiscated and sent to Mexico City, he had little trouble acquiring more. Such was the strength of his reputation among the commerce-minded Frenchmen.

When Ramon warned him against doing so, St. Denis replied that he was no longer a French citizen, but a Spanish one. He even had a Spanish wife to prove it. Unless he was very much mistaken, she was pregnant with a Spanish baby.

While St. Denis and his party were in Mobile, the Spaniards continued to build missions. Nuestra Señora de los Ais was built farther east than the other four, and San Miguel de Linares de los Adaes was constructed only twenty-one miles from Natchitoches. It was planned as a post for watching French activities. Presidio Nuestra Señora de los Dolores de los Tejas was established at the western end of the mission chain. Its presence would ensure that neither the French nor the Indians would dislodge the Spaniards this time.

His task completed, Ramon and a small group of soldiers returned to San Juan Bautista. St. Denis accompanied them, bringing fourteen bundles listed as his worldly possessions. He claimed they were to set up housekeeping with his wife and baby daughter, Luisa Margarita. Undoubtedly, they were for trade.

And St. Denis's charm and luck had run out.

They arrived at the Presidio del Rio Grande in April 1717. Captain Domingo Ramon immediately ordered St. Denis's arrest. The goods were confiscated as trade goods. St. Denis appealed to Manuela's grandfather, insisting that he was a Spanish citizen. Diego Ramon, who had not favored St. Denis from the beginning, ruled that no one, Spanish citizen or Frenchman, was allowed to import foreign goods. Manuela tried to intercede for her husband, but her kinsmen were adamant.

From a humble room in the presidio, St. Denis sent a letter to the viceroy. That succeeded only in getting him into worse trouble. Linares had returned to Spain. In his place was the Baltazar de Zuniga, Marquis de Valero and Duke de Arion.

At the same time, the new viceroy received letters denouncing St. Denis. One came from the commandant at Pensacola in Spanish Florida, Gregorio Salinas, who denounced St. Denis for speaking the Texas languages, for living among them in Spanish territory for nearly half a year, and for bringing livestock back from Texas in 1713. Another letter arrived from the governor of Coahuila. Seizing his chance to avenge the loss of Manuela, Alarcon swore that St. Denis had entered Texas for the sole purpose of introducing illegal French goods into Spanish territories. Both letters recommended that St. Denis' be imprisoned as a threat to the sovereignty of New Spain.

By order of the new viceroy, St. Denis was transported under guard to Mexico City and there thrown into prison.

Fortunately, he had more friends than enemies. Father Hidalgo and his fellows all wrote letters praising his work and naming him a good friend to Spain.

When their letters to the viceroy went unheeded, they wrote directly to the King of Spain. On February 24, 1719, a decree was issued by no less than the royal person himself pardoning St. Denis. The only stipulation to his freedom was that he had to agree to take his wife and live in Guatemala, thereby removing his influence on the Indians of Texas.

Neither pardon nor stipulation affected St. Denis. On September 5, 1718, he had managed to talk his way out of his cell. From there he stole a horse and galloped out of Mexico City.

Traveling fast and alone, he made his way back to the Rio Grande. Whether he stopped at San Juan Bautista to make contact with Manuela is not known. What is known is that he crossed the Rio Grande and followed El Camino Real home to Natchitoches.

Smarting from the loss, Valero decided to place Texas under the command of the governor of Coahuila, Don Martin Alarcon. The new governor was ordered to move the capital. He was to take residence in a new presidio to be built in the heart of Texas—San Antonio de Bexar. A bitter man, Alarcon's oppression of all the people under him created great hardships among the Texans, both Indians and Europeans alike. It set the rules for treatment of all non-Spaniards for the next century. In 1832 and 1833 one of the demands of the Anglo-Celtic colonists of Texas to the government in Mexico City was the separation of Texas from Coahuila.

By the same decree Valero established a new mission on the San Antonio River only a short distance from the presidio. It was named in his honor—San Antonio de Valero. People who lived and worked around it called it by the name of the groves of white-barked trees that stood tall around it—Alamo.

St. Denis arrived home in Natchitoches February 24, 1719. For nearly six years he had worked for the French, for the church, and ultimately for the Indians of Texas. He had accomplished much—the Spanish and the Indians in the East Texas missions had no choice but to trade regularly for the contraband goods of the French.

His success in bringing this about through his "diplomatic mission" to New Spain earned him a commission as captain of the presidio of Natchitoches. Louis XV, the new King of France, knighted him a Chevalier of St. Louis.

Later that same year the War of the Spanish Succession broke out in Europe between France and Spain. St. Denis and six soldiers from Natchitoches marched to Nuestra Señora de los Dolores de los Tejas, the presidio he had been instrumental in founding. Courteously but firmly, they expelled the priests and soldiers from the area. When his country called, St. Denis never hesitated to follow its drum.

All the Spaniards in East Texas retreated to San Antonio de Bexar, where four other missions were built.

In 1721 Valero allowed Manuela and her two children to join her husband. The St. Denises had at least two more babies and lived together happily at Natchitoches. There he made an enormous fortune in contraband trade with the Indians and some of the Spaniards who had returned to live in and around the missions and presidios his influence had helped to found.

He brought trade and prosperity to Texas even as he saw the French boundary slip away from the Red to the Sabine River. In part his civilizing influence on all the people made Texas a desirable place to settle after the depression following the War of 1812 in the new United States of America.

Moses and Stephen F. Austin certainly thought so.

From time to time battles broke out between his traders and the Spanish, but they were minor and of little importance. He always won. As has been stated—he was a fighter. But he almost never fought. Fighting brought about loss of life and the destruction of property. Where was the profit there?

He stands as a man whose courage and single-mindedness, whose attention to duty, whose cleverness and diplomacy make him almost unique in the annals of Texas history. A hero with the truly formidable weapon of reason.

Kind and thoughtful to his last days, in January of 1743 he wrote to the Comte de Maurepas at Versailles. He could no longer perform his duties as commandant at Natchitoches. With death whispering at his shoulder, he asked permission to retire with his wife and children to New Spain. Manuela was only forty-six years old. He reasoned she had too long to live among strangers.

His request was denied. Even infirm, St. Denis was too valuable to Louisiana in a nominal position of command.

He died at Natchitoches on June 11, 1744. Manuela lived on in the fine house he had built for her until her death April 16, 1758.

* * * * *

The site where St. Denis's house stood is now the Fine Arts Building on the campus of Northwestern State University of Louisiana in Natchitoches. St. Denis's widow is buried in the American Cemetery whose earliest grave is 1717.

Fort Saint Jean Baptiste, the wooden fortification as well as its chapel, has been reconstructed on the Cane Riverfront. A bust of St. Denis marks the beginning of the historic district. Various festivals are held in and around the town every year. A marker close at hand announces the beginning of El Camino Real, the highway St. Denis followed from Texas and Mexico.

West of Natchitoches is Los Adaes Historic Park, site of one of the Spanish forts St. Denis caused to be built in 1717. Los Adaes was the capital of Spanish Texas until 1773. A visitor center has artifacts—arrowheads, eating utensils, and bottles—unearthed from the site.

The War Chief

Quanah Parker

Had the Fates instead of the Furies been present at the time of his birth, Quanah Parker should have been hailed as what he indeed proved to be—an extraordinary individual whose life was a thread of pure gold. Indeed, his life was the very essence of Greek tragedy. His name might have been Oedipus or Orestes, except that he refused to blind himself or let his enemies drive him into exile. Instead, he stared fate in the face until he mastered it with a dark, mature heroism. Dark it was—and dipped deep in irony—and bitterly affecting his very existence and that of all his blood kin for generations.

Born around the middle of the nineteenth century on the windswept prairies of the Panhandle, Quanah Parker can be said to be the truest Texan of all. Until the appearance of this son of a Comanche war chief from the Llano Estacado and the blonde granddaughter of a Baptist lay preacher from Virginia, all Texas heroes began their lives in foreign countries or distant states.

His mother was Cynthia Ann Parker, Texas's most tragic heroine. His grandfather was Elder John Parker, a "hard-shell" Baptist, who in 1834 took his clan of some thirty souls up the Navasota River, where he founded Parker's Fort approximately thirty-five miles east of the present city of Waco. "Hard-shells" were stubborn, self-reliant people who did not invite other Baptists, much less other Christians, to take communion with them. So far as they were concerned most other people were bound straight for Hell.

On May 19, 1836, only two months after the fearful massacres at Alamo and Goliad and less than a month after the truly astonishing and unexpected victory at San Jacinto, all of Texas was in disarray. The settlers who had not fled before Santa Anna's advancing army were unprotected. A Comanche raiding party, probably led by the war chief of the Quahadi tribe, Peta Nocona, swept down on the isolated fort. They stabbed, scalped, and mutilated John Parker. His wife "Granny" was stripped naked, pinned to the ground with a lance, and raped. His two youngest grandchildren, Cynthia Ann and John, along with two young women, Rachel Plummer with her small son and Elizabeth Kellogg, were borne away on horseback to *Comancheria*.

"Granny" Parker pulled the lance from her flesh and crawled back inside the fort. She survived, as did many of her other children and grandchildren. The fate of Cynthia Ann and John was unknown until Elizabeth Kellogg was sold to General Sam Houston for $150. She had been a captive with various tribes for seven months. To her knowledge the Parker children were alive and being treated well.

When Rachel Plummer was ransomed, eighteen months after her captivity and enslavement, she reported much the same thing. The children including her son James had been adopted and initiated into the tribe. They had quickly learned to speak the Uto-Aztecan language of their captors. They dressed like them and ate the tough buffalo meat roasted over the cookfires. They had forgotten their own language and their God.

How Granny Parker must have cringed at the thought of her pretty, modest granddaughter riding bareback and astride at breakneck speed over the sun-bleached Texas prairie. As matriarch of the clan, she did not allow the rest of the Parkers, with their strong family ties, to forget their kin living and growing up among the godless Comanches. Headed by this truly indomitable woman, no Parker would rest until the children were returned.

They would not come face to face with Cynthia Ann for almost a quarter of a century.

The Parker children and young Jacob Plummer were welcomed joyfully into the Comanche nation. They became one with the Nermernuh, the People.

For six years the Texas Rangers and the army of the Republic of Texas sought the famous children. In 1842 John Parker was located. He was then twelve. His only close ties were with his sister, who had just become the wife of the great war chief Peta Nocona, the man who had in all likelihood slain her grandfather. John did not want to be brought home to live among strangers whom he could no longer understand. He stayed with the Parkers only until he could steal a horse and ride away. A solitary figure, he moved across the plains searching for Cynthia Ann. Texan and Comanche left him alone with a sort of awed respect. He had declared himself a man. He walked his own path. He belonged to them both, yet he belonged to neither.

He could not find his sister.

Rather than risk losing his wife, Peta Nocona took her along with his Quahadis, whose name meant Antelope, into the relative safety of the vast reaches of the Staked Plains. Eventually, John married a Mexican girl who had been a slave among the Comanches. The two settled in the desert south of the Rio Grande. He never saw Cynthia Ann again.

The Republic of Texas ceased to exist in 1845. Annexed to the United States of America, it gave up part of its Indian lands, which its settlers dared not enter, and turned the Indian problem over to the federal government. A string of forts was built beginning with Fort Martin Scott and Fort Croghan in 1848 and followed swiftly in 1849 by Fort Gates, Fort Inge, Fort Duncan, Fort Gates, and Fort Worth. The idea was to put a ring around *Comancheria*. But how could one ring so vast a land with so determined and fierce a people?

Negotiations between delegations from Washington and chiefs of the various tribes began throughout the West.

Cynthia Ann was seen from time to time by Army officers at these Indian Councils. As the only wife of the great war chief Nocona, she accompanied him everywhere. With her blue eyes and long blonde hair, she was easy to catch sight of. Eventually she covered her hair with mud and buffalo dung and kept her eyes lowered in an effort to hide herself.

But she was too famous. The rewards were too great. Comancheros, the despised traders who moved back and forth between the white and Indian world, saw her and tried to buy her. American businessmen tried to find her. Her story appeared in Eastern newspapers. Her rescue became a secret ambition of every young man who became a Texas Ranger.

Even though she was aware that she was important to a great many people beyond Peta Nocona's tipi, Cynthia Ann never tried to escape. She adapted perfectly to his way of life and became a good and loving wife to the war chief. By every account he was right to value her and be extremely proud of her.

Thanks to good diet and good health for the first decade of her life, she became an exception among Comanche wives. The hard life of constant riding, backbreaking toil, and limited diet took its toll on the Comanche females in particular. Many women simply failed to conceive. Among those who did, miscarriages were frequent. One child per family was common. Two children were considered a great blessing. Cynthia Ann bore Nocona three children—an unusual number among the Comanche nation. He was envied by every other man.

Indomitable "Granny" Parker's granddaughter was given the name Naduah. She named her first tall son Quanah. His name meant "fragrance." In later years, Texas historians would say—erroneously—that it referred to his body odor, characteristic of Anglo-Celts rather than Indians. His brother was named Pecos or Peanut; his sister was Topsanah or Flower. Altogether, they were as happy as any family anywhere in the world could be.

Comanches loved and cherished their children. Their lives on the Staked Plains, moving swiftly on horseback, following the great herds of buffalo, must have been thrilling and fulfilling. Quanah would have been rocked by the motion of a horse within days of his birth. His mother undoubtedly carried him on a cradle board strapped to her back. From there he could see the other members of his tribe riding behind him in long lines and family groups and smiling at him. He could look out over the prairie, watch the buzzards floating lazily in the burning blue sky, see the dust devils whirl across the horizon, inhale the sharp creosote smell after the sudden shower.

And ride they did—for their very lives.

In 1849 Nocona had good reason to move the Quahadi as fast as he could push them. Like prairie fires, deadly plagues were sweeping across the Great Plains. They ravaged the other Comanche tribes—the Nakoni, the Kotsoteka, and the Yamparika. Half the fierce Pernatekas died, their tribal structure and way of life completely destroyed. Every Indian tribe from the Rio Grande to the Canadian border was affected. Epidemics of smallpox and syphilis had appeared earlier in the century, but not to the extent that they now descended.

Discovery of gold in California had brought the Americans from the eastern cities as well as immigrants from Europe by the scores. With their hysteria for gold, they brought the diseases of civilization, which the strongest Comanche could not fight. Asian cholera and a more virulent strain of smallpox—unaffected by the sweat lodge, the rites of purification, the prayers and incantations—killed probably more than half of the Indians west of the Mississippi.

In the end the survivors lived because they were forced to abandon the dead and dying. The social framework of their lives was destroyed as well. The psychological depredations to their morale and emotions created a fatalism that contributed mightily to their defeat.

Only the Quahadis, whose chief had isolated them in a remote corner of southeastern Colorado, survived with their tribal structure intact. They survived the white man's diseases because of the presence among them of a white woman—Cynthia Ann Parker. The Greeks would have appreciated the irony.

By the time Quanah was three or four his father strapped him onto a saddle on a gentle mare. Then the youngster looked ahead of him. His vision, like his mother's, would probably have been sharper than his father's, for contrary to popular belief, the eyesight of most Indians was weak compared to that of the Anglo-Celts of Texas.

When Quanah's legs grew long, he rode bareback. At that time his fun really began. For hours he and the other Comanche boys practiced tricks that would have thrilled any circus that Barnum and Bailey ever presented in their rings. At first he learned to pick up objects from the ground while his mount traveled at full speed. As he grew older and stronger, the objects grew heavier and bulkier until the day when he could swing up the body of the heaviest man.

To rescue a fallen comrade was the greatest obligation of a Comanche warrior. This attention and respect for the bodies of the dead would contribute to the downfall of the Comanche nation, yet the People could not entirely abandon their beliefs. To leave a man on the field of battle to be mutilated and scalped by enemies was a disgrace.

Quanah learned another trick that spread the fame of the Comanche horsemen throughout North America and even to Europe. He learned to ride with one leg hooked over the horse's backbone. He would slip a loop around his own neck and under his arm. This was attached to the saddle cantle or braided into his horse's mane. Hanging on the side away from the enemy, he had both his hands free for shooting beneath his horse's neck.

Of course, the horse had to be trained for such exploits. Quanah, the son of a great war chief, would have had many fine mounts of his own to train. His father would have seen that his son had the best horses and would have taken great pride in him. His mother would have loved him dearly, for he took the place of her brother John, whom she missed.

Meanwhile, fear and animosity turned to pure hatred on the part of the Texans for the Comanches and all other Indians as well. The ring of forts stretched farther. Fort Davis, Fort Stockton, and Fort Griffin were only a few. The war raged. The newspapers printed exhortations to kill the Indians wherever they were found. Comanches in particular were the enemies of the Texans.

Then in 1860 Nocona led a war party back into what was then called Parker County, near the ruins of the old fort. The Parker tragedy was about to come full circle.

When the Comanches withdrew, Nocona was pursued by Ranger Captain Lawrence Sullivan Ross, who was determined to teach them a "Texas" lesson. His call for volunteers recruited a band of more than sixty riders—Tonkawa scouts, twenty troopers from the Second Cavalry, and a large group of angry citizen volunteers.

Into *Comancheria* he rode, into the teeth of a howling "blue" norther. On December 17 he found the Comanche camp—on the Pease River, not far from the present town named for Quanah. In a howling windstorm, Sul Ross attacked. The resulting victory was not all he sought but immeasurably greater than he had hoped for. The Texans opened fire, taking the camp by surprise. In the hail of bullets, men, women, and children were dropped where they stood or fled screaming. Quanah, who was probably ten at the time, and his brother, Pecos, were among those who escaped into the brush.

What happened when the rangers rode down into the camp is not clear. Sul Ross shot a man trying to protect the women. He was sure the man was Peta Nocona, although later all the survivors swore that the man was a Mexican slave. The women fled in all directions. The Texans kept firing—bent on extermination. Memories of Comanche cruelties to white women were uppermost in their minds.

In the midst of the melee, Naduah's blanket blew off. She was carrying a baby and—more important—her hair was yellow.

Ranger Charles Goodnight, who later would found one of the great cattle ranches in the Palo Duro Canyon, spotted her hair and then her blue eyes. He grabbed hold of her when she tried to run away. "Don't shoot!" he yelled. "She's white."

Though she fought fiercely, she was hampered by the eighteen-month-old baby girl in her arms. When she was finally subdued, she managed to remember her name. "M-m-me! Me, Cynthia."

Sul Ross listed the identity of the women's protector as Cynthia Ann's husband, Peta Nocona. He was probably correct. Peta Nocona was never seen again. The Ranger captain considered the raid only a qualified success. He had exacted revenge for the raid in Parker County, but many of the warriors were away hunting. He took his blue-eyed captive back to civilization where she was positively identified as Cynthia Ann Parker. He was hailed as a hero. Her rescue made him so famous that he was later elected governor of Texas.

What happened to Cynthia Ann was much worse than what happened to her lonely brother. She was taken back into the Parker family—who expected her to be glad to see them. Though they did everything they could to care for her and treat her with loving kindness, they had no sympathy for her godless Indian ways. Because of her fame, the state of Texas voted her a pension of $100 a year and a league of land. Yet she was a prisoner. When she tried to escape as her brother had, her family placed her under guard.

Topsanah died at age four of a disease of civilization. For tragic Cynthia Ann, the last reason for living was gone. She scarified her breast in self-mutilation, prayed to the spirits of the Comanches, and starved herself to death.

If Nocona was indeed killed that day, then the young Quanah lost the love and guidance of both mother and father in one fell swoop. He might have been as young as nine. He could not have been more than twelve or thirteen. Within a year, his younger brother, Pecos, died of one of the diseases so rampant in the Comanche camps.

Word reached Quanah on the death of his mother and sister the next year. Only he remained—tall, strong, intelligent, an independent character. With a broken heart. A fierce heart. Within five years, probably before he was twenty, Quanah Parker became the acknowledged leader of the Quahadi tribe. His great-grandmother and his grandmother, his cousins and his uncles, all remained at Parker's Fort. Their story came to represent the fate of people who came in contact with the fierce Comanches. They were the living embodiments of the American axiom recited mantra-like for the rest of the century. "The only good Indian is a dead Indian."

Ironically, while regarding the Parkers as tragic, Texans took a certain perverse pride in the existence on the Llano Estacado of one of their own. They always referred to him by his double name—Quanah Parker. As his fame spread, they attributed all his good qualities and many of his fierce fighting ways to his mother's family. Blood, they said, would always tell.

But whose blood was telling?

Quanah had great need of intelligence, courage, and strength. The Comanches had good reason to believe that no treaty would ever be kept—no promise would not be broken. They remembered—as had all the Indians in the Southwest—the burning of the cornfields and villages of all the peaceful Indians of east Texas July 25, 1839. Shawnees, Cherokees, Caddoans, Creeks, and many more were chased across the Red River into much less fertile land designated Indian Territory. Then on March 19, 1840, in San Antonio, the chiefs as well as many tribesmen of the mighty Pehnahterkuh Comanches were lured into a trap and slaughtered in the Council House Fight.

For the Comanche there could be no peace, no treaty, no truce. For them there was only a fight to the death—which they could not win.

Along about this time, a story is told that Quanah Parker's uncles came searching for him after his mother's death. She is supposed to have told them about her tall son while she taught them a few words of Comanche. Armed with those and the sheer determination that marked all Parker doings, they rode into the camp of the Quahadis under a flag of truce. Ten Bears, the civil chief, allowed them to talk with their nephew. The Comanche could understand the call of blood. After the death of a father, the next of kin were supposed to take responsibility for the family.

Quanah may have even gone back with them for a few weeks, breaking horses for them and demonstrating his considerable skills that they did not possess. Whether this meeting actually took place or whether it is only a story told by people who wished it might have happened, we shall never know. Perhaps after watching Cynthia Ann's tragedy play to its end, the Parkers wished they would have done so.

The next certain appearance of Quanah Parker was at Blanco Canyon. In 1869 the Texas frontier was approximately where it had been in 1849, but its days were numbered. Raising beef for the eastern market had become profitable. People living in the bigger cities could no longer grow their own food. The iron rails built to take gold-seekers to California could pick up a herd of beef cattle on the way back and transport it live to the Chicago slaughterhouses without an appreciable loss of weight. Suddenly the Llano Estacado became desirable.

But before the ranches it could sustain could be developed, the ranchers had to get rid of the Comanches, who had gone into the beef business themselves. They would raid past the ring of forts and steal beef from small ranchers. Driving it back into *Comancheria*, they would trade it or sell it to the Comancheros for guns and ammunition.

The solution was obviously to push all the Indians off their lands, onto reservations where they could be forgotten. After the Civil War, Congress abolished the corrupt, incompetent Office of Indian Affairs and created the Indian Bureau within the Interior Department. The nation that put "In God We Trust" on its money reasoned that the Indians should be taught about the true God through missionaries. Lawrie Tatum, a Quaker, was put in charge of the Fort Sill reservation agency. There Comanches, Kiowas, and Apaches, all ancient enemies, were expected to become friends and Quakers in the bargain. Although Tatum knew nothing about his work, God had called him to it. To his credit he was honest, and he totally disapproved of the use of force against any of the tribes.

Unfortunately, he quickly became disillusioned. The Quahadis, with their half-white chief, refused to come to the reservation. He had expected them to be most co-operative and most receptive to conversion to the Quaker faith. In fact, he expected them all to become Friends.

By 1871 Tatum had lost all hope, and Texas governor Edmund J. Davis had lost all faith in the Indian Bureau. He was the Reconstruction governor—one of the most unpopular governors Texas ever had—in a state that was ninety percent ex-Confederates. His solution to the Comanche problem was Colonel Ranald S. Mackenzie and the Fourth Cavalry, who had come to Texas on the orders of General William Tecumseh Sherman.

The fame of Mackenzie's mostly black troopers in dealing with the Indians quickly spread across the Southwest. The "buffalo soldiers," as they were called, were earning respect among the warriors they fought against. In October 1871 they moved onto the Llano Estacado—into the territory Texas called *Comancheria*.

Colonel Ranald Slidell Mackenzie from the West Point Class of '62 was promoted seven times and wounded four during the Civil War. One of the injuries was loss of half his hand. One left a permanent limp. With his Negro cavalry, which he had made into the best military instrument in the Army of the West, he expected to be just as successful in Texas.

He was about to meet Quanah Parker, whose Quahadi Comanches would force Mackenzie to rewrite his book of military tactics. In 1871 Quanah might have been twenty-one years old. He was leader by default, for the old war chiefs were dead. Perhaps his mother's genes had helped to immunize him from the diseases. No question was raised about his parentage, however. The tribe followed him because he was the leader with the fierce heart.

Out on the prairies, the cavalry became the hunted rather than the hunter. Mackenzie quickly discovered Civil War tactics would not work against Quanah, who had not attended West Point and therefore used strategies different from those developed in Europe as far back as the Middle Ages.

Quanah knew that the United States had unlimited numbers of men to throw against him, whereas the Comanche could not afford to lose one warrior. Therefore he kept his men hovering just below the horizon line. His favorite points of attack were the picket lines and the camps. He would lead a lightning raid at dawn, killing the sentries and stampeding the horses.

Himself a horse soldier without equal, Quanah knew the cavalryman afoot was virtually ineffective. Therefore, the mounts were always his main targets. Even with double and triple guards and sharpshooters ordered to fire at will at the bobbing, racing targets, the cavalry lost mounts.

The troopers "helled and damned" the Comanches who refused to ride upright in the saddles, but ducked down behind their mounts and fired repeating rifles from beneath the horse's necks. Mackenzie was forced to split his forces to guard his mounts.

When the Quahadis did charge, they did not charge directly at the army to give them proper shots. The warriors would sweep down off the ridges in a wide inverted V-formation. Instead of charging head-on, the ends of the V would come faster, sweeping around behind the column of troopers so the buffalo soldiers couldn't charge them. If they tried, the Indians simply swerved their horses and galloped away at an angle.

The saber was a useless weapon. Its advantage came in a charge against a massed foe who could be slashed both right and left as the horse galloped into the melee. The Comanches would not stand and fight. The buffalo soldiers were not trained to deal with attackers one on one. No one got close enough to use the "long knife."

Equally ineffective was the hollow square, where the troopers dropped to the ground and fired into the mass. Again the Comanches swerved and the volleys did little damage.

Finally, if the cavalry tried to ride them down, the Comanche ponies, carrying lightly clad warriors with their legs entwined in a rawhide surcingle, could easily outrun the heavier cavalry mounts carrying a wool, leather, and brass uniformed soldier, heavily armed, with a fifty-pound saddle and pack.

The final humiliation came when one of Quanah's raids succeeded beyond even the war chief's dreams. A swift attack at dawn managed to cut the picket lines and get away with most of Mackenzie's horses. The Comanches galloped away with whoops of triumph, leaving the troopers to follow their colonel back on a litter with a Comanche arrow in him. Another time they had to follow him on a thirty-mile hike back to Fort Belknap on the banks of the Brazos. Despite the minie ball—a Civil War souvenir—behind his left kneecap, Mackenzie walked with them until he realized that his men were slowing their steps to match his.

While Quanah bought himself another wife with the horses he captured, Mackenzie analyzed the situation. He had never really joined the battle with his enemy. They had merely brushed against each other in action after action. Mackenzie realized he had no idea how much damage he had managed to do in the "brushes," for the Quahadis always retrieved their dead and wounded before breaking off the attack. The year 1871 had been a waste of time and effort resulting in the loss of men, equipment, and valuable animals. Mackenzie retired from the field.

Even so, victory was hollow. Quanah had to have known what was happening. The buffalo were disappearing at an alarming rate. In 1870 the American tanneries had developed a process that made the hides valuable. In 1872 not the government but the leather industry insured their demise. Raw hides brought $3.75 apiece in the industrial market. A subsidiary enterprise began—the hide hunters.

The speed with which the buffalo were slaughtered must have been a surprise even to the men who slaughtered them. Thousands of men found employment and income. Millions of buffalo robes were sold. Seven million pounds of bison tongues were shipped from Dodge City, Kansas, to be served as table delicacies as far east as Delmonico's in New York City. The rest of the millions of carcasses were left to rot on the prairie, which even today bears their bones.

The technology was hideous in its efficiency. The .50 caliber Sharps rifle, firing a 600-grain bullet driven by 125 grains of black powder, could knock down a full-grown bison at long range. Instead of fleeing like deer or antelope, the herd did not move, perceiving no danger from the noise. A skilled hunter, concealed, with his gun resting on a tripod half a mile away, could shoot an entire herd without moving himself. As many as fifteen skinners would then roll in on big wagons while the hunter would move on. The vultures and coyotes gorged until they could eat no more, and still the slaughter went on.

The Comanches as well as the Southern Cheyenne, the Kiowa, the Kiowa-Apache, and the Arapahoe saw their deaths written in the bones. Desperate, as the physical world disintegrated around them, they turned to the spiritual world. Magic must help them. Their own medicine men seemed helpless. They tried the magic of other tribes.

At about that time a young man appeared at Quanah's side. His name was Isa-Tai which meant Little Wolf. Such messiahs are recorded social phenomena when societies decay and begin to disappear. When "nothing but God" is left, someone rises to spread the message to the people. In the case of Isa-Tai, they eagerly embraced his deception.

Isa-Tai claimed that he was impregnable. Since Iron Shirt, chiefs and warriors seeking to bolster their importance had claimed the same thing. However, he claimed he had ascended above the clouds where he had communed with the Great Spirit, who had told him how to make paint that would turn away bullets. He promised to make such paint before the battle and give it to the warriors, so they too would be impregnable. If this were not enough, he claimed he could bring warriors back from the dead if reinforcements were needed to drive the white man away.

Most important, he had predicted the disappearance of a comet that had frightened the Plains tribes for many months. He also predicted a summer-long drought that did occur thereafter. Only when these things came to pass did Quanah, who must have inherited a pragmatic streak from his mother, agree to a council.

In the hard spring of 1874, the Plains tribes came together to listen to what Isa-Tai preached. Purification, he demanded. The Comanche needed to make great medicine. He demanded that they hold a tribal Sun Dance. That particular ritual, famous among the Kiowa, the Cheyenne, and the Sioux, was not part of the Comanche religion.

Borrowing magic even farther afield, Isa-Tai selected members of the tribe to dress as Mudmen from the Navaho and Hopi religion and caper among the participants and strike at them with whips.

Doubts of Isa-Tai's power must have been in Quanah's mind because he refused to permit the Comanches to torture themselves with stakes driven through their pectoral muscles. Nor did he allow them to fast or go without water for the five-day period. Perhaps the son of Cynthia Ann was already looking away from the dying spirit world of the Comanche and into the pragmatic world of the white man.

Nevertheless, according to directions, a lodge was constructed in four ceremonial days in the manner of the Cheyenne. A freshly killed buffalo was mounted on the center pole. With the symbol of what they most wanted to save, the Quahadi performed the ritual of desperation—with dancing, prayer, and a symbolic battle ending in victory—to save the Comanche way of life.

The whole ritual lasted more than a week. At the end, Quanah led the Comanches to a meeting with the other Plains tribes. At daybreak on June 27, 1874, they attacked the encroaching buffalo hunters at a small settlement built beside William Bent's old trading fort. On the South Fork of the Canadian in Hutchinson County, Texas, stood Adobe Walls. The hide hunters were the focal point of the attack. Their destruction was to be the starting point of a war of extermination—a war of salvation.

The battle was indeed the starting point toward extermination. Again, the Greeks would have appreciated the irony.

Five or six miles east of Adobe Walls, the Indians camped. Accounts of the numbers vary from a thousand to seven hundred. Quanah was elected the battle chief of the united tribes of Cheyennes, Comanches, and Kiowas. With Isa-Tai's direction they made magic paint with which they painted their bodies and in some cases the bodies of their horses as well. Some authorities say it was yellow. Some say it was a blue paint flecked with yellow. Isa-Tai determined to paint his entire body with his magic paint and ride naked with them.

Twenty-six white hide hunters and one white woman were in the saloon, the sutler's store, and the hide warehouse constructed near the dilapidated fort. Though it had been abandoned in 1844, its adobe walls were still five or six feet thick. It would serve, if need be, as a fort of last resort. During the night a roof beam had cracked in the saloon, so everyone had gotten up to repair it. The work had turned into a party encouraged by free whiskey from the proprietor Hanrahan, who had moved in to do business with the hide hunters.

The attack began with—of all things—a bugle call for the charge sounded by a black bugler, possibly a deserter from Mackenzie's cavalry.

Unfortunately for the Indians, the hide hunters were awake and somewhat drunk—too drunk to take into account the hopeless odds—too drunk to be afraid. But not so drunk they could not shoot. More important, they were all armed with new large-bore, long-range buffalo rifles. They were seasoned and calm—some of the best sharpshooters the world had ever produced. The sutler's store had a large supply of ammunition.

Although neither the saloon nor the store were built to be defended, the buffalo hunters made do with what they had. They piled sacks of flour and grain against the doors and windows and rested the deadly guns on them.

Isa-Tai had promised that the Sun Dance would turn away the bullets. He had promised that the whites would be asleep and the fort would fall easily. Three Cheyennes, one the son of Chief Stone Calf, and a Comanche were shot off their horses in the first charge. To their credit, they did not falter at what must have looked like a betrayal. Quanah's courage led them on.

Two freighters asleep in a wagon outside were dragged out and killed along with their big St. Bernard dog. They were scalped and cut to pieces in an orgy of bloodletting—a ritual sacrifice for triumph and revenge. Billy Dixon, whose feat was to become a legend, was one of the defenders. Bat Masterson, who would later go on to marshal with Wyatt Earp in Arizona, was there also. He reported that several of the hunters understood the bugle calls, so the defenders were primed and ready before each charge.

In the midst of the hail of bullets that met them at each effort, Horse Back, an old man and the last civil chief of the Comanches, was killed. Quanah's horse was killed beneath him, and he was shot in the back by a spent bullet. Wounded again as he tried to crawl away, he saved himself by burrowing behind a rotting buffalo carcass, which stopped the bullets that would have finished him off.

Demoralized, the attackers were forced to pull back to what they believed was a safe distance, but from there they could not loot the warehouse and retrieve food and more ammunition for their Henry repeaters. As they moved farther away, the hide hunters adjusted their sights and continued firing. The bugler was killed. The battle was over.

Angry Cheyennes, who had suffered the most grievous losses, began to taunt Isa-Tai, who had covered his naked body and that of his horse with the magic paint. They called him coward since he had watched the action from afar. Apparently, he was not far enough. A chief next to him was shot dead, and Isa-Tai's horse was shot out from under him.

When the young medicine man tried to blame the Cheyennes for "breaking the medicine," one of them struck him savagely with a quirt and led the others away.

By four o'clock in the afternoon, the battle was over. It had taught the Plains tribes a terrible lesson. There was no medicine. Extermination was inevitable. Although they continued to fight gallantly if sporadically through the summer, the alliance that might have aided them when they sued for peace was broken.

Isa-Tai had many years to live in disgrace. When white men asked the translation of his name, they were not told he was Little Wolf. Thereafter, he was Coyote Droppings.

The end did not come quite yet. The Indians had gotten away with many horses. They continued to be seen at great distances from the old fort. On July 2 Billy Dixon loaded up his big Sharps Fifty and shot an Indian off his horse at a distance of a mile. Actually it measured 1538 yards, but to the warrior's companions, that single death represented the greatest magic. There was no escape.

Winter came early to the Staked Plains in 1874. A cold wet norther roared down on September 24. Most of the Comanche, Kiowa, and Cheyenne were snug in the Palo Duro Canyon when it struck.

On September 28 the Fourth Cavalry, still under the command of the relentless Ranald Mackenzie, arrived at the edge of the canyon. Below them—unaware they were in a trap—were the winter lodges of Quanah's people.

Palo Duro Canyon is one hundred twenty miles long and in some places the floor is a thousand feet deep. Streams run through it—the Prairie Dog Town Fork of the Red River is formed by the Palo Duro and Tierra Blanco Creeks. Wood for fires and arrow shafts grows in abundance there. The horses were allowed to roam where they would since it was unlikely they would climb out of the canyon and into the teeth of the norther.

When Mackenzie attacked, the alarm was given too late. Quanah's people were forced to flee down the canyon with scarcely any weapons and only the clothes on their backs.

The warriors set up a heavy covering fire so the women and children could escape. When the noncombatants were out of harm's way, the warriors had no choice but to follow them. They could not save their horses.

Mackenzie did not even try to pursue. He had what he had come for. The European tactic of winter warfare would do the rest. Napoleon's troops retreating from Moscow would have understood. Mackenzie gave orders to burn all the tepees and supplies. What the Tonkawas did not loot—huge stocks of flour, sugar, blankets, meat, and repeating rifles and ammunition—everything for survival for the approaching winter—was burned.

Fourteen hundred twenty-four horses were rounded up. The next day Mackenzie drove them back to his camp at Tule Canyon. After separating the horses that were branded cavalry mounts and allowing the Tonkawa scouts to take what they wanted, he ordered the rest shot. In a thunderous roar, 1,048 shrieking, plunging animals were destroyed. The action won the war even as it destroyed Mackenzie's career. To the cavalry-idolizing United States and especially to the horse-loving Texans, the act was awful barbarism.

The Quahadis unhorsed were pitiable. They could not fight or find food. They could not even carry the supplies they had managed to rescue. Their trails were strewn with their abandoned possessions.

Within days the first faint-hearted groups straggled back to the reservations. The others Mackenzie continued to pursue as fiercely as the Greeks' hideous Furies tormented the damned.

The Kiowas under Lone Wolf surrendered in February 1875. The Cheyenne led by Stone Calf, a broken and defeated man, came in March.

Only Quanah, now war chief, medicine chief, and civil chief of the Quahadis, remained to lead a remnant of his once proud people up onto the Canadian River and see them through the winter. They would wait one more year for the buffalo.

When the spring came, the buffalo did not migrate northward. They were too few and too scattered. Perhaps they no longer knew the way. The mighty herd bulls and the big herd cows were all dead. Yearlings and calves could find forage where they were.

The hunters discovered too late their trade was gone. America had hunted to the brink of extinction its greatest beast.

Sergeant John Charlton, who had scouted the Palo Duro Canyon and found the Indian encampment, came to find Quanah and the remnants of the Quahadis on the Canadian. The U.S. government terms were implacable: Return to the reservation at Fort Sill in the land north of the Red River, set aside as Indian Territory, or face extermination.

Mackenzie had new orders—to hunt those who did not surrender to the last person.

In June of 1875 Quanah Parker led all the Comanche remnants out of Texas and into Fort Sill. Nearly a thousand people came with him to join the six hundred already there. The number of Comanche enrolled was 1,597. They were the last of the people who had numbered in the hundreds of thousands just a quarter of a century before.

The first treaties proposed a decade before had called for three million acres to be set aside for reservation, but that number was quickly reduced. There were not enough Indians to utilize such acreages. Despite all the chiefs could do and say, the lands were apportioned to individuals, 160 prairie acres each. In many cases white men married Indian women to get their acreages. The tribal system was broken forever. The Indian was forced to live according to Anglo-American way.

Quanah Parker, because he was the son of the tragic Cynthia Ann and because of his relationship to a powerful Texas family, fared better than almost anyone. His mixed blood allowed the Texans to be proud of him. He was respected and given the freedom that the rest of his tribe did not have because, in the eyes of some very powerful people, he was a Texas hero. His legend grew.

Perhaps there was some truth in what they said. Wily and pragmatic, as his people were not, he was able to assimilate more easily. Likewise, he was a relatively young man in his mid-thirties, flexible in his thinking and able to adjust to the culture shocks that followed one after another. In humiliation and defeat, he became a true hero—one who was able to lead the people in the way that would save their lives.

He became the spokesman for not only the Comanches but also for other tribes in the Indian Territory. Recognizing his co-operation and respectful of his strength, the federal agents named him chief of the Comanches though they had no right to do so. The tribe would probably have chosen him at any rate. No one else was alive to assume the title.

As chief, Quanah did many things that angered and many things that pleased the few elders remaining. What he did, he did with courage that put many to shame. Quanah frequently dressed in white men's clothing. They were angered. He absolutely refused to cut his braids. They were pleased. He kept seven wives, among them the widows of some of his friends who had died in battle, as was right and proper for a Comanche to do. He left the old ways of hunting and riding to become a cattle rancher, living in a twenty-two-room wooden house with bedrooms for all his many dependents.

He learned English quickly, traveled to Washington, D.C., and became friends with President Teddy Roosevelt, who came to Fort Sill to hunt with him. To increase tribal capital, he leased grazing lands to white cattlemen and collected rents like a white landlord. Though members of his tribe criticized him initially, they came to see the canniness of it when those very ranchers rose up to defend their leases and preserve the Comanche grazing lands against federal encroachment.

He was able to get a copy of a photograph taken of his dead mother and baby sister and kept it with him at all times. His well-publicized affection for his white family moved many Texans to think of him as a fine man and accept him as an equal. In this way he was named to important liaison positions in the white world. He was appointed a judge of tribal court where he approved the establishment of a Comanche police force. In 1902 he became the deputy sheriff of Lawton, Oklahoma.

He became the supreme assimilationist, an advocate of co-operation with whites for cultural transformation. He set the standards by example. He supported the construction of schools on the reservation lands and sent his children to them. When they were old enough, he sent them to boarding schools off the reservation, where they could grow up in the Anglo-American culture.

He refused to become a Christian, even though one of his sons, White Parker, became a Methodist minister. Quanah was a member of the peyote-eating Native American Church. Many credit this church and Quanah's good sense with keeping the Comanches from following the Sioux and the Cheyenne into the terrible Ghost Dance religion and culture.

Perhaps Quanah reminded his people of Isa-Tai and the failure of magic that had carried with it so much suffering and so many deaths. Be that as it may, the Comanche did not take part in the last great wars of retribution that cost so many lives in the 1890s.

Instead, Quanah showed the way to become a capitalist. Through shrewd investments, he became a very wealthy man, perhaps the wealthiest Indian in America at that time. A town in Texas was named for him and a railroad bore his name. He became a rancher and advised other Comanches to do so as well. The old ways could never come again. They should take care of themselves and learn the new ways. They must not go into paths that would result in their deaths and the deaths of their children. Each man must strive to live the best life he could without shame.

Quanah's heroism required that he abandon all pride and struggle to find a new way of life. He saw the end of the Comanche as a people, but he wanted them to live on as individuals. He lived to see his people and those they married come to be proud of their Comanche heritage while they lived in the American way.

In 1910 he moved the bodies of his mother and sister to Post Oak Mission Cemetery where he spoke at their funeral service. He recalled how much he had loved his mother. Did his voice tremble at the thoughts of her separated from him for so long? He must have remembered his father and the long lonely life that he, their son, had lived. He spoke of how his mother had loved the Indian life and not wanted to return. At the end he said that all people were the same anyway with the same god. He felt himself able to love all people.

On February 23, 1911, he died at his home in Oklahoma. He was buried in full Comanche regalia in Post Oak Mission Cemetery beside his mother and sister.

His monument bears one of the most famous inscriptions in the history of the West:

Resting here until day breaks and darkness disappears
is Quanah Parker, Last Chief of the Comanches.
Died Feb. 21, 1911, Age 64 Years.

* * * * *

Quanah Parker's grave as well as his mother's can be visited at Fort Sill, Oklahoma.

Texas, the outdoor musical drama, plays nightly during the summer in Palo Duro Canyon south of Amarillo. Quanah Parker is a character and his role in Texas history is recounted.

A replica of John Parker's log blockhouse and stockade are constructed in Old Fort Parker State Historical Park north of Groesbeck, Texas, on Texas Highway 14. In the Limestone County Historical Museum in Groesbeck, memorabilia from the fort and family are on display.

Today all the Parker descendants, both Indian and white, come together from time to time at the fort in loving family reunions.

The Alamo

Why It Happened

On the wind-swept prairies of central Texas in San Antonio, the most Mexican of towns, a small band of rebels took a stand inside a crumbling Spanish mission. The complex of buildings was largely indefensible. Most of the men wore no identifiable uniforms. They furnished their own weapons and in some cases their own ammunition. They had no real reason to be there. Indeed some of them had just arrived in the state. They flew the flag of the government they were rebelling against with but one small change.

Yet they stayed.

The army arrayed against them was, by contrast, huge. It was the best army in the Western Hemisphere commanded by the most ruthless general, a man who took no prisoners. They had no chance of defeating it. They had no chance of survival.

Yet they stayed.

Until the very hours before the actual attack, they could have abandoned their hopeless position and lived to fight another day. Ways lay open in all directions. By ones and twos, in small groups, even in organized retreat, they could have gone. No blame would have fallen upon their heads. No history would have condemned them as cowards.

Yet they stayed—

—and became the quintessence of courage. Their leaders became the synonyms for heroes. Their sacrifice became acceptable and good for all young men and women who lived in Texas from that day to this. They were the scions and at the same time the richest progenitors of the dynasty of courage.

Even today, we have to ask why.

Texas did not especially want to be free of Mexico. The Mexican Constitution written in 1824 was patterned after the Constitution of the United States with the exception of freedom of religion, deemed unnecessary since Catholicism was considered the only religion. The document divided Mexico into thirteen autonomous states. The central government was to be supported by twenty percent import duties on all foreign goods.

Texas was not satisfied with the constitution, but it would do. What they really sought was to be let alone—to be a self-governing commonwealth—although few in the state could voice their desires so gracefully. Rather they opined that they didn't want to be taxed to pay for a government a thousand miles away in Mexico City that wasn't doing "a dang thing" for them, and they didn't want to pay duties on goods imported from the United States where most of their business and family connections were.

The more farseeing amongst them, Stephen F. Austin, for example, recognized a bad situation in the making. Texas was joined in statehood with Coahuila. In the joint state legislature, she had only one vote out of a dozen. To Anglo-Texans, taxation without representation was an abomination.

In the final analysis politics is usually about economics.

Only when the Mexican government realized that Texas was its fastest-growing and most prosperous agricultural province did it decide to make the land pay off. For six years it had ignored the vast territory six weeks away from Mexico City by fast horse.

At first by little encroachments, the Mexican government began to exercise its muscle. It set up customhouses and levied taxes. These irritated the Texans, but still not enough to bring about revolution. The levies were easy to ignore. Smuggling was almost too easy. The ships came and went at all hours from Galveston and Brownsville and all ports in between.

Furthermore, the government was quickly collapsing into political anarchy as one president after another assumed the chair only to be deposed usually by forceful and humiliating means. Not so the bureaucracy behind the men. In just six years it had entrenched itself and taken as its cause to bring the separate thirteen states under national authority where their disparate wealth could be properly equalized and dispersed. Texas was a shining though distant star, rich and glowing.

Far away and defiant, it thumbed its nose at its lawful tax collectors. Looking back on the situation from the twenty-first-century perspective, one sees no moral high ground. Mexico certainly had the right to levy taxes and expect loyalty and compliance by its citizens. The Texans had a right to be free to build the society that would enable them to prosper. The result was a conflict of cultures. There is no right or wrong.

The Constitution of 1824 had—in just a few years—become a meaningless rag. The conservatives or Centralists wanted a strong government, controlling everything that happened in every state in Mexico. The liberals or Federalists wanted a narrow central government with power in the hands of the people and the states, but the wind was no longer blowing in their direction. The parties could not agree, nor could they compromise.

Suddenly, the army was the source of order; the general of the armies stepped into the seat of power at first supporting the president, then letting him fall. The strongest general believed he was destined to be *el caudillo*—the boss. The proper government for Mexico would be a *caudillaje*—boss rule. He was Antonio Lopez de Santa Anna Perez de Lebro.

No George Washington of Mexico, he saw himself as the Napoleon of the West. When he seized the presidency and held it through the middle of the nineteenth century, he cost Mexico the chance to take her place as a second great power on the North American continent, a fit rival for the nation it disliked most throughout most of the century.

That chance never came again. In nationalistic disarray, Mexico became a pawn of European powers, a country deeply divided, corrupted and demoralized by military rule imposed by garrisons of Federales. Mexico lost Texas, California, New Mexico, and Arizona, as well as the stability of representative government that must be supported and maintained by an informed and ever-growing middle class.

It should have been different. Mexico was discovered and established before the United States. Her wealth was extensive, her resources as great. She had to defeat a world power like England not once but twice. When she won her own independence from Spain fifty years later, she had the model of the United States constitution to guide her to a workable representative government. She failed to establish it.

We can only guess what position Mexico might have assumed in NATO and in the United Nations in the twentieth century were it not for the political carnage of the nineteenth.

Three men can be said to have planted the seeds of revolution in the hearts of Anglo-Texans. They were part of the Spanish elite, who had remained in power even when their viceroy and many of their countrymen had gone home. They were Anti-American to their very bones. Rather than enter into close co-operation with their rising neighbor to the north, they chose to create rivalry between the two nations. They were General Don Jose Maria Tornel, General Don Manuel Mier y Teran, and the Mexican Minister of Foreign Relations, Don Lucas Alaman.

The recommendations they made to the Mexican Congress were adopted into policy although not part of the stated policy.

1. To settle Mexican convicts in Texas.

2. To introduce colonists from nations where English was not the language.

3. To place Texas directly under the control of the central government and dispatch spies to observe and report.

These along with the Edict of April 6, 1830, drove a killing wedge between Anglo-Texas and Mexico. The decree went one step farther than one of the recommendations. It specifically forbade further immigration into Texas, and it limited trade to Mexico proper. It was designed to curtail the Texas economy and to stop any further settlers coming from the United States—a

Mexico for the Mexicans ethnocentrism. Only with other states of Mexico could Texas trade. Only from the other states of Mexico could people emigrate.

Immigration and foreign trade had become the lifeblood of the state. They meant more stores, more towns, more commerce, more cotton ginned and exported, more manufactured goods imported, more capital accumulated. The edict stopped all that. At the same time it separated families, for fathers and brothers had come to the savage land first expecting to send for their wives and sweethearts, children and old people later.

To enforce the edict, Texas was placed under the command of General Don Manuel Mier y Teran, who hated Americans with a determined iciness. Immediately, soldiers—released convicts—were stationed at Nacogdoches, at Anahuac on Galveston Bay, at Velasco at the mouth of the Brazos, and at La Bahia in Goliad. The garrison was increased at San Antonio de Bexar, whom its citizens as well as the rest of Texas referred to simply as Bexar (pronounced "bear").

No people on the face of the earth could have hated military rule worse than Anglo-Americans. The battle of New Orleans in 1815 seemed like yesterday. Some Texans had fought in it. Most had close affiliations with Louisiana. No one knew whether it had finished England's territorial aspirations. The British lion might roar again at any moment.

The Mexican convicts looked like "foreign" soldiers. They were undisciplined, poorly equipped, and obnoxious. They looked and behaved like exactly what they were. Their commanding officers were imperious dons, easily recognizable as remnants of the Spanish monarchy still acting above everyone else. Moreover, they made no efforts to control their troops. In places without billets, they quartered their soldiers in the homes of citizenry.

The ethnic differences between the Mexican officers and the Mexican soldiery were as real and as recognizable as the difference between the Texans and the soldiers. It was a racism most peculiar to the eighteenth and nineteenth centuries, whose vestiges survive today. The Spaniards and the Texans looked down on and despised those of mixed blood—the *mestizos*. They made no attempt to put a kind face on their feelings.

Neither Spaniards nor Texans recognized the fact that the *mestizos* hated back just as virulently. Their hatred for the time being focused on the Anglo-Texans, who were taller and much lighter skinned. They spoke a different language. They practiced markedly different customs. The Texans might have conformed to laws they understood, but they would never submit to domination from a race they regarded as inferior.

The situation was a powder keg.

At Anahuac in 1832, a redheaded firebrand lawyer from Alabama struck the match. He was William Barret Travis. His friends and his enemies, whom he had in equal numbers, called him Buck. In May he got himself arrested by garrison captain Juan Bradburn.

The situation was quickly turning from smoldering resentment to a brush fire of hostile emotion. Ninety men gathered to attack the garrison. They were serious enough to send for cannons.

The situation at Anahuac was never really defused because before actual negotiations could begin, the garrison was called away and Bradburn resigned. A revolution of another sort was taking place in Mexico. General Antonio Lopez de Santa Anna was taking control of the supreme government.

The Texans thought to appeal to Santa Anna for redress and perhaps a return to their commonwealth status. They appealed to the one man whom the Mexicans respected, the man who understood them. The Texans appealed to their most respected leader, Stephen F. Austin.

In January 1821 his father, Moses, had obtained a Royal Commission to settle three hundred families in Texas. When Moses died, Stephen had taken the job for himself. It was, after all, a business opportunity. By the end of the year Don Estevan Austin was the Great Empresario, moving families onto some of the richest country in Texas—the bottomland between the Brazos and Colorado Rivers along Louis St. Denis's old Camino Real. It was perfect for Austin's solid citizens—planters and their attendant occupations that constituted their goods and services. His headquarters at San Felipe de Austin quickly became a sort of capital for Anglo-Americans coming to Texas.

By the time of Mexico's revolution against Spain, twenty thousand Anglo-Americans and their slaves had come to Texas. They exceeded the Mexican population by five to one.

Other empresarios had followed Austin. Some colonies had succeeded. Some had failed. Austin's colony set the example. He was the leader who swiftly became by default the most important man in Texas. He was the liaison between Texas and Mexico. He spoke to the *criollos*, that is, the native-born Spaniards, as an equal. The Mexicans recognized him as a patron. The Texans appealed to him to go to Mexico City to set their case before Santa Anna.

Though ill, Don Estevan Austin undertook the journey on April 22, 1833, to bring their case to the House of Deputies. Arriving in Mexico City, he cooled his heels for six months. The government had other more pressing problems closer to home. Politics was in turmoil. Asiatic cholera was in the city, killing hundreds daily and spreading throughout the countryside.

Frustrated, unable to effect any substantial negotiations, Austin started back home in December 1833. He was arrested in Saltillo and taken back to the capital. There he was imprisoned in the ancient Prison of the Inquisition. He was held *incommunicado*—no books, no writing materials, no visitors. Even walks in the courtyard were denied. It was solitary confinement. All efforts from Texas failed to free him. The only promise was that he would be released on bail on Christmas Day, 1834.

An innocent man was in prison. The government of Mexico had become a dictatorship. Who knew what horrors might be visited on the Texans?

While Austin sat in solitary, a new face appeared on the Texas scene. Sam Houston, a protege of U.S. President Andrew Jackson, came to Texas. Although he was not a legal resident, uneasy Americans saw him as the new direction Texas should take. They wanted to be part of the United States of America. He was made chairman of the constitutional committee of Texas even though he was not a legal resident.

Mexican historians believe to this day that he was the spearhead of a well-conceived plot to take Texas from Mexico. Although this cannot be proved, it is not easy to deny.

In April 1834 Santa Anna took over the government of Mexico. He dissolved the republican congress. He dismissed all the cabinet ministers and abolished all the state legislatures. In October 1835 the Constitution of 1824 was officially voided.

When Zacatecas revolted against the idea of a standing army, Santa Anna's regular army, the largest standing army in the Western hemisphere, defeated and destroyed the force of five thousand. He took no prisoners and permitted his troops to rape and plunder the state capital.

So long as he was in the vicinity, he sent his brother-in-law, General Martin Perfecto de Cos, to break up the government of Coahuila. The Mexicans with anti-government sentiments flew across the Rio Grande—carrying more stories of pillage and murder.

Since 1830 another ten thousand Anglo-Americans had entered Texas. Probably most of them had come with the idea that war was brewing and that Texas would soon be part of the United States. Their chance as they saw it was to speed that process as fast as possible.

Cos moved to Matamoros and ordered the arrest of the fugitive Coahuilans as well as several men, including William Barret Travis, who had caused trouble for the commander at Bexar.

What did Austin think? What would Austin do? became the burning questions. But no one could answer. Austin was illegally imprisoned in Mexico City. At last on July 13, 1835, Austin was released under a general amnesty. Before he could leave the vicinity of Mexico City, he had to seek permission from Santa Anna. With his trust in the government completely destroyed, Austin was given a passport to take ship to New Orleans.

His health broken, his anger hot after eighteen months in a Mexican prison, he wrote a letter to his cousin. Texas must be fully Americanized. He hinted that it should come under the

American flag. He was sure that Santa Anna would move against Texas in the spring or summer of 1836. He advised that the trouble be kept damped until a flood of American immigration would increase Texan numbers.

"A great immigration from Kentucky, Tennessee, etc., each man with a rifle...would be of great use to us—very great indeed...." With enough Kentucky and Tennessee rifles in Texas, Austin had no fear of Santa Anna and his Mexicans.

With these in mind, he sent forth the call for immigration and rode back across the Sabine toward the Brazos. In Texas he issued a call for a consultation of all Anglo-Texans. At San Felipe, he took the chair as colonel of militia. When Cos crossed the Rio Grande bound for Bexar, Austin put out a general call for a stand to arms. "War is our only resource. There is no other remedy. We must defend our rights, ourselves, and our country by force of arms."

The defenders at the Alamo only a few months later were simply answering the call.

And so they stayed.

The Hellbound Spirit

James Bowie

The epidemic cholera that brought down the government in Mexico City in 1833 destroyed Jim Bowie. His death at the Alamo must have come as a release to him. According to author Lon Tinkle, his beautiful, aristocratic wife Ursula de Veramendi, his little daughter and infant son, and his mother-in-law and father-in-law had died within the space of three days.

Tears coursed "down his cheeks while lamenting her untimely death." He blamed himself because he had moved her to the clear mountain air of Monclova, where the Veramendi's had a summer home, where she and the babies would be safe. He heard the terrible news when he was staying in plague-ravaged Natchez, Mississippi, where the disease never touched him.

The life he chose for himself in the time he had left never gave him a chance to recover from his loss. He had always been a hell-raiser. Now he lived intent not only on raising hell but in getting there as quickly possible. The Texas Revolution seemed the ideal vehicle.

The forty-one-year-old Bowie was a seasoned and dangerous fighter. He stood six-feet-one with the broad shoulders of a man who had done manual labor in his early years. He had thick auburn hair and blue-gray eyes. The Mexicans called them "killer's eyes." Moreover, he was highly intelligent and reasonably well educated.

A fight was exactly what he was seeking, preferably to the death. The fighting brewing in Texas would be fierce, perhaps hand-to-hand. He savored the thought of meeting it with his legendary knife. With a mirthless smile twisting his lips, he returned to Texas.

James Bowie was born in Logan County, Kentucky, in 1795, one of three brothers. At about nineteen, he settled on Bayou Boeuf in Rapides Parish, Louisiana. There he worked in a desultory manner, farming a bit, logging a bit. The life was dissatisfying to him. He quickly came to the conclusion that he would never get rich at those sorts of things. He took every opportunity to find things that would make him so.

His brothers, Rezin and John, joined him there in an enterprise that held more promise of fortune. Their lack of conscience assured those in the vicinity that the three were bound straight for hell.

In their early twenties they made a deal with the pirate king Jean Lafitte to smuggle slaves through Texas into Louisiana. Recent law had made bringing slaves into the United States illegal. However, owned slaves could be bought and sold. Every Southerner, whose economy depended to some extent on slavery, regarded the contradictory regulations as hypocritical and generally stupid.

Although they made $65,000 in profits from slave trading and everyone knew in essence what they were doing, the Bowie brothers suffered no ostracism. They bought a sugar plantation. Rather than be content merely to raise crops, they built a steam mill for grinding sugar cane. The first in the state, it made them another $90,000 profit.

John served three terms in the Arkansas state legislature. Rezin served the same number in the Louisiana legislature where he gained fame as an orator. Jim was still dissatisfied. He wanted a different kind of adventure. Land-hungry and money-hungry, he looked toward the Texas frontier.

Bowie must have been an amazing man to know. Besides his obvious spirit of entrepreneurship, he possessed a chameleon-like talent with all groups of people. He was able to fit easily into the best society. Supposedly at about that time, his brother Rezin made and gave Jim the knife that became a legend. With that and Bowie's truly frightening reputation, he was

respected and admired by the wildest, toughest men on the American frontiers. Well-mannered and charming, he was invited into the homes of the gentle, loving ladies of the proud Creole society of the towns and plantations.

Acceptance by the one should have ruled out the other, but Bowie was welcomed everywhere. The fact is that he lived in a violent society. Law enforcement was generally not available. Civilized, intelligent men considered Bowie a paragon among them and quite sound in his actions.

His killer eyes were not just for show. He was a killer. He was rumored to have killed the son of Jean Lafitte, who is supposed to have double-crossed him. On the fabled sandbar duel, fought in the middle of the Mississippi at Natchez, he was serving as second to General Cuny who was facing Colonel Crain. The duelists fired into the air and exchanged handshakes. To the many surprised witnesses, everything seemed over.

Suddenly Crain pulled out two more pistols. He killed Cuny and wounded Bowie. In the general melee that followed, Bowie leaped to catch Crain to kill him. Major Norris Wright, Crain's second and Bowie's sworn enemy, rushed at Bowie with a sword cane. Already wounded Bowie fell to his knees. Then with his fabulous knife, he gutted Wright, stabbing all the way through his abdomen into his backbone. A friend of Wright's came after Bowie with another sword cane. With a knife reputed to have a double-edged, curved point, Bowie slashed the unlucky man crosswise in the stomach. No one else bothered Bowie.

While Bowie was recovering from his wounds, legend has it that he credited the knife with saving his life. He wanted to honor the blade. He had it polished and set into an ivory handle mounted with silver. Its sheath he had mounted with silver also and wore it on his belt wherever he went.

The story spread. Knife makers seized the opportunity to make a weapon such as they had heard tell of. It was duplicated numberless times for those who could afford it. The ideal was a short butcher knife forged out of the best available steel. The blade was narrowed and double-edged at least two inches from the point and curved more than ordinary knives—hence the nickname "Arkansas toothpick." The handle was heavier than that of other knives, often made of horn, and guarded from the blade like a small sword. Most important, the blade, guard, and handle had to be properly balanced, so it could be thrown a maximum distance with deadly effect.

It was both economical and practical for skinning, cutting up meat, hammering, and performing a multitude of other services. Moreover, it would not misfire as pistols often did. The weapon became very desirable, but relatively few could be handmade in the proscribed manner. Ironically, an English company undertook a profitable new line of trade—manufacturing Bowie knives for the American frontier. Whatever the truths or myths surrounding it and its owner, it became the favorite weapon of the backwoods South until the arrival of the six-shooter.

Not only the knife, but the credited and documented duel added to Bowie's legend. Stories of other duels were told more and more fantastic. How many of the tales were real and how many were "tall" will never be known. He is supposed to have survived fierce fights with his wrist bound to that of his opponent. He is supposed to have fought a man while he and his adversary clenched corners of a handkerchief between their teeth. He is supposed to have ridden alligators, won sit-down knife fights on logs in the Mississippi River, fought Indians, sailed with pirates, and caught runaway slaves.

People stared at him wherever he went—saying that he had never lost a fight, nor had he ever started one. His hellbound spirit probably loved every minute of the adulation.

While his brothers married, became settled family men, and entered politics, he left for Texas in 1828. He announced he was searching for the fabled San Saba mine, reputed to contain both gold and silver. Prospectors and treasure hunters continued to hunt for it for generations after his death. When asked, they said they were searching for Jim Bowie's lost mine.

How much he actually searched is open to speculation. Shortly after he arrived in Texas, clothed in his glittering reputation, Stephen F. Austin introduced him to Juan Veramendi, the vice-governor of Coahuila y Tejas, whose place of residence was in Bexar. Veramendi took an instant liking to the strapping fortune hunter who was interested in the same things Veramendi was—land and wealth.

Bowie took an instant liking to the vice-governor's beautiful daughter, who was kin to most of the aristocrats in the combined states. Shortly thereafter, he rejoined the Catholic Church in a public ceremony and became a Mexican citizen. With his new citizenship and his father-in-law's sponsorship, he was able to obtain almost a million Texas acres. (Other Texas colonists were limited to one league—4,428.4 acres.)

On April 23, 1831, he married Ursula de Veramendi. He lied about his age on the marriage license, listing himself as thirty when in fact he was thirty-five. He misrepresented his wealth in the United States as a quarter of a million dollars, although nearly a hundred thousand of that was merely paper money from fraudulent land schemes that he shared with his brothers. In the marriage contract he promised to provide fifteen thousand dollars, money which he did not have in hand, for a dowry for Ursula if he should die before her.

The wedding was a glorious one as befitted people of wealth and circumstance. The honeymoon, paid for by Veramendi and by Ursula's grandmother, was a luxurious trip to New Orleans and Natchez, where he introduced her to his friends.

Everyone admired her. Those who knew him best believed him to be truly in love. He had never pursued women. Indeed, he had had an "excessive reverence for them."

"Bowie was supremely happy with her," wrote his good friend Captain William G. Hunt. "Very devoted and more like a kind and tender lover than the terrible duelist..."

They returned to Texas to live in a wing of Veramendi palace. Though he could have lived the life of the idle rich, he was soon riding over Texas searching for more land to buy and incidentally the San Saba Mine. He always returned to her. Some sources say she bore two children. They were supremely happy. He signed his papers "Santiago Bowie." His father-in-law treated him like a son. Together they opened a cotton textile mill in Saltillo. If they had been allowed to continue, who knows what changes in history they might have made. Instead, cholera wiped out the entire Veramendi family and with them the better part of Bowie's life.

Except for a brief retreat to Louisiana, he remained in Texas—searching not for gold but for the reason why he had not died. Perhaps searching for the swiftest way to do so.

He gambled, he drank, he lost money, he lost friends, he sold land that he had once prized so highly. A man obsessed, he did everything to expunge the memories and the painful pictures of what might have been.

When the revolution actually began, he embraced it like a savior. Perhaps as a citizen of Mexico, he would have been accepted by the Mexican politicians as one of their own. Perhaps not. Many members of the centralist party would have taken exception to him. He was, after all, a former citizen of the United States. Physically and psychologically different from them, he would have stood out among them and he would have made them constantly aware of his own opinions.

Santa Anna might have found it politically expedient to destroy Jim Bowie. He was *el caudillo*. He took no prisoners.

In the fall of 1835, Bowie took the lead in throwing Santa Anna's brother-in-law Cos out of Bexar. The dictator's brother-in-law had marched north from Matamoros to Goliad. There he left a small detachment to hold the presidio of La Bahia, which he rightly considered the Mexican army's route from the Gulf. He arrived as Bexar and assumed command from Colonel Domingo Ugartechea, a man of unquestioned courage.

The area southeast of Bexar over which Cos passed was swarming with riflemen, some of them the Kentuckians and Tennessean that Austin had called for. Jim Bowie was among them. After a skirmish Ugartechea retired the army, reasoning that his troops had no idea how to fight these undisciplined, ragtag cowards, who fired from cover then faded into the brush to find another vantage point.

All Mexican troops were withdrawn into the town of San Antonio. Within its environs stood a ruined mission. The Alamo was under siege for the first time. Jim Bowie was one of the men in charge of the Texans.

In November 26, 1835, a vicious little fight ensued between the Texans led by Bowie and Cos's foragers desperately searching for grass for their horses. The Texans won, but they were without cannon to blast through the Alamo's walls and could not continue to maintain a siege indefinitely.

On December 4 the Texan army was already loaded to retreat to Gonzales when a Mexican deserter was captured. Interrogated by several officers, he told them that Cos's army was hungry and disheartened. Bexar could be taken easily.

While others hesitated, an old Texan *empresario* agent shouted, "Who will go with old Ben Milam into San Antonio? Who will go with old Ben Milam into San Antonio?"

The response was instant. It spread like a current through the men awaiting the order to march away. Why retreat when they could capture the city? It took five days of house-to-house and man-to-man fighting. The Mexicans were dumbfounded. Like all successful armies, they were experienced in assault rather than defense. House to house, plaza by plaza, the Texas rifles sniped from rooftops, from doorways, from behind window curtains, and through lacy iron grillwork.

Ben Milam was killed on the third day and buried in the courtyard of the Veramendi house that now belonged to Jim Bowie by inheritance. He took his place in the dynasty of Texas heroes while others raised the standard that he had borne for such a brief time.

On December 10, 1835, Cos surrendered eleven hundred officers and men and his fortress, the Alamo.

Many in Texas made the mistake of believing that with this brilliant victory of 350 over 1,100, the battle was over. Cos was allowed to sign a covenant of surrender and march his men back across the border.

The new government of Texas no longer had Stephen F. Austin at its head. On November 24 he had been named an emissary to the United States to obtain volunteers, guns, and money. Sam Houston was named general of an army that was little more than a handful of volunteers. Worried men, avaricious men, disappointed men, men with all their wealth in Texas, men with their homes and families in Mexico—all met to decide what to do—whether to stay with Mexico or declare themselves independent.

For a month the debate continued. Some favored attacking Matamoros. Some favored declaring themselves a separate state, though few had the least idea what to do beyond that point. Some talked of joining the United States. Some suggested the most moderate course, simply to do nothing but return to the Constitution of 1824.

Sam Houston, who had actual military experience, opposed an invasion of Mexico. He reluctantly spoke in favor of a raid on Matamoros, but only if Jim Bowie commanded the troop. A lightning raid stood a good chance of having a psychological effect on an approaching army. It would be particularly effective with Bowie at its head. His fearsome reputation would command the respect of all of northern Mexico.

The council fell apart, fighting among themselves, splintering into partisan divisions, squabbling like children. A man named Smith was elected governor although he was little known beyond the body. Without Austin to moderate, the government of Texas simply disappeared.

When Houston remembered Santa Anna's conquest of Zacatecas, the general felt a chill of apprehension. At Bexar Cos had been caught by surprise. He would remain beyond the Rio Grande, Houston reasoned, just long enough to lick his wounds and gather reinforcements. Indeed, Santa Anna himself would consider the rout at Bexar an insult. He could and probably would come to Texas. Houston thought a policy of retreat was the only way possible to avoid terrible bloodshed.

On January 17, 1836, Houston sent newly commissioned Colonel James Bowie to Bexar to strip the presidio of cannon and ammunition and as much of the fortification as he could manage.

On February 2, 1836, Jim Bowie wrote a letter to Henry Smith, the provisional head of the provisional government of Texas. In so doing he countermanded Sam Houston's direct order.

"The salvation of Texas depends in great measure on keeping Bexar out of the hands of the enemy...If it was in the possession of Santa Anna, there is no stronghold from which to repel him in the march to the Sabine...We will rather die in these ditches than give them up to the enemy."

If Jim Bowie was hellbound, the Alamo was the closest to the final darkness he was going to find.

The Politician

David Crockett

Stephen F. Austin's invitation to men from Kentucky and Tennessee to come with the rifles had brought one of America's famous frontiersman—David Crockett, a former U. S. Congressman, an old man of fifty to be sure, but a man whose reputation for shooting straight was as legendary as any in the world. Like the other two colonels at the Alamo he stood over six feet tall. His hair was black, but he had the same gray-blue "killer eyes" as Bowie.

He was born on August 17, 1786, near Limestone Springs in northeastern Tennessee just as George Washington was about to begin his first term as president of the United States. Davy grew up in an era when a man with a long rifle could shoot a squirrel at fifty yards. Such a man was valuable. He had an important skill. The most significant event in his young life was the American Revolution. All a man needed to do was be able to shoot.

At the age of twelve or thirteen, he was sent to school for the first time. After four days he played truant. When his father punished him, he ran away from home and hired himself to a neighbor who was about to drive a herd of cattle to Virginia. When he returned to his father's tavern three years later, he was almost a man. Only one of his sisters recognized him.

Perhaps a look at life in a more civilized state had somewhat changed his ideas about books. He arranged to work two days a week for the schoolmaster in exchange for room and board and a little learning. His father was in debt, so Davy worked to help the family. For six months he worked and went to school. Those six months were all the formal schooling he ever had.

His ignorance hurt him very soon. He fell in love with a Quaker girl who rejected him because of his lack of education. Still he never went back. Though he is supposed to have written several books, they were probably merely told to an amanuensis who finished them off in what would have been considered appropriate style.

In 1806 he married Polly Finley, a descendant of Macbeth, King of Scotland. Her parents objected strongly because of his ignorance and his lack of ambition. When Polly insisted, they gave the couple two cows each with a calf. With Davy's horse the couple were set for farming.

Of course, Davy hated anything having to do with plowing and planting. He wanted what was over the horizon, what was beyond his reach, what he could never have. In 1812 he joined General Andrew Jackson's army as a private to go off to Florida to fight in the bloody Creek Indian War that culminated in the battle of Horseshoe Bend, Alabama.

When food ran out for Jackson's troops, Davy hunted along the line of march. Every bird and animal that moved in the forest fell to Davy's dead aim. In eight or nine months he is said to have killed 105 bears. During this campaign, when soldiers from all the United States could carry the stories back to their homes, he became a national legend.

He returned home after the Creek War to find his wife ill. She died shortly thereafter, and he married the widow of a comrade who had been killed in Florida. Though his new wife had a farm that earned her a comfortable living, Crockett persuaded her to move westward.

He had a glib tongue and a rich store of folksy sayings that charmed everyone who heard them. He hated farming, he did not care for soldiering. What he really liked was talking. Obviously, politics would come easy for him. He was chosen magistrate of the Shoal Creek community even though he had no knowledge of the law, except what he termed in his stump speeches "natural law."

Assuming the job, he discovered that he really needed to learn to write. In his first months, he ordered his constable to make out the warrants while he practiced "by care and attention" until he could write a legible hand.

Armed with his new knowledge, he was still nobody's fool. He kept his new learning to himself believing that it would dispel the image that had won him the election. What people had elected was a backwoodsman, an unsophisticated son of nature who would "be sure [he] was right, then go ahead." They trusted what they believed was his honesty and his shrewd simplicity. They loved his coonskin cap and his good-hearted antics. They applauded his butchery of the language and his corny jokes.

Next, he served as a colonel in the state militia. Then in 1821 and 1823 he was elected to the state legislature. There he began to run afoul of U.S. Senator Andrew Jackson, who expected that everyone in his home state would think as he did. Davy let his constituency know that he opposed Jackson's Indian Bill and earned Jackson's eternal enmity.

The Jackson political machine blocked his third term for the state legislature. Ironically, his defeat became a catapult into national prominence as an anti-Jackson man. Members of John Quincy Adams's party sponsored him. The United States watched with interest as two war heroes from Tennessee faced off.

In 1824 Crockett won a seat in the House of Representatives while Jackson lost the presidency to John Quincy Adams. Crockett won again in 1826. For four years he had a wonderful time. Standing well over six feet tall, in a buckskin shirt and leggings topped off by a coonskin cap, he cut a memorable comic figure. Washington laughed. The papers quoted his homespun wit. His promise was that he would vote for anything that was good for the union, even if someone in his own home state might be discomfitted by it.

Evidently, enough were. He lost to Jackson's man in 1828 when the Jackson political machine swept President John Quincy Adams and most of the Congress from office. To the horror of everyone in the town, Jackson proceeded to institute the "spoils system." Out with the old; in with the new. The whole Washingtonian bureaucracy was out of a job.

Though Crockett regained his seat in 1830, he found politics had lost its charm. He was a rough and tumble backwoodsman. He believed in a stand-up fight. On his fourth run for Congress, he had lost to a mudslinging machine. Disillusioned and angry, he decided he had had enough.

No one knows whether Davy Crockett came to Texas to answer Stephen F. Austin's call to arms. In a letter to his brother-in-law written October 31, 1835, he speaks of starting for Texas the next day, but nothing about the plea that Austin was already issuing. He writes that he planned "to explore Texas well."

The next letter to his son and daughter was mailed from Nacogdoches January 9, 1836. He planned to send for them and his wife later. He had heard much land was available for twelve and a half cents an acre. Back in the United States land purchased from the public domain cost $1.25. Though he could have seen little of Texas, he speaks of it as "the garden spot of the world...good land, plenty of timber, good mill streams, good range,...game a plenty."

Whether he had heard Austin's call or not, he and his Tennessee riflemen, numbering about a dozen, enrolled as volunteers for six months. The citizens of Nacogdoches had heard of him. They welcomed him as if he were a visiting dignitary. Men clapped him on the back and shook his hand. Women invited him to dinner.

They took the oath of allegiance to the provisional government of Texas, as well as any future republican government that might be declared at the end of this revolution. Actually, Davy was excited about the prospect of fighting in a revolution. He had been born too late for the first one.

They planned to set out for the Rio Grande. He wrote to his children, "I had rather be in my present situation than to be elected to a seat in Congress for life. I am in great hopes of making a fortune for myself and family..."

He went on to say that he had little doubt that he would be elected a member of whatever committee was formed to write the constitution when the time came. No one can doubt that he planned to make his fortune in Texas.

The American Revolution had made George Washington president. The War of 1812 had done the same for Crockett's hated rival Andrew Jackson. Crockett was no fool though he acted the court jester. He was only fifty years old. Jackson was sixty-one when he took the oath of office.

Did David Crockett see the prairies of Texas as the broad path he would take to the White House? No matter.

On February 9 he arrived at the Alamo.

He was immediately offered the rank of colonel since he had held that title in the Tennessee militia. He declined, saying he would function well as a private. "Here I am, Colonel," he said to Travis. "Assign me to some place, and I and my 'Tennessee boys' will defend it all right."

Some of them noted that he looked older than they expected. All that vitality, all that legend should be attributed to a much younger man. They quickly forgot about that when they had a chance to know his magnetic personality. Through the middle of February in Bexar, he kept everyone amused telling tall tales and jokes. On the day of George Washington's birthday, he held the Texans spellbound with his folksy southern oratory honoring the first president. All through the night of February 22, he was the life of the *fandango*, pulling out his fiddle to scratch out a tune, dancing a jig, carrying on outrageously as everyone laughed and applauded. The corn whisky and Mexican *mescal* flowed freely. What a night they all had!

The next morning the tolling of the bell in the San Fernando Church tower awakened them to a painful reality. Within four hours Santa Anna's glittering army spread across the horizon.

The Firebrand

William Barret Travis

One of the fiercest members of the War Party was the hot-headed lawyer William Barret Travis. Many thought he was a fool. Stephen F. Austin was frankly afraid for Travis to have a position of importance in the army or the government. He was too quick to act. His impulsiveness could lead to disaster for the citizens of Texas.

The sons of South Carolina had a reputation for being hot-headed. One of its favorite sons Senator and later Vice-President John C. Calhoun had long borne the name of War Hawk. Buck Travis seemed destined to follow in his footsteps.

He was born near Red Banks, Edgefield County, South Carolina, on August 9, 1809. One of his friends was James Butler Bonham, who either came with him or followed him to Texas. When Travis was nine, the family moved to Alabama where he attended the school founded by his uncle. It was staunchly Baptist as was the whole Travis family. Later he taught school, not an uncommon occupation for a young man who was reading for the law.

He was undoubtedly handsome, though no contemporary pictures exist of him. The likeness in this book is taken from heroic portraits done of him years after his death. Supposedly the artist consulted with people who knew him, but the accuracy of the portrayal is doubtful.

He was well-spoken with a soft Southern drawl that belied his excitable personality. He stood over six feet tall. Like Bowie he had red hair, a more truthful barometer of his temperament. Also like Bowie he had the gray-blue eyes of a killer. While neither eye nor hair color is an indicator of the man, in Travis's case by coincidence both had hit the mark. In him all elements combined together to make a man of heroic mold who flung himself at everything he did with disquieting passion.

He read for the law with Judge James Dellett at Claiborne, Alabama, took his exam, was admitted to the bar, and began practice before his twentieth birthday. On October 20, 1828, he married Rosanna Cato, who had been one of his pupils. The daughter of a prosperous farming family, she was sixteen years old, not an uncommon age for a girl to be married in those days. Their son Charles Edward Travis was born in August of the following year, the appropriate time for a first birth to occur given the presumed ardor of the bride and groom and the absence of birth control devices of any kind.

Despite these favorable circumstances, the marriage was unhappy. Whether the two were simply incompatible, or whether another person came between them is unknown.

A persistent rumor has followed Travis through many historical and biographical works. The firebrand lawyer came to believe Rosanna had taken a lover whom he then shot. Under questioning Travis is supposed to have confessed his deed to Judge James Dellett. The judge then supposedly gave him three choices. He could keep his mouth shut. He could confess to the world, bring scandal to his wife and her family, and take his chances in court. Or he could go to Texas.

What is known and documented is that by the spring of 1831, Travis was deeply in debt. A recent scrutiny of Judge Dellett's papers has revealed notes that he had no choice but to prosecute his former pupil if Travis had stayed in Alabama. The result would have been disgrace and a sentence to a debtor's prison.

While the papers are persuasive in and of themselves, they may not tell the entire story. If Travis did kill the man who had dishonored his wife, in all likelihood his friend and mentor Dellett would have done much to protect him. The judge knew his papers would be open to scrutiny at some time after his death. How much safer to include in his records the

comparatively forgivable charge of indebtedness, than to name Travis a murderer.

We shall never know. What we know is Travis left, mounted his horse, and swam it across the Alabama River leaving behind his pregnant wife and his two-year-old son whom he loved above all things. He chose Texas—and glory.

He hung out his shingle in Anahuac. In letters to Rosanna, he promised to send for her and Charles. He kept a diary that has come to us so we know much of his thoughts during his years in Texas. Though his sense of justice was strong—as will be shown—his Baptist conscience seemed remarkably quiet in matters of personal behavior.

Shortly after Travis's arrival, a new customs collector established a post at Anahuac. Captain Juan Bradburn, a renegade Kentuckian whom the rest of the town considered a traitor, arrived with 150 men to give teeth to his orders to collect the taxes the Texans had so far refused to pay.

First, Travis argued with the captain. Then he insulted him. When he did not respond, Travis and a co-conspirator named Patrick Jack manufactured false messages about plots and revolts. These they sent to Bradburn, hoping to goad him into a foolish response.

His response was not what they had hoped for. He declared five leagues of the Texas coast in both directions under martial law and arrested Travis and Jack. He held them for fifty days without trial.

Rebellion blossomed. William Jack, Patrick's brother, rode to San Felipe de Austin only to find that the Great Empresario was in Saltillo, Coahuila. Unable to get the ear of Stephen F. Austin, Jack walked the streets telling anyone who would listen that Bradburn must go.

Insurrection followed as disgruntled men assembled all over the area. While the captain at Anahuac was much hated (What tax collector is loved?), another group focused their anger on Bradburn—men who had come to Texas after the Decree of 1830 and failed to get land. They made a potent army. The actual war was postponed when Colonel Don Jose de las Piedras arrived from Nacogdoches. Instead of fighting, he negotiated with the dissidents and released Travis and Jack.

Bradburn resigned.

Travis moved his law practice from Anahuac to San Felipe de Austin where he could be a part of the great doings he was sure would soon be happening in Texas.

He kept a commonplace book in which he wrote his thoughts. People who love to write find the book helps them to organize and make sense out of their lives as well as plan for the future. The love and practice of writing stood him in good stead in the Alamo. The world is a richer place for what William Barret Travis wrote in those thirteen immortal days.

He also kept a diary in which he recorded his daily activities, many of which do not bear repeating. Though separated from his wife, he did not let his Baptist conscience get in his way. For example, on March 21, 1834, he wrote that he had spent a pleasant day—in *"la sociedad de mi inamorata."* On other days he listed going out to buy whiskey.

He kept a list of the books he read, perhaps developing literary aspirations. He read widely from the king of romantic novelists Sir Walter Scott. He read straight history from Herodotus to Napoleon. His knowledge of liberal arts probably surpassed any man in Texas at that time.

Meanwhile, his marriage deteriorated. His letters to his wife and hers to him evidently grew more hostile. Rosanna wanted him to come home. He wanted her to send him his son along with a divorce. He loved children. He was always buying candy for those in town. He even tried to buy Sunday School literature for them, only to discover San Felipe de Austin had no Bible to buy.

He met and began to keep company with Rebecca Cummins, a farmer's daughter who went swimming with him, spent the night with him on many occasions, and knew all about his wife and his efforts to divorce her.

In the fall of 1835, Rosanna brought the two children to Texas to see their father. She had hoped for a reconciliation, but he met her in the company of Rebecca Cummins. Embarrassed and distressed, she made no effort to discuss anything.

He wrote her a letter that allowed her to obtain a divorce when she returned to Alabama. Then she left, taking her daughter with her. The arrangement must have been traumatic for everyone. Charles Edward Travis, now six, remained behind with his father although the boy could have had no memory of him. He had only a short time with his father before Travis entered Texas politics. He boarded the boy with a friend, David Ayres. Travis visited him on his way to Bexar in February.

Rosanna obtained her divorce and married again only two weeks before the Alamo attack. When news came that Travis had been killed, Charles Edward was sent back to his mother and stepfather where he lived with the newly married couple in New Orleans. Travis's son became a lawyer, and in 1848 he returned to Texas where he later became a captain in the Texas Rangers.

Travis came to command the Alamo under orders from Smith, whose recruiting officer he had been at San Felipe de Austin. Having been designated a lieutenant colonel in Smith's nonexistent army, Travis presumed he was to command at the Alamo.

Bowie had arrived ahead of him and assumed command. It placed Travis in a very uncomfortable position. Bowie, whose authority came from General Sam Houston, knew the Mexicans in the town while Travis did not. Bowie spoke their language fluently while Travis had only a smattering of it and stood by looking ignorant while they discussed serious matters. When Travis tried to issue an order, everyone looked sideways to Bowie waiting for the nod of approval.

Neither of these proud men had any intention of giving an inch. How would the history of the Alamo, indeed of Texas, have been different if only one had been there? The stand-off between two proud men would not have occurred. Bowie knew the conditions of the countryside. He knew Santa Anna could and would march overland in winter. He had intelligence that Santa Anna was only eight miles away.

Perhaps Bowie was already having doubts about his original decision. The Alamo compound was built and expanded in the eighteenth century around the original mission to protect the people of the town from short-lived Indian attacks. The garrison was supposed to ride out and drive the marauders off. Then everybody would go home.

It was not meant to be defended against a long siege. Moreover, Bowie had made no effort to supply the place. No food or medical supplies had been stocked. Perhaps in the back of his mind was the idea that all the ammunition and cannon in the fort could be used to blow it up rather than let it fall in Santa Anna's hands.

When Travis rode into Bexar he was accompanied by approximately three dozen men, including his friend James Butler Bonham. Travis was ten years younger than Bowie and a hothead willing and eager to assert his authority. He was angry at finding the older man there and ignored Bowie's advice. By his very bearing he denigrated Bowie's importance, his status, his reputation as a fighter. So they remained toe to toe, the firebrand lawyer and the hellbound widower who had no real reason to live. Together they entered the presidio.

Probably as they looked around them, they were not slow to realize that the place was really not the place for any of them. It was not built to defend.

Today reports of the dimensions of the place are conflicting. So much of it was destroyed. Contradictions came from Mexican and Texan sources, and for many years no one tried to make drawings of it or reconstruct it. The part that remains today—that is, the famous chapel—occupied only a corner of the entire compound. At the time it was a ruin. Its roof had caved in. Debris filled its apse and nave. But its walls were four feet thick and twenty-two feet high. It sat behind a four-foot-high inner wall and court. A man could make his last stand there, rest a rifle on that wall, and fire at an enemy charging toward him.

Not so the rest of the presidio. The outer walls were built in a rectangle that covered two or three acres depending on which description one reads. The chapel and the two-story mission convent beside it occupied one of the narrow sides.

The entire inner court was approximately one hundred fifty-four yards long by fifty-four yards wide. Three sides were made up of a long stone wall about three feet thick. It stood between nine and twelve feet high with small adobe rooms, facing into the court. There were few windows and no defensive rifle slots or any other means to fire through those walls. The cannon could be placed on platforms around the walls, but their thickness kept defenders from kneeling or crouching behind them to shoot except at the beginning of a charge. Too soon, the attackers would run in under the guns. When they did, the only way the defenders could continue to fire at them was to stand on top of the wall and shoot down. Then their entire bodies were exposed to sharpshooters back in the lines.

The main entrance onto the court was a ten-foot-wide porte cochere, through a stockade. The porte cochere divided the stockade with the soldiers' quarters on one side and the fort prison on the other. A stockade gate—eight feet wide—made another entrance at the point where the south wall turned inward to become a well-barricaded stockade fence.

Travis probably missed much of the indefensible qualities of the place. He was too new at the business of fighting, for all his firebrand reputation. Bowie did not try to offer any advice. It would not have been welcomed, and besides he had already taken the stand that the Alamo must be saved. It was the key to Anglo-American Texas. He would not back down in front of the young upstart.

On the night of Washington's birthday *fandango*, Bowie had come to Travis with disturbing correspondence. Travis refused to listen or read the written message. He turned his shoulder because he was dancing "with the most beautiful lady in Bexar." Even in a position of command, Travis would be interested in the ladies.

Bowie posted a lookout on the bell tower of San Fernando Church. The next morning when the sun was well up, the man began to toll the bell. Bright and glittering as a parade, Santa Anna's cavalry came over the horizon.

On the afternoon of the twenty-third, Travis ordered his defiant troop of 150 men into the Alamo and closed its gates behind them. Like Jim Bowie before him, he had made his decision. He would rather die than abandon this town he considered to be the key to Texas.

Santa Anna marched into Bexar unopposed.

Victory or Death

The withdrawal into the Alamo was not made in an orderly fashion. Near panic set in as the men scrambled from the places they had spent the night, most of them shaking off the effects of the *fandango*. Some came half-dressed. The first order sent them scurrying in all directions to find food. No one had thought to stock the fort with victuals.

They broke into deserted houses around the town and appropriated eighty to ninety bushels of corn by Travis's own estimate. At the same time they rounded up twenty or thirty head of cattle and drove them inside.

While Travis was fairly certain the siege would be lifted in three or four days, he did not want anyone hungry. Singly and in groups, they made their way into the Alamo until 150 were inside. Then Travis ordered the gates closed.

The waiting began.

Its proper name was San Antonio de Valero, named in part for the eighteenth-century Spanish viceroy who had been so fearful of St. Denis's encroachment into the territory. This same viceroy had commanded that it be built as part of a presidio to keep the immigration of such Frenchmen from occurring.

People referred to it then as the Alamo. They called it the same thing when the tatterdemalion troop of Texans took refuge in it. Captain Almaron Dickinson, one of the artillerymen, brought his twenty-two-year-old wife, Susannah, and their fifteen-month-old daughter into it. On the afternoon of the twenty-third he had come galloping down the street. Before she could protest or even think, he took the baby in one arm and pulled her up behind him. By going with him, she became the only Anglo-American woman in the Alamo. It was the most dangerous place in the state, but he had left her no choice.

All day Santa Anna's glittering army continued to arrive. The dragoons in their red short coats and bright blue trousers were the most elegant sight the Texans had ever seen. Their helmets were black decorated with horsehair plumes. The strong sunlight reflected off their lances, pennons, sabres, carbines, and holster pistols.

Their leader General Andrade was garbed in an indigo blue jacket with gold epaulets and red frogging. His indigo blue trousers also had red slashing. A fearsome sight, he carried his sabre upright as he rode toward the Alamo. The sunlight burned off its curved blade as well as the silver guards on his stirrups. The Texans passed their spyglasses back and forth among them, too amazed to do more than stare at a vision of European royal opulence they had never even imagined.

Then Santa Anna's cannons moved into position and began to fire. All afternoon and all night on February 23, the cannonade continued. The dictator's strategy was sound. Many defenders would have been so demoralized by continuous noise and explosions that they would have surrendered without a fight. Perhaps it might even have worked had he not raised a red flag from the tower of San Fernando Church.

The red flag meant what it always meant—NO QUARTER.

Travis wanted to answer the flag with a shot from an eighteen-pounder, but Bowie sent a messenger before the cannon could be fired. Older and infinitely wiser, he was not foolish enough to think they had a chance against an army that had been arriving for twenty-four hours and still kept coming. What were the terms of surrender?

The answer came back: Unconditional surrender.

Jim Bowie shook his head. He knew perhaps better than anyone else. Bexar was going to be Zacatecas all over again.

In utter defiance of both Santa Anna and Jim Bowie, Travis ordered the eighteen-pounder fired and ran up a flag. No one is sure exactly where the flag flew, but a good guess would have been the chapel. It was the tallest building and it sat on the southeast corner closest to the arriving army.

The sight of it must have made Santa Anna furious. It was his own flag, the red, white, and green flag of Mexico, with one addition calculated to make the Napoleon of West furious. It stood straight out from the pole on the harsh wind of a blue norther. On its white background were large black numbers clearly legible—"1824."

On the morning of February 24 the cannons were being rolled into place on top of the ramparts and general strengthening of the Alamo's fortifications was taking place on every side. Sometime during this activity, Jim Bowie—the original commander, Sam Houston's man, the hellbound spirit who had refused to destroy the presidio and retreat—resigned his commission.

A tale told for many years was that he was taking an active part in shoring up the defenses when he was grievously injured in a fall. The details of the fall, while well documented, are now believed to have been merely a tale.

The truth is probably much simpler. Bowie had been ill for years, perhaps stemming from the time when he was stabbed in the chest during the duel on the sandbar. A punctured lung with a possible infection of longstanding could quickly have become pneumonia. He was forty-one and for the past three years had had little reason to take care of himself. In the bitter cold of the Texas February, perhaps his iron will could no longer command his weakened body. Whatever the cause, he suddenly grew markedly worse.

Like the hero he was, he did not ask to be taken outside the walls. With his Mexican citizenship, Santa Anna might have allowed Bowie to be carried to the Veramendi palace where he could die in peace. Instead, he took to his bed inside the Alamo, where he suffered through the next seven days. By one account he was already dead when the walls were breached. A more likely tale is that Davy Crockett brought him a brace of loaded pistols, which he kept at hand. The hellbound spirit with the killer eyes would have scorned to die in bed.

While the fortifications were being readied, Travis was writing a letter, the first of many pleas for reinforcements. It shows the tenor of the man as nothing else could. It has been called the "sublimest document in American history."

To the People of Texas and All Americans in the world
—Fellow Citizens and Compatriots: I am besieged . . . I
have sustained a continual Bombardment and cannonade for 24 hours and have not lost a man. The
enemy has demanded a surrender at discretion, otherwise, the garrison are to be put to the sword, if the
fort is taken. I have answered the demand with a cannon shot, and our flag still waves probably from the
walls. I shall never surrender or retreat. Then, I call
upon you in the name of Liberty, of patriotism, and
every thing dear to the American character, to come to
our aid with all dispatch. The enemy is receiving reinforcements daily and will no doubt increase to three
or four thousand in four or five days. If this call is
neglected, I am determined to sustain myself as long
as possible and die like a soldier who never forgets
what is due his own honor and that of his country.
VICTORY OR DEATH.

> William Barret Travis
> Lt. Col. Comdt.

P. S.
The Lord is on our side. When the enemy appeared in
sight we had not three bushels of corn. We have since
found in deserted houses 80 to 90 bushels and got
into the walls 20 or 30 heads of Beeves.

> Travis

The message was entrusted to Captain Albert Martin, who
picked the fastest horse inside the Alamo for his mount. Under
cover of darkness he dashed out along the water ditch and safely
made his way onto the road to his hometown, Gonzales, where
the revolution had actually begun. Once there he passed the letter on to another courier to carry it to Governor Henry Smith,
who governed nothing and commanded no one. To give Smith a
small measure of credit, he tried to raise some reinforcements
but failed.

The night of February 25, Santa Anna threw everything he had at the Alamo—grenades, grapeshot, canister. The command now was Travis's. Travis had only himself to blame for all the mistakes, and he was the only one who could rectify them. As he watched sleepless, he damned himself for overlooking the obvious. The houses along the river, in some cases hardly more than *jacales* of sticks and brush, would provide cover for the soldiers. They were already using them for cover for the cannon.

Travis sent two young men who could run fast to set them afire. Every man in the Alamo watched from the walls. When the fires started, the Texans cheered. When the young men dashed back unscathed, morale strengthened.

Travis wrote a letter to Houston in which he praised their deed and begged for reinforcements. "Do hasten aid on to me as rapidly as possible, from the superior number of the enemy, it will be impossible for us to keep them out much longer. If they overpower us, we fall a sacrifice at the shrine of our country, and we hope posterity and our country will do our memory justice. Give me help, oh my Country!"

He really expected help to come within a day or two. He closed again with the words that had become his mantra, "Victory or Death!"

Albert Martin managed to raise thirty-two men at Gonzales. Under cover of darkness on the fourth day of the siege, they sneaked through the Mexican lines to join their comrades. Their arrival kept spirits high. They were cheered, even though their number was disappointingly small. Surely, Fannin could not be far behind. But they were the only reinforcements to come. They set the final number of defenders at 182.

The Mexican army besieging the Alamo outnumbered the defenders by over three to one, with more reinforcements en route from the south.

Santa Anna had already ratified his Texas policy with his rubberstamp congress in Mexico City. Every colonist who had taken part in the rebellion was to be executed or exiled. The Texans would pay for all the cost of the campaign by giving up their cleared and improved lands, which in turn would be allotted to the soldiers who had won the glorious victory.

It was a splendid plan. It cost neither dictator nor government a peso. After the state was cleansed, no Norte Americano would ever be permitted to enter Texas again. Soldiers loyal to Santa Anna would settle Mexico's northernmost state. All desired results would be accomplished.

On the fifth day of the siege, every Texan's eye was trained on the distant horizon to the east and north. In every mind's eye was the sight of Sam Houston riding at the head of an army just over the horizon and James Fannin coming from Goliad with all his men and more cannon.

Thoroughly discouraged now, Travis called his friend James Butler Bonham to his side. He needed Bonham, whom he had known since childhood. Bonham was surely his touchstone, his brother in all but blood. In fact, they were the same height and looked something alike, although Bonham's hair was black. Some part of Travis must have known that the battle could begin any day, and they would not last for more than a few hours, if that long. He must have reminded himself that Bonham would not be here if not for him. Perhaps he sent his friend away to spare his life.

Bonham was to impress two things upon Fannin. The first was that the enemy was receiving reinforcements daily, while the Texans had received none. The second, and perhaps more important, was that Fannin and the men from Goliad could still get through the gates. For five days men had been going in and out of the Alamo bringing in supplies. As yet, no one had been killed.

Bonham promised he would return with the word—with Fannin right behind him.

Another blue norther dropped the temperature and made life miserable for the thousands of Mexicans camped out on the bare plain and the hundred or so Texans in the Alamo, who did not dare burn wood to keep warm for fear they might need it later.

Inside the infirmary Bowie got steadily worse. Joe, Travis's servant, reported later that the sick man was burning with fever and unable to lift his head from the pillow. He coughed every few minutes and the pain racked his ribs. Crockett came to visit with him and left two pistols at his side.

Meanwhile, Travis had located Santa Anna's headquarters. He ordered two twelve-pounders to fire at the place. The first missed the building, but the second came right in. A near miss that had it found its target would have changed everything, especially Mexico herself. Unfortunately, Santa Anna was not there at the time.

On March 2 a new convention of Texas delegates met at Washington-on-the-Brazos, 150 miles northeast of Bexar. They ignored Governor Smith and his council and came to a quick conclusion that they must declare themselves an independent state. They voted unanimously to do so. The job of writing the document was given to George Childress, who pulled out his copy of Thomas Jefferson's work of sixty years before. Changing words and details to fit the time and place, he penned the Texas Declaration of Independence. At the bottom, according to tradition, he affixed a sort of seal using one of his cufflinks—a lone star.

The convention wanted to adjourn at that moment and go to the aid of the Alamo, but Sam Houston shouted them down. The Alamo was in its present straits because Texas had not made a government. They must use the time Travis, Bowie, and Crockett were buying them to make one. They stayed—and that night Houston got drunker than he ever had been before. Bonham returned with the message—Fannin was not coming. Travis's heart broke but not his courage. On March 3 John W. Smith, no relation to the governor of the council, crawled out through the Mexican lines at midnight. He carried Travis's last messages, one to his friend David Ayres, who was taking care of his son. "Take care of my little boy. . . . if the country should be lost and I perish, he will have nothing but the proud recollection that he is the son of a man who died for his country."

The second was to the government of Texas. He called for a declaration of independence so the men might understand what they were fighting for. He, of course, did not know—nor did any among them—that it had already been written. Travis's last bitter words were, "...my bones shall reproach my country for her neglect....My respects to all friends, confusion to all enemies."

In the words of Hamlet, "The rest is silence."

Whatever occurred inside during the next two days is legend. Stories of a line in the sand, of Bowie asking that his cot be moved across it, of one man deserting are wonderful stories, but not one of the noncombatants who survived the Alamo ever told them. Such doings if they actually happened are the doings of men. Women and children were not part of their heroism.

During that time, some or perhaps all could have slipped away. The lines were not tightly drawn, the circle around the fort was much too wide to be covered adequately by Santa Anna's troops, who posted only the usual guards. But no guards reported any activity. No shots were fired at fleeing figures.

Travis's men were probably sick from nervous as well as physical exhaustion. The constant shelling continued. No one could sleep.

On March 4 Santa Anna called a commanders' conference. They were divided. Some wanted to wait for the arrival of two twelve-pound siege guns. With these the walls could be breached completely. Cos warned against the fire from the Texans' rifles. He had seen it firsthand back in January. Colonel Almonte warned that the cost would be high.

Santa Anna did not want to wait.

Then on March 5 a small breach was battered in the Alamo east wall. The orders were issued that night. Everyone was ordered to his place at 4 A.M. Blankets were left behind. No one was to fall asleep.

The army arrayed against the Alamo was approximately two thousand men. Divided into columns of attack were three hundred fifty men led by General Cos, Duque leading four hundred men, Romero's four hundred, Morales's column of one hundred twenty-five, and Sesma's three hundred seventy mounted cavalry. Santa Anna held his Zapadores Battalion of four hundred men in reserve.

The best Mexico had to offer—seasoned veterans, smart, brave, armed with bayonets and flintlock muskets—had to charge across an open field carrying siege ladders, because the walls were to be assaulted from all sides. Hampered as they were, some only managed a few strides before they were killed. Their return fire was fruitless because their flintlock muskets were inaccurate except at very close range.

Still, no military strategist of the day could have faulted the charge, except the British. The Americans with their tradition of marksmanship learned to shoot when they were boys of six of seven. If a boy missed, his family usually went hungry. At New Orleans the Redcoats had faced those boys grown to manhood taking cover behind breastworks of cotton bales. In typically understated fashion, the British reported their losses as "unacceptable."

The horror of the Alamo is that possibly if Fannin had come, if they had had four or five hundred reinforcements, they really could have won.

Santa Anna's regimental bands blared "El Deguello," a Moorish tune from Spain. Its title means "The Throat-slashing." The trumpets called the troops to their feet on all four sides of the Alamo.

Men on both sides heard Travis yell one coherent order. "The Mexicans are upon us—give 'em Hell!"

The first ranks went down as if a scythe had cut them off at the knees. The second went down as well. Officers screamed and fell where they stood.

The first assault fell back and died without reaching the walls. The Texans sent up a ragged cheer.

As though their cheer were a signal, the second assault came. There were fewer Texans to meet it this time and less ammunition. Ladders went up the walls. They were pushed back, but to do so the Texans had to stand on the walls and fire down into the faces coming for them.

At this point most of the Mexican musketry was missing its targets. Some of it even cleared the walls and hit Mexicans charging from the opposite sides. Unfortunately, too many found their mark. Texan dead lay beneath the walls on both sides.

A new wave of Mexican officers had spotted the weak points where the walls were the least defended. On the north wall the ladders went up and stayed up. The soldiers surged into the compound. The first wave fell on top of the walls, but on they came like water through a breached dike.

Now the defenders no longer fought to win. Winning was impossible. They had no thought but kill—charge into the ranks of the Mexican soldiery and destroy as many as possible. The Mexicans had never seen such savagery before. Most of the Texans were taller, with longer arms and broader shoulders. They used their empty rifles like clubs, swinging them with crushing force until the oaken stocks shattered. They drew their tomahawks and knives to chop and slash. They used their fists and boots and heads to smash and kick and butt.

A killing frenzy gripped both sides. For the Texans, sheer numbers destroyed them where they stood. Then their dead bodies were mutilated by hundreds of wounds. Stories were told of unusual heroism, of the death throes of Bowie, Travis, and Crockett, but they are after all stories. No one knows the truth because everyone was killed or killing. As each man tore into the Alamo, he stabbed and slashed at the bodies until the Texan dead were unrecognizable. At nine o'clock, March 6, 1836, five hours after the assault had begun, the Alamo had fallen.

Susannah Dickinson, the twenty-two-year-old widow, was certain of only one thing. She saw Bowie's body tossed aloft on a dozen bayonets. Santa Anna sent for her. As she carried her baby out of the chapel, a bullet struck her right leg. She had to be helped to Santa Anna's quarters.

While she sipped coffee and someone dressed her wound, Santa Anna composed a letter to the people of Texas. Susannah Dickinson was to be his messenger. With cruel purpose he put her on a horse accompanied by a Negro and set her out on the northeast road. A moving representation of what awaited any family man who opposed the General-in-Chief of the Army of Operations of the Mexican Republic, she was supposed to strike terror into Texas hearts. She was found by Houston's invaluable scouts Deaf Smith, Henry Karnes, and R. E. Handy.

The words of the enemy tell the whole story. Mexican General Vincent Filisola: "On our opinion the blood of our soldiers as well as that of the enemy was shed in vain, for the mere gratification of the inconsiderate, puerile and guilty vanity of reconquering Bexar by force of arms, and through a bloody contest... The massacres of the Alamo convinced the rebels that no peaceable settlement could be expected, and that they must conquer, or die, or abandon the fruits of ten years of sweat and labor, together with their fondest hopes for the future."

Among the Mexicans, the ghosts of Bowie, Crockett, Bonham, Dickinson, and Travis and all the rest spawned the legend of the "diablos Tejanos," the Texan devils who can slay and wound six hundred. A third of Santa Anna's assault force was gone—forever.

As the survivors piled up the bodies of their friends and comrades, every soldier must have thought, what if the Texas numbers had been closer to six hundred instead of two hundred. Every soldier must have dreaded vengeance.

With the example of the Alamo before them, no Texans could surrender. The courage of the Alamo created the necessity for courage in the hearts of every man and boy who left the Runaway Scrape and rallied with Sam Houston on the plain of San Jacinto. Their courage was the standard by which all Texans measure themselves.

So it has been—and so it will be.

The Captain

John Coffee Hays

"Me and Red Wing not afraid to go to hell together," commented Chief Flacco of the Lipan Apaches, who was a scout for the Texas Rangers in the days of the Republic. Then he arrived at his point of comparison. "Captain Jack heap brave; not afraid to go to hell by himself."

In the pantheon of Texas heroes, John Coffee Hays stands on one of the tallest peaks. He literally became a legend in his own time, "a gentleman of purest character." He was like no other, incredibly brave without seeming to be so. Indeed, he was one of those few men who was conscious of neither fear nor courage. Therefore, he was free to act in the way that seemed the most intelligent to him. His actions assumed mythic proportions and his fame spread through no efforts of his own. From the Mississippi to the Pacific, generals, governors, and at least one president of the United States spoke his name in admiring tones.

So impressive was he that for almost the whole of the nineteenth century, every Texas Ranger wanted to be "like Jack Hays."

A man with outstanding qualities, three stand out above all the rest. First, he was no talker—the archetype for the strong, silent man of the West, who rode into town, did the job he was expected to do, and rode out again determined to avoid any embarrassing demonstrations of gratitude or praise. Second, he was a born fighter who did not seem to be one even when riding through some of the wildest country that God ever created.

Perhaps he regarded himself as something quite different—as a man who had a dirty job to do—and did it because it *was* his job. Third, he was a superb psychologist who instinctively acted and spoke in such a manner that both friend and foe acted as he wanted them to act.

He rode into the new Republic of Texas late in 1836, just one of the crowd of people from the United States coming for the cheap land, seeking the opportunities despite the dangers that accompanied it. He was twenty-one years of age with no immediate family and no prospects. Within two years President Mirabeau B. Lamar had appointed him captain of the Rangers based at San Antonio. Evidently, he was the type of man who drew attention almost in spite of himself.

The fact that he did so is a little surprising. No six-footer like the heroes of the Alamo and San Jacinto, he stood only about five foot eight or nine. He never weighed more than one hundred fifty pounds. On short campaign rations, his lean body would become little more than skin, bone, and muscle. He had reddish-brown hair and unprepossessing hazel eyes. John Salmon Ford, who was his contemporary, remarked that a compliment would make Hays blush.

He was born January 28, 1817, in Little Cedar Lick in Wilson County, Tennessee. Not far away stood the boyhood home of Sam Houston. Rachel Jackson was his mother's aunt. Future President Andrew Jackson bought the Hermitage from Hays's grandfather, who had served with him in the Indian wars. Young Hays was named John Coffee for one of Jackson's trusted officers.

His childhood would be the envy of any boy alive today. From his parents' farm he was allowed to roam freely through the forests and fields of Tennessee. He mastered riding and shooting and had become a credible athlete before his idyll ended. When he was sixteen, both parents died of yellow fever.

The family farm was sold and he went to live on his uncle's plantation in Mississippi. His uncle evidently took little interest in his charge. Young Hays took a job as a land surveyor. He saved his money until he had enough to study for a year at Davidson's

Academy in Nashville. Ambitious and extremely bright, he wanted to go from there to West Point, but his uncle refused to send him.

At nineteen, he realized that he would have to make his own opportunities. He left the plantation for New Orleans where he and others from his state joined with volunteers from Kentucky,

Mississippi, and Louisiana in answer to Stephen F. Austin's call for help.

The group arrived too late for the battle of San Jacinto. Still, he enlisted for a six-month stint as a private in the new army of the Republic of Texas. He was assigned to a reconnaissance patrol, whose first major assignment was to bury the remains of Fannin's 352 men shot down at Goliad. What he thought of the massacre is not known. Certainly, no man—especially a young and impressionable one—could perform such a duty and remain unscathed.

Anglo-Texans as a group were appalled by the brutality of Santa Anna's orders to shoot down unarmed men who—while they had surrendered unconditionally—at least did so under the impression that they would be accorded the honors of war. According to the statements of survivors and some reports from the Mexican army, General Don Jose Urrea promised that he would intercede. Urrea did write *El Presidente*, but the reply was the death sentence.

Hays, above all, would not have understood such cruelty. Modeling himself after Jackson and Houston, two of the most honorable warriors the United States had yet produced, he could only have been appalled. His attitudes toward Mexicans and later Indians could not help but be affected by what he saw firsthand.

Furloughed after six months, he left the army. In February 1840 he surveyed the boundaries of Travis County where Austin, the new capital of Texas, was then located. Texas President Mirabeau B. Lamar had moved it despite Sam Houston's fierce objections. The "Raven" fought hard to keep the government in the town named for him close to the scene of his greatest victory.

Thereafter Hays is supposed to have joined a company of rangers begun by Erastus (Deaf) Smith and Henry W. Karnes. These two were Houston's most valuable scouts. They also had tales to tell of Mexican brutality. They were the ones who came across Mrs. Susannah Dickinson and her baby Angelina when Santa Anna had set her and a black slave stumbling out on the road from the Alamo. Hays could not have learned from two more excellent teachers. The scouts were exceptional fighters as well as canny frontiersmen. From them he would have learned how to fight and, more important, how to survive.

The Republic of Texas had to fight on two sides if it was to survive. All of Mexico hated the tall, blonde, uncivilized barbarians whom they called *los diablos Tejanos*. The Mexican people were humiliated by their own defeat by a vastly inferior force. The *criollos* among them were embarrassed by their leader Santa Anna and their inability to create a workable democratic government for themselves while they watched the United States of America grow and prosper. Mexico growled and clawed at Texas's southern border.

On the west was *Comancheria*, the land of implacable people, fierce warriors whose pillage-rape-and-burn raids harassed the colonists and threatened everything they tried to build. The Comanches prowled along the rim of the Cap Rock, armed with the best weapons they could make, trade for, and steal. Their lightning invasions kept every family in constant fear.

The settlers had a right to be afraid. Texas could not afford a standing army. Her farmers and ranchers lived too far apart to gather into effective militias. The government felt obligated to provide some form of protection. How to do so was the question. With virtually no money at its disposal, it permitted the citizens to protect themselves by organizing "ranging companies" such as those begun in the days of Austin's colony.

The term Ranger actually came from the United States where it referred to Indian fighters. They were the kind of men who ranged widely, seeking out and carrying the war to the enemy. To engage the Comanches, they faced foes twice as fierce as even the Mohawk or Huron dared to be.

A part of the problem arose from the fact that Americans were—by and large—not horsemen. Unlike the Spaniards, who considered the horse part of their equipment, the English colonists coming to America generally brought dairy cattle, pigs, and fowl with them. A horse was impractical because it gave neither milk nor eggs and could not be eaten. Moreover, a cow could pull a plow just about as well.

While the settlers did come to ride horseback as more and more of the plantation owners were able to import blooded stock, they were hardly cavalrymen. They were certainly no match for the Comanche warriors, universally acknowledged as some of the greatest riders in the world.

Their weapons also presented a disadvantage. Kentucky rifles fired a single shot and then required a new charge, during which time-consuming process—usually about a minute—the shooter was totally vulnerable. Furthermore, reloading was almost impossible to accomplish on horseback.

Texas needed men who could ride and shoot from horseback, men whose sole job was search and destroy. Their solution was the Texas Rangers. Therefore, from 1836 throughout the nineteenth century, the history of Texas, particularly, and the West as a whole was the story of these intrepid, resourceful men.

They were unique—a paramilitary force authorized by the government and supported by the state when it could scrape together some money. Texas never had sufficient funds to pay these men as they should have been paid or equip them as they should have been equipped.

The pay, a mere thirty dollars a month, came irregularly. The company commander, usually with the rank of captain, at first received seventy-five dollars a month. Within a month he was raised to $150 when it was reported that he usually furnished the ammunition for his men. They furnished their own guns and mounts—horses, mules, mustangs, whatever they could find. They had no thought of uniforms. No badge was issued for over half a century. With no quartermaster to furnish food, they were expected to shoot wild game and live off the land. Their tour was more or less permanent because the danger never ceased. They were hailed with thanksgiving when they first appeared to rescue citizens in danger. When they had disposed of the danger, the good citizens complained that the Rangers sometimes shot the livestock to feed themselves.

Nobody loves a policeman, except when he is desperately needed.

They had nothing but pride and their duty as they saw it. They were extremely adventurous, extremely brave, extremely young. They were all volunteers—Knights of the Lone Star—in a state that bred heroism as if it were a holy calling. The ghosts of the Alamo and the victims of Goliad imbued them. Though there were never more than a few hundred and as many as half their number might be killed in a single year, they became the most colorful, efficient, and deadly band of irregulars the world has ever seen. In the process they won everlasting fame. To this very day, when a Texas Ranger appears on the scene, people murmur and stare and stand back in awe.

The man who more than any other made them what they were was Jack Hays. In 1839 he had been spying with Henry Karnes in a company organized to uncover word of suspected Indian and Mexican invasions. Lamar was well pleased with Hays's work, and in 1840 he made Hays a captain of a company that was supposed to spy on enemies in San Antonio and farther south. He was twenty-three.

In August of 1840 his company's first engagement occurred at Plum Creek assisting several other companies. While he did not distinguish himself, the battle was deemed a victory for Texas.

The Rangers gathered to intercept a force of four hundred Comanche that had raided the small town of Linnville within thirty miles of the Gulf of Mexico. The measure of how fearless the Indians were and how ineffective the ordinary farmers and ranchers were against them is the distance they had boldly galloped across the state.

On August 11 about two hundred Rangers and citizen volunteers waited in ambush at Plum Creek. The Comanches were flushed with success and probably had been drinking part of the loot from John Linn's store. They had decked themselves in ridiculous fashions in garments looted from the store. They were driving two thousand stolen horses and mules. The scalps of twenty murdered Texans dangled from their belts. The Rangers opened fire and then charged. Their superior fire power and the element of surprise won the battle.

Courage, once it is proved, becomes the norm. The Alamo had taught the Ranger volunteers how to behave. In a sense everyone of them had signed on to continue the battle. They never disappointed the people of Texas. Hays himself undoubtedly slipped into the heroic mode of behavior without even realizing the change that was occurring in his character. The first time made the second time easier. He survived, and the next time survival was easier. He led others to win, and the next time winning was easier. When the enemies fled in defeat, the next time they fled more quickly.

Hays's first battle was only the beginning of a decade of service. At Canon de Ugalde, at Bandera Pass, and at Painted Rock, he fought the Comanches.

To recount all the battles would take a book devoted entirely to him. Yet to leave these early adventures without recounting the one that contributed the most to his legend would be a disservice to this history. The engagements listed above were all in the company of Rangers and other Texan volunteers. In one instance John Hays found himself alone. He was with a party of fifteen or twenty men surveying boundaries in Gillespie County near the town of Fredericksburg. In the early days Rangers had to hold other jobs to support themselves if they wanted more than a hand-to-mouth existence.

He was in the vicinity of Enchanted Rock, an escarpment of solid granite. It covers an entire section of land (640 acres) and rises four to five hundred feet above the Edwards Plateau that Texans usually refer to as the Hill Country. The rock's name comes from an Indian legend concerning a small band of fierce and clever warriors. They used the rock as a fort, successfully defending themselves against the hostile tribes that surrounded them. They were few in number and eventually they died or perhaps were overcome by superior numbers.

The ghosts of the warriors are said to hold the rock even to the present day. Thereafter, other Indians came there in defiance and practiced religious rites. Enchanted Rock has the dimensions to accommodate large groups of participants. It has a fairly flat top covering two or three acres with a few shallow depressions on its surface. The execution of prisoners as well as sacrifices to appease angry gods were said to have occurred there. People were thrown or pushed to their deaths from its height.

Hays was riding close to the rock when he was attacked. Whooping and yelling, the Indians pursued him. It is said they recognized him, or perhaps they were simply attacking any hated Texan they found alone and therefore easy prey. He made straight for the Rock, lashing his tiring horse, arrows and a few bullets flying around him. At its base he dismounted and scrambled up the scarp to the top.

The Indians pursued him, anxious for his scalp. He stationed himself in one of the depressions. When the first Indian's face popped over the edge of the rock, Hays reared up and aimed his rifle at him. Terrified, the Indian ducked back. For several minutes Hays played this bluff. Finally, as his tormentors were becoming more daring, he shot one. Not taking the time to load the rifle, he drew his precious Paterson Colt five-shot revolver. When two Indians popped up almost immediately, sure that he would be struggling frantically to load, he shot them both.

For several minutes nobody came near him. When the next one came, Hays had reloaded and was ready. The upshot of the encounter was that Hays held a hundred Indians off for an hour. When he was finally rescued by his surveying party, he still had a shot or two left. His cool behavior in the face of overwhelming odds with a terrible death waiting below, the psychological handling of the enemy, and the martialing of his very limited resources were the talk of Texas.

As his legend grew, he attracted men of legendary caliber: Ben McCulloch and his brother Henry, fellow Tennessean of unquestioned bravery, who became captains themselves. Samuel L. Walker, the man linked to the efficient Walker Colt, whose modifications he suggested to gunsmith Samuel Colt. Leander McNelly, who would sit down to eat among his own men as friendly as can be but who would have instantly shot any one of them who disobeyed a combat order. William A. "Bigfoot" Wallace, who "dipped deep" for life and came back from the failed Mier Expedition with a great hatred in his soul for any-thing Mexican. Peter Hansborough Bell, later elected governor of Texas.

A more dangerous situation for the infant republic was stir-ring south of the border where all was tragi-comedy. In 1836 Santa Anna had been released by President Andrew Jackson to make his way back to Mexico. In 1838 the loser at San Jacinto buckled on his long saber and galloped off to Veracruz to fight off the blockading French fleet. Santa Anna arrived to find things quiet and the ships standing offshore. In the midst of his nap, a French raiding party entered the town. On hearing the noise, he sprang to his feet and raced out through the streets in his underwear, brandishing his saber. By the time he found clothes and a horse, the French were rowing away. In subse-quent firing he was struck below the knee. He lost his leg, but became the "Hero of Veracruz." San Jacinto was forgotten. The ultimate result was that by 1841 Jack Hays and the Rangers had to fight the invading Mexican soldiers of General Woll and drive them back to the Rio Grande.

In March 1842 General Rafael Vasquez was ordered by the Mexican government to capture San Antonio. Marching quickly overland from the Rio Grande, he met little initial resistance so that he might indeed write in his dispatches that he had obeyed the orders. Within forty-eight hours Vasquez realized that his position was untenable. He would be surrounded by hostile, vengeful forces in a very short time. His supply line would be cut off. He marched back, with Hays and his Ranger company of about a hundred sniping at his troops every foot of the way.

One result of these invasions was that the Texas government came to realize the war with Mexico was not over. They needed more Rangers. Hays's one company was expanded to three whose job was to protect the southwest frontier. San Antonio was their official headquarters. The captains of each company were given extraordinary powers that many elected governors and even those of higher authority did not have. The scope of these powers was dictatorial but hardly unreasonable given the state of undeclared war that prevailed.

Twenty-five-year-old Jack Hays or any other Ranger captain could exchange prisoners with Mexico as if he were a diplomat. He could establish trade with Mexico as if he were a president. He could declare martial law if he deemed the situation desperate enough. He and his troops could ride into any town or county, demand that the officials step aside, and command the citizenry to carry out their orders. Hays could summarily execute felons without a trial or even a hearing. Many bandits, cattle rustlers, and Comancheros were shot down or hanged high at the scene of their capture. Much of the negative reputation that accompanies the legend comes from these last two powers.

People today tend to forget the times were desperate. Desperate times call for desperate men.

And desperate men need desperate weapons.

One final and decisive weapon won the Texas West. In February 1836 twenty-one-year-old Samuel Colt had taken out a patent on a revolving pistol. In 1838 in Paterson, New Jersey, he began the manufacture of his new weapon in sizes ranging from .22 to .50 caliber. The .34 caliber with a four-and-one-half-inch octagon barrel had a concealed trigger that dropped into place when the gun was cocked.

Almost immediately Colt was in despair. He could find no market for such a gun in the East. Civilians did not need it on the streets of Boston or New York. He tried to interest the military, but it was still committed to the rifle for infantry in the European way. They regarded their cavalry as a showy but inefficient part of the overall force and maintained them largely for the sake of tradition.

The Texas Rangers saw the significance of the Colt revolver all right. A pair of arms dealers from Texas happened along, snapped up every one Colt had made for a reputed twenty-eight dollars apiece, and took them back to Texas where they sold the weapons for two hundred dollars apiece. Every Ranger who could not afford the weapon tried to beg or borrow one. If all else failed, stealing remained an option. The gun became known as the Texas Colt.

Such excitement for such a faulty mechanism! Since it had been designed for civilians, its .34 caliber was too light for the military. It had no trigger guard. Loading required it be broken into three component parts, which made it devilishly difficult on a galloping horse. It really wasn't practical except that it shot *six times*.

Texans never called it a revolver. It was the six-shooter or six-gun and the name of Colt became world famous. Its worth was proved on the Pedernales River where Jack Hays became the first man to use it in a running fight. Jumped by a party of about seventy Comanches, Hays with only fourteen men realized that running was futile. With their backs to the enemy, they would be ridden down and picked off one by one. Instead, he ordered his men to wheel their horses and ride straight at the Comanches. The war whoops turned to howls of pain as fifteen men, each with a loaded rifle and six-shooter, had over a hundred shots to fire. Hays lost several Rangers, but he killed thirty Indians before they fled in terror. The gun was significant for another reason. It proved to the Rangers, the Indians, and the rest of Texas that they could whip the Comanche on horseback.

Another engagement in the same year saw Hays attacked by a superior force. This time he did not hesitate. At his command his men fired a fusillade from their rifles, then drew their six-shooters.

"Charge!" Hays yelled, leading his men close enough for hand-to-hand combat. The Comanches, who had never known white men to do anything but run until they were safe inside the walls of a fort, were off-balance from the beginning. "Powder-burn 'em!" Hays thundered as they rode between the ranks of Comanches, firing their six-shooters at range close enough for a shot to go completely through one Indian's body and wound another.

The Comanches fled with Hays chasing them for three miles. Some of the Rangers managed to load in the saddle, and the shooting never seemed to stop.

Later a Comanche war chief moaned that he would never fight "Yack" Hays again. He "has a shot for every finger on the hand."

Hays readily admitted that his success was due to the six-shooter, but the thing had to be made better. Around the campfires and in the bunkhouses, Texas Rangers were cussing and discussing the merits of the weapon. With his head filled with their ideas, sometime after 1840 Ranger Captain Samuel H. Walker went East to look up Samuel Colt, who lived in New York City.

Young Mr. Colt was delighted to meet young Captain Walker. The meeting changed the way wars were fought, forever. The days of the single shot weapon were numbered. Walker told Colt that his pistols were the best yet seen, but the Texas Rangers had some improvements in mind. The Connecticut-born Colt was more than accommodating. He took Walker to his Paterson plant. Out of this visit came the world's first martial revolver—the world-famous Walker Colt.

It was first and foremost a horseman's weapon. It had a heavy strong frame able to withstand wear and rough usage, as in clubbing someone who was "not worth shooting." The grip had a natural curve that fitted well into a large hand. It had a sturdy trigger guard so it could be worn in the belt and drawn from it. It had excellent balance, and its caliber was .44, large enough to drop an enemy or a malefactor in his tracks. Its modifications and improvements made it the ultimate weapon of its time. It was to kill more men than any other handgun ever made.

Though Samuel Colt had to file for bankruptcy in 1842, he never really gave up his trade. From time to time for five years when no Colts were manufactured, hard-eyed men—some Rangers, some outlaws—would ride up from Texas and get him to make one for them. He ended up giving away his own.

Meanwhile, the undeclared state of war continued. On January 23, 1844, Captain Hays was authorized to raise a company of mounted gunmen to act as Rangers on the western and southwestern frontier. Their primary duty would be to provide protection from the Mexicans who were raiding Texas almost on a daily basis. Another company was raised at Corpus Christi in 1844. In February 1845 four more companies were stationed at Goliad in central Texas as well as farther north on the Brazos in Robertson and Milam Counties.

The command remained at Bexar. The captains of these respective posts were under orders "to scour the frontiers of their respective counties, [to] protect them from incursions..." When the call to arms came to protect the citizens from Mexican invasions and Indian depredations, they were to come together for such "...emergencies to be under the command of Captain Hays."

The legend grew that "one Ranger was worth five or six Indians." And so they were, but not for the reason that they were any better men. The Comanches were some of the most skillful of cavalrymen. Their tactics could not be faulted. Their lack of weaponry made the difference.

In 1846 the Mexican War began for the entire United States, not just for Texas. A lame duck Congress, under the advisement of President John Tyler, passed a joint resolution annexing the sovereign nation of Texas to the United States of America. The incoming President James K. Polk was left with the unpleasant prospect of fighting a war no one really wanted to fight.

The northern senators had long objected to the admission of Texas to the Union. It was a slave state that could be counted on to upset the balance of power that existed in the legislative branch of the government. Only the threat of Texas's being annexed by England, thereby placing a British presence on both the north and the south borders of the United States, was able to persuade enough votes.

The generals appointed to fight the war were Zachary Taylor, "Old Rough and Ready," and Winfield Scott, "Old Fuss and Feathers."

Both felt that politics had saddled them with the Texans. Neither one of them cared for these irregulars, but they had no choice but to use them. By the end of the war, both thoroughly detested them. Not so much, of course, as the Mexicans did.

Toward the end of the war *los diablos Tejanos* had become *los Tejanos sangrientos*—the bloodthirsty Texans.

Initially Hays and his Rangers were called by General Zachary Taylor at Fort Brown to raise five thousand Texas volunteers, two regiments of infantry and two of cavalry. Hays enlisted as a private but was elected to colonel in one jump. His command was the First Regiment of Texas Mounted Riflemen. Its nucleus was, of course, Hays's Rangers. They excited the public with their glamorous reputation. The press referred to them as the Texas Rangers.

Within days Hays's officers, among them Ben McCulloch, Sam Big Foot Wallace, and John S. Ford, went to General Zachary Taylor and demanded a thousand of something called a Colt. The general allowed it. He considered the small order negligible in comparison to the amount of equipment necessary to outfit his U.S. infantry. He wanted nothing newfangled for them. They knew their mission—to march steadily and implacably across country and fight when they arrived at their destination. Almost as slow-moving were his dragoons, the mounted infantry, who would ride up to the battle, then dismount and fight it. Taylor wanted Hays's Rangers to stay out of the way.

Samuel H. Walker was sent again to New York to find Samuel Colt and give him an order for one thousand six-shooters, two for each of the new "Texas Rangers." Colt had no models left. He had to design a new one, now known as the "Old Army Type," and had Eli Whitney's cotton gin company manufacture weapons according to the new specifications. Colt lost three thousand dollars but negotiated for the one thing that made his name and his fortune worldwide. Every one of the weapons bore the hallmark *Address Samuel Colt, New York*. When the Texas Rangers reached Veracruz, the weapons were distributed to them by "Rip" Ford.

Zachary Taylor also found he had no one else to use except the Rangers for scouting activities. Politics reared its head in his professional life. He was a Whig whose party was currently in the minority. He had been sent to Texas while his rival Winfield Scott, a Democrat perceived to have great political potential, had been tapped for the honor and the glory of going in at Veracruz. Those who thought wars were made to be won should take note of the salutary lesson that follows. The prize was the fame that victory would bring and a possible presidential nomination somewhere down the line.

Taylor fought two deciding battles in Texas, then sent a troop of Rangers, led by Ben McCulloch, to find the best route to Monterrey. His orders were that no unarmed Mexican citizens were to be molested. Taylor found he wasted his breath. The Ranger captain and several of his men had been a prisoner of the Mexicans after the failure of the tragic Mier Expedition.

When questioned, the Texans reported that "villains [who] were found shot or hung up in the chaparral [had been] tortured by conscience for the many evil deeds they had committed, [and] had recklessly laid violent hands upon their own lives!"

Taylor confessed thereafter that he could not stop the Texans. They were insubordinate and lawless even though they were the best soldiers among the volunteers. He was furious when they celebrated July 4 by drinking two horse-buckets full of whiskey and roasting Mexican pigs and chickens "accidentally" shot down while they were firing salutes to honor the day.

Hays's force left Matamoros on August 9, 1846, to work itself across the Mexican countryside on a mule-buying expedition. The mounted dragoons had no mules, and Taylor's officers had not been able to buy any. They did not know the country or the language. They could not deal with the people. Jack Hays rode out with his Rangers and came back with all the mules Taylor wanted.

Gritting his teeth in frustration, Taylor was forced to send Hays and McCulloch out to be his eyes and ears. Later they proved to be his right and left arms as well. On the march to Monterrey in September, McCulloch and his rangers rode at the head of one column. Hays and his men, at the head of the other. To a man they were eager for the fight. They had come seeking revenge for the Alamo, and on the way they intended to behave accordingly.

The mountains above Monterrey with the famous Silla del Cielo (Seat of the Sky) were within sight of Taylor's force of six thousand. "Old Rough and Ready" ordered the Rangers to "form the advance of the army tomorrow, and to move at sunrise."

The Mexican cavalry, supported by infantry, rode out to arrange themselves for battle, beautifully uniformed, mounted on the finest horseflesh, as they had ten years before in front of the Alamo. Their commander gave the order to set lances.

Ben McCulloch did not wait for the order from the commander of his column. Yelling in a voice that echoed off the mountains, he charged. The Texans followed—into a violent melee where every rule of combat up to that time was violated. Screaming like a berserker, Ben McCulloch rode down everything in his path. The Rangers fought at close range with lances, swords, knives, and above all the deadly six-shooters. At the end a hundred Mexican bodies, their commander among them, lay dead in their beautiful uniforms. The rest were fleeing for their lives to Saltillo.

The battle of Monterrey was notable for three things. It was not a decisive battle because Taylor refused to press the advantage. He gave the Mexicans an eight-week truce in which to regroup. While Taylor negotiated a truce, his near victory was disapproved by his government. He was not supposed to win. President Polk's Democrat administration did not want a Whig victorious. Winfield Scott was sent to the Rio Grande to commandeer Taylor's best troops and lead them on the planned Veracruz expedition, which would end in the capture of Santa Anna and Mexico City. His victory would secure him the next presidency. Taylor was ordered to remain in Monterrey and hold a defensive position.

Hays's Texans' six-month enlistment was up. They went home in disgust. They had also been notable for three things. They were overwhelmingly effective when they were allowed to fight. They inspired terror in the territory's civilians because of their fearsome reputations. They were easily identified by their colorful dress, in particular the stars they wore, which they pinned everywhere on their coats, hats, saddles.

When they marched away, the news spread like wildfire. On January 3, 1847, their absence changed history and indirectly elected a president of the United States. With its "eyes and ears" gone, the U.S. Army's lines of communication collapsed. Couriers were killed and their dispatches delivered directly to General Santa Anna.

Of particular importance was a dispatch sent by Scott to Taylor. It was carried by a Lieutenant John Richey. He was roped out of the saddle and cruelly murdered. The dispatch contained the information that Taylor was to be abandoned at Monterrey. Santa Anna set out with the best force in the Mexican army to give Mexico the popular victory it craved.

Meanwhile, General Winfield Scott landed at Veracruz in March 1847. Marching overland, fighting as he went, he rolled up victory after victory. He never knew and therefore never credited his success with the fact that the best army and the best general were on their way to Monterrey. He arrived in the capital on September 14. He had no Rangers nor any cavalry.

Meanwhile, Hays had returned to San Antonio. His duty was still to the people of Texas. He was granted permission to organize the Second Unit of the First Texas Mounted Riflemen. He also took time to marry Susan Calvert. Now a family man, he looked forward to whipping his unit into shape and then retiring. Meanwhile, Winfield Scott found himself with his lines of communication cut from Mexico City to Veracruz. The country was beautiful—forests, gorges, passes, upper plateaus—infested with the new Mexican opposition to the Americanos—*guerrillas*. *Rancheros* and *hacendados* had become the wagers of the "little war."

Americans recognized the war—it was the one they had waged and won against the British half a century before. Supplies and reinforcements were getting through with greatest difficulty if at all. Their carriers were decimated on each march. Scott was beset and besieged. His situation was fast becoming untenable.

On July 17, 1847, President James K. Polk wrote in his diary that he had insisted that Jack Hays be given the job of keeping the road open between Mexico City and the sea. The Army might protest and the politicians might fume and call him traitor, but James K. Polk had been handed a war, not necessarily of his own making. He did not intend to be the first president in American history to lose one.

In September Colonel Jack Hays and his new regiment of a thousand mounted Texans arrived via ship at Veracruz. Awaiting them were the arms they had requested almost two years before. Samuel Colt's thousand new "Army" revolvers were distributed joyfully by Captain John S. Ford.

The regiment was composed of real Rangers, not a conglomerate force of Americans. As they mounted, everyone stared. Instead of uniforms they wore an odd assortment of clothes. Most wore red or blue shirts, but they had adopted a wide variety of headgear—everything from caps of leather or fur to fedoras. As usual they had armed themselves before they came. In addition to the new Colts, they were hung with a regular arsenal. In their saddle boots were short rifles or shotguns. They generally had one or two holster pistols, an old Colt revolver in addition to the new one, and a Bowie knife. Only Hays was dressed as if he were on serious, if not military, business. Though he had been part of a Texan fighting force in one way or another for eleven years, he was a mere thirty years old. He is reported to have worn a black leather cap, black trousers, and a short, close-fitting blue jacket without a sign of an insignia or stripe. One of the army officers described him as having a sun-browned, clean-shaven face and gaunt cheeks—"more like a boy than a man."

The Rangers made it a point to look as ferocious as possible; practically all of them, with the exception of Colonel Hays, wore long beards and mustaches.

Nevertheless, they were mustered into Lane's Brigade where Samuel Walker had been impressed to lead a troop of U.S. dragoons. As they moved toward Puebla, the thousand Texans awed and terrified the population. For the very first time, the Mexicans in the interior of the country had a chance to see what had killed so many of their kind at the Alamo, what had defeated them so thoroughly at San Jacinto, what had now overrun them. The reputation that preceded them was confirmed—"a sort of semi-civilized half man, half devil, with a slight mixture of lion and snapping turtle." Women crossed themselves and children ran in terror as if they beheld "a more holy horror...than of the evil saint himself," wrote Lieutenant Ebenezer Dumont describing the Texans' effect on the people.

Unfortunately, leading the attack on the town of Huamantla on the way to Pucbla, Samuel Walker was shot dead. His troops wept bitter tears over his body, and his death strengthened the Texans' hatred of every Mexican man they encountered.

Hays's Rangers took Walker's place and moved his men to Puebla where he broke the siege. Then he cut a wide swath of destruction, terror, and probably revenge southwest through the mountains to rescue twenty-one Americans being held prisoner at Izucar de Matamoros. At the same time he relieved the Mexicans of enough supplies, ammunition, and horses to fully equip their former prisoners. Taking *guerrilla* warfare to the *guerrillas* considerably lessened the *rancheros'* taste for the adventure.

When the Rangers rode into the groveling towns, "they rode, some sideways, some upright, some by the reverse flank, some face to the rear, some on horses, some on asses, some on mustangs, some on mules. On they came, rag, tag, and bobtail, pell-mell, helter-skelter, the head of one covered with a clouched hat, that of another with a towering cocked hat, a third bare-headed, while twenty others had caps made of the skins of every variety of wild and tame beasts; the dog, the cat, the bear, the coon, the wildcat...and each cap had a tail hanging to it." Many believed that the tail belonged to the devil Texans rather than to the animal.

Their reputation suffered even more because they were so undisciplined and so brutal. They were men who understood as few others in the U.S. Army seemed to do, that the purpose of the army was to kill. Too many regular officers considered that rules and gentlemanly formalities were to be observed. They deplored the barbaric way the Texans assumed the role of judge, jury, and executioner. Mixed with their self-righteousness was green-eyed jealousy that forced them to admit that the Texans were the best soldiers both Scott and Taylor had.

In Mexico City, Hays's Rangers behaved as if they were above the law. When they were not performing their duties on a variety of expeditions against *guerrillas* in the vicinity, they were strolling the town and creating problems wherever they went. One of them shot a man dead for throwing a stone at him. In one of the disreputable quarters of town, one of their number was murdered. The company to which he belonged rode into the quarter and shot the place to pieces. Eighty Mexican bodies ended up in the morgue.

Afraid of adverse publicity affecting his already teetering career, no less than Winfield Scott himself called Hays in to account. The colonel faced the general down with the calm reply that no one could "impose" on the Texas Rangers. Scott dropped the matter.

They were almost always outnumbered. Yet they never lost. Their enemies were deathly afraid of them as well as of the deadly Colt pistols they carried. They were undisciplined except when commanded by their own officers.

In the end Hays controlled his Rangers so that they let a messenger pass through their lines on the night of January 21, 1848. When they pulled him from his carriage, he produced a safe-conduct pass bearing General Scott's signature. The Texans demanded that they be allowed to kill him. General Lane, Hays's superior officer, ordered him to let the man go.

The messenger carried the safe-conduct pass to Santa Anna. That evening when the Rangers rode into Tehuacan, Santa Anna's apartments were deserted. The Texans had missed him by minutes.

In ransacking the apartment they found a cane. "Its staff was of polished iron. Its pedestal was of gold, tipped with steel. Its head was an eagle blazing with diamonds, rubies, sapphires, emeralds—an immense diamond in the eagle's beak, jewels in his claws, diamonds everywhere. The cane was a marvel of beauty." So described witness Doctor D. Wooster.

"Give it to Colonel Jack!" the Texans instantly chorused.

Hays accepted the cane with a shy smile. Later Major William H. Polk wished to send it to his brother the president. Hays gave it up, telling him to say it was from the Texas Rangers.

Later they did have a chance to kill Santa Anna, but Hays talked them out of it by saying that if they did so, they would dishonor Texas. All agreed that Santa Anna's life was not worth the honor of Texas.

While Scott was fumbling at Mexico City, Zachary Taylor, his troops led by Ben McCullough, was winning a decisive victory at Buena Vista outside Monterrey. Shortly thereafter, he was carried down the Rio Grande by Texas riverboat to his "manifest destiny." He became the Whig party candidate and won the presidency. Winfield Scott passed into history. The Mexican War ended thereafter with the Treaty of Guadalupe Hidalgo. By its terms Mexico lost the states that became California, Arizona, and New Mexico.

In a burst of ingratitude, Zachary Taylor condemned the Texans for their tactics and their lawlessness. He issued public condemnation of them. The Texans cared little for his pettiness. They had used the war to even a few scores.

The same year that Taylor rode to fame and Scott to obscurity, Hays's service to the Rangers ended. He had a wife now and their first child was on the way. He had done his duty to Texas. His duty lay now with his family. At thirty-one he needed to establish himself in a profession that would provide for them.

The businessmen of San Antonio wanted to establish trade with El Paso, through the Mexican state of Chihuahua and other points west. At that time the trade routes to the Pacific Ocean ran through Missouri. Texan entrepreneurs wanted one established for Texas. Hundreds of miles of unexplored land lay from El Paso westward. The Texas government was willing to help fund the expedition because they wished to know where to build forts to keep the Comanche at bay.

Hays was the first and only choice to lead the "Chihuahua-El Paso Pioneer Expedition." He employed seventy-two men: thirty-five citizens from San Antonio and Fredericksburg, thirty-five Rangers, and two guides and interpreters. The purpose was to mark out a road between San Antonio and Chihuahua.

The expedition was a disaster that proved a route through Mexico was unfeasible. In the great Chihuahuan Desert they found little water and so little food they were reduced to eating mustang meat and pack mules. Samuel Maverick, one of the businessmen who made the trip, reported that the guides did not know the territory as they had claimed. The entire expedition was lost for a time in the desert.

They returned to the Texan side of the Rio Grande and made their way to Ben Leaton's fort in the Big Bend on a site that had been Mission El Apostol Santiago in 1684 and El Fortin de San Jose in 1710. There they ate and rested for sixteen days.

Hays, who was never a fool, made the decision not to try to travel into Chihuahua. The others lacked the discipline of his Rangers. The expedition split into three parties. Twenty-eight men marched directly back to San Antonio. The two other groups went into Mexico and north to Santa Fe. Most of those men died of exposure and starvation.

True to his hire, Hays reported that the route through the Big Bend and northern Mexico was impracticable. The best route for a wagon road, he contended, was north from San Antonio to the San Saba and thence through the Concho country to the Pecos.

Hays's opinion was not well received. He retired shortly thereafter and left for California. Locating near the present city of Oakland, he was doing well financially. In 1848 James K. Polk offered him an appointment as commissioner of Indian affairs in the newly acquired Gila River country.

Ultimately, he helped to build the city of Oakland. He and his wife had three boys and three girls, only two of which, John Coffee and Elizabeth, lived to be adults. He remained very popular and famous. In his deprecatory way, Jack Hays wanted the fame to be forgotten, but somehow he always drew a crowd. He quickly learned that if he drove a buggy to town rather than ride a horse, many people wouldn't recognize him.

He died at sixty-six on his ranch near Oakland on April 21, 1883. His will assigned all his property to his wife and son and requested a simple private funeral. The citizens of California demanded an opportunity to pay their respects. Finally, Susan Hays relented. The city of Oakland staged a partial military funeral, the most elaborate the city had ever seen.

More than any of the men who followed him, Hays's character determined the nature of the organization he did so much to establish. Today, his merciless code seems harsh and inhumane. To indict Hays for his adherence to his code makes it possible to lose sight of the essential quality of the man—mild in appearance and demeanor and yet as tough and self-reliant as the conditions under which he lived demanded.

The need for a hero presupposes an amoral world. Texas in the nineteenth century was such a world where three cultures clashed with little or no basis for understanding each other. The hero, for good or evil, brings his brand of morality and sets things to rights. Such a man was Jack Hays. An unassuming man with a hero's job to do, he came into a state reeling from the horrendous massacres at the Alamo and Goliad. Despite the turnaround victory at San Jacinto, it was a state weakened by its losses and its fears. He and his men gave it a foundation of law and order upon which it could build its own system.

Sam Houston was right. "You may rely on the gallant Hays and his companions."

* * * * *

Pictures and memorabilia of John Coffee Hays and the rest of his brave band fill the walls and display cases of the Texas Ranger Hall of Fame and Museum in Waco, Texas.

Enchanted Rock, scene of his miraculous single combat, is a state park in Gillespie County north of Fredericksburg on State Highway 965.

The Renaissance Man

John Salmon Ford

In 1847 the adjutant of the First Regiment of Texas Mounted Riflemen (Second Unit) was sent to Veracruz with Winfield Scott's army. John Salmon Ford, a doctor who had taken down his shingle to publish a newspaper, had enlisted as a private because he wanted to be in the action. His education, his skills, and his ability to organize had won him an almost immediate promotion to lieutenant. He had been part of the amphibious landing at Veracruz. He had marched overland with Scott to Mexico City.

From headquarters in the captured city, one of his duties was to prepare the casualty lists and notify the next-of-kin with a properly sympathetic and carefully hand-copied letter. A God-fearing and serious-minded man, he at first closed the lists and the letters with the reverent words "Rest in Peace." As the casualties mounted, the constraints of time required that he abbreviate where possible. At the bottom of each letter, after his signature, he took to printing R.I.P.

One of his fellow Rangers saw it and gave him a nickname that stayed with him through bloody battles, terrible wars, humiliating defeats, and brilliant victories.

"Old Rip."

Of all the men who fought for Texas, Rip Ford had arguably the finest mind. His education, both formal and self-taught, enlightened him and enabled him to see beyond the frenzied present to catch a glimpse of the future. He understood better than most what Texas was about and what she would come to be despite her fierce and violent history. A soldier, a physician, a journalist, a lawyer, a public servant, a legislator, an autobiographer and chronicler of the times, he made sense of Texas.

He was born in the Greenville District of South Carolina, May 26, 1815. The family fortunes took an upturn shortly thereafter in 1817 with the move to Lincoln County in southern Tennessee where his father took over the running and eventually the ownership of a plantation.

From his earliest recollections, Ford loved to learn. He attended a one-room school that taught a limited eight-year curriculum. So avid a student was he that he completed its entire course—spelling, arithmetic, and reading the Bible and the classics in five years. He borrowed and read all the books the teacher owned as well as all that his neighbors in nearby Shelbyville owned. At sixteen he was qualified to teach school.

He did not want to teach, and he had already decided that he did not want to farm. His father's profession had no appeal for him. He studied medicine with the local doctor, James G. Barksdale, in Shelbyville. In those days potential doctors "read medicine." No medical schools existed west of the Alleghenies. He met and married Mary Davis. The couple had twins, a boy and a girl. When their marriage ended in divorce, Mary took custody of his son, and Ford left his daughter with his parents while he heeded Stephen F. Austin's call for reinforcements for Texas.

He arrived in July 1836, too late to help Sam Houston at the battle of San Jacinto. From that time when he was twenty-one until his death sixty-one years later in 1897, he witnessed, lived, and wrote the history of Texas. He was the only man among all the lone star heroes to be involved in a major way in every military and political action of the nineteenth century.

He settled in San Augustine, a small town between the Sabine and the Angelina Rivers, in East Texas. Just twenty-one years old, he set about the practice of medicine. At first he made only night calls for folk too poor to pay the fees of the established doctor. He was compassionate and generous with his time, his medical knowledge, and his advice. He taught Sunday school, thereby winning approval and more prosperous clients

among the church-goers. He wrote and acted in local plays. He served in the local militia company, formed to fight some Indians who were raiding local farmsteads. On these skirmishes he met Jack Hays, a fellow Tennessean, who made little impression on him. Hays appeared too unprepossessing to possibly be much of an Indian fighter—though he was gaining some reputation

Sometime during the next five years, Ford decided he would rather be a lawyer. He read for the law and passed the East Texas bar exam. He ran for the Congress of the Republic of Texas but lost to Sam Houston. In 1844 he was elected since Sam Houston had gone on to be president of the Republic.

He continued to read voraciously and was always avidly interested in everything. He discovered he had opinions that he hated to keep to himself. In 1845 he became a journalist for the *Texas National Register*, published at Washington-on-the-Brazos. He discovered that he loved writing. With the help of partner Mike Cronican and the money he had made from doctoring and lawyering, he purchased the paper and moved it to Austin, where he could be in the thick of things in politics. At the same time he married a fragile young woman named Louisa Swisher.

Ford's *Register* was strongly pro-Houston. His bias in favor of the hero of San Jacinto, whom many citizens cursed as the "damned old drunk Cherokee," earned him the outright hatred of many Austin citizens. He paid no attention to the calumny and the death threats. He changed the name of the paper to the *Texas Democrat*, and in March 1845 he and Cronican began publishing it semiweekly. It became the foremost liberal press in Texas, and shortly thereafter they were awarded the contract as the official state printer.

In May the Democratic party elected Ford to the state central committee.

Then all the excitement, all the sense of being in the thick of things stopped. His wife Louisa fell ill. He doctored her himself, hardly leaving her bedside, writing nothing, attending no meetings. When she died in August 1845, he mourned her deeply, swearing that he would never practice medicine again. For the first and only time in his life, nothing interested him.

Around him the newly annexed state of Texas was in turmoil. Savage internal arguments raged among citizens struggling to save their places in the constantly shifting political and economic climate. At her southern and western borders, Mexicans and Comanches raided at will.

After a long period of isolation, he flung himself into public service. Politics, journalism, speechmaking, meeting with committees, all occupied his time to the exclusion of grief or any private life. When his daughter, mother, and father came from Tennessee to live with him, he was still so stricken that he couldn't accept the love they brought him.

When the first call came from Jack Hays for volunteers to fill ten companies to be known as the First Regiment, Texas Mounted Riflemen, Ford stayed in Austin. He had family responsibilities. He was a newspaperman whose place was at his desk, stirring up popular support for the war. Still, his spirit stirred within him as the Texans under Ben McCulloch and Jack Hays were commended for the capture of Monterrey.

The next year when Hays had returned to Texas, President Polk singled him out to raise a second regiment. Ford had buried his grief. He was one of the first in line to join. On July 7, 1847, he enlisted as a private but was immediately promoted to lieutenant. His skills were too valuable to waste in the line. He was transferred to Hays's staff as regimental adjutant.

The Texas Rangers with Jack Hays at their head and John Ford as their adjutant landed at Veracruz with Winfield Scott. During that infernally hot summer of 1847, Ford issued a thousand Walker Colts to the regiment.

Though they had been designed by Samuel Colt as per Ranger Samuel Walker's directions and suggestions, most of the recruits didn't know how to use the heavy, long-barreled weapons. A few put the conical bullets in backwards. When that happened, the first shot burst the cylinder. When a "Greeny" spilled powder around the revolving cylinder while reloading, all six shots exploded at once. Ford recalled that one forgot what sort of weapon he was holding and tried to clean and oil it after firing one shot *while the other five chambers were loaded*. The hard luck of a few taught the many, and the regiment became unstoppable with the six-shooter or six-gun. It was the weapon they would make famous. It would make them famous in turn.

Ford longed for combat. On the march inland to Mexico City, he begged for and received permission to lead a spy company whose duty was to search out enemy *guerrilla* units. The fighters of the "little war," the *guerrilleros*, plotted constantly how to wreak havoc on the American lines. Ford spent the fall discovering small parties and riding them down at full gallop with his six-shooter drawn and ready for action.

He paid a heavy price for his field experience. Over the 260-mile march to the capital, he caught malaria, a disease that never left him. Throughout his life it would come upon him and set him reeling in the saddle. He would treat himself with quinine and ride on. Only on one or two rare occasions did he allow it to put him out of action.

Mexico City was in chaos when they arrived. The *leperos*, a huge gang of thieves and murderers, had taken advantage of the governmental chaos to terrify the city. Nightly, American soldiers including those led by Zachary Taylor and Winfield Scott were being attacked and wounded or killed. Worse for the city was that its good citizens were suffering also. The Mexican police were ineffective. Whether from incompetence or choice is unknown. Probably from a combination of both.

In retaliation for the injuries and deaths among their numbers, the Texans, who had been called *"los Diablos Tejanos,"* the Texan Devils, became *"los Tejanos Sangrientos,"* the bloodthirsty Texans. The brutal gangs were no match in street fighting against Bowie knives and six-shooters. After the Texans killed about eighty, the *leperos* simply melted back into the general population. Ironically, the Texans' brutal success earned them enmity from the citizens who had been terrorized as well as from American occupation troops.

Through all the fighting, the killing, and the dying, Ford proved his ruthlessness and his willingness to order the wild Texans to battle. When violence was called for, he did not hesitate to employ bloody-minded brutality and fight-to-the-finish stubbornness. At the same time, he found he preferred reason and intrigue to violence. The Mexicans with whom he dealt never understood him. Therefore, they feared him.

The Treaty of Guadalupe Hidalgo was signed February 2, 1848. The Rangers except for Hays and Ford were mustered out and sent home immediately. The regulars under Taylor and Scott had suffered quite enough embarrassments by comparison.

When Colonel Hays and Captain Ford returned to Texas on May 10, they were greeted at Port Lavaca as heroes because of their success in leading the Texan Devils.

On May 14, 1848, Ford was mustered out. He returned to the newspaper with a feeling of dismay. His life would never be the same. He had spent too much time in the company of Jack Hays. He found he ached to make history rather than write about it. He sold his interest in the *Democrat* and petitioned the state to organize a ranger company.

His request was denied ostensibly because of a lack of state funds, but in part because of the lack of favor accorded the Texas Rangers by the Washington political system. Both Zachary Taylor and Winfield Scott had been overshadowed by the Texans' insubordination as well as their success in irregular activities. Both Whigs and Democrats wanted no more heroic Texans swaying votes one way or another.

John S. Ford retired to his home and family to read military history and tactics. His reputation, however, ensured that he didn't stay home very long. In 1849 the California gold rush created a need among Texas businessmen to secure a practical route to California. Restless for something to do, Ford and Indian Agent Robert Simpson Neighbors blazed a trail from San Antonio to El Paso.

They rode north to Waco, then west with friendly Indians and a respectable entourage of white men. In fifty-five days they covered the round trip of twelve hundred miles. Ford, the writer, kept a detailed account with maps, which he drew himself using some surveying experience he had picked up in his many endeavors. For decades it was known as the Ford-Neighbors Trail. He was the first to recommend a railroad track following the thirty-second parallel, which was subsequently built.

Returning from his expedition, he found the people of Texas in as much jeopardy as they had been during the days of the Republic. While Texas Rangers had been fighting in Mexico, the Comanches had stepped up their attacks. After the signing of the treaty, Mexican raids had become a constant thing as bandits robbed and murdered settlers north of the Rio Grande. All along the southern and western borders of Texas, citizens were suffering terribly.

In response to the angry demands of many with political clout, General G. M. Brooke, commander of the Texas Military District of the U.S. Army, authorized the formation of three ranger companies at federal expense.

The redoubtable Jack Hays and his wife had left Texas for Oakland, California, where he had settled down with a government appointment as the new Indian commissioner in the Gila River country.

Old Rip Ford was one of the logical choices after Hays. When his chance came, he knew he had been waiting all his life for the opportunity. He would have his own company of seventy-five men, men to train, to whip into shape, to create a fighting unit as Jack Hays had done. The U.S. government provided percussion rifles, pistols, holsters, and ammunition. Each Ranger was expected to furnish his own horse, saddle, bridle, halter, and lariat. The pay was $23.50 monthly.

Ford was assigned to a duty station just south of Corpus Christi in the disputed area of Texas. The section between the Nueces River and the Rio Grande, called variously the Wild Horse Desert or Nueces Strip, was still claimed by Mexico. Raids were subjecting Texas settlements along the Rio Grande to constant harassment. The herds of the great ranchers Richard King and Mifflin Kenedy were being rustled wholesale and driven into Mexico. Ford and his Rangers provided protection for the citizens of Brownsville and assistance to the Kinenos, who worked for King. In exchange King furnished many of the remounts for the Rangers who risked their lives for the ranch.

Ford's Rangers spent the next two years as a subsidiary branch of the regular Army. His Company was mustered for only six months, but so strong was their loyalty to Ford that they re-upped three times. They became known as "Ford's Old Company." Midway through his tour on May 12, 1850, his troop engaged in a bitter hand-to-hand battle with Comanches on the upper reaches of the Nueces. The fighting was stab and hack and shoot at close range. The Rangers won, but the battle was not without cost. Private David Steele was killed. Ford's horse on which he led the charge was brought down by an arrow, which Ford subsequently believed was poisoned. Another arrow also possibly tipped with poison grazed Ford's right hand. He lost partial use of his arm for the next six years.

"Ford's Old Company" was disbanded at Laredo September 23, 1851. The Nueces Strip was still being raided by hostile Indians and Mexican bandits, but their depredations were less bold, less overt. The Comanche had troubles of their own dealing with the streams of gold-seekers headed for California. Mexico was troubled by internal strife and economic near-ruin.

Seeking a new cause to lend his skills to, Ford became personally involved in politics across the border. Jose Maria Jesus Carbajal, a Texan born in San Antonio and educated at Bethany College, Virginia, sought to free his section of Mexico from military domination. From his residence in Camargo, he tried to establish an independent state to be called the Republic of the Rio Grande. Among his adherents were Jose de los Santos Benavides and John S. Ford. Unfortunately for Carbajal, the time was not right. His dream ended with the three of them retreating across the river with undignified haste. Benavides returned to Laredo, and Ford escaped back to Austin and into politics.

He bought another newspaper, the *South Western American*. A staunch if sometimes unreasoning Democrat, he damned the Republican Party as an un-American institution. He supported slavery, state-backed railroads, and temperance. He called for a permanent Ranger service to protect people all along the border even in the new territories acquired from the Treaty of Guadalupe Hidalgo.

His views were popular enough that in December of 1853 he was elected mayor of Austin. He promptly fired the town marshal for being drunk in the streets and took over the man's job. The people of Austin discovered they had more than they voted for in Ford, who is supposed to have stared down one drunken gunfighter. Rather than shoot the man, Ford scared him out of town.

After a year in which his impulsive behavior made him unpopular, he returned to the newspaper business. His voice became the *Texas State Times*, which he built into the largest weekly in the state except for the famous *Galveston News*, published all through the revolution and the republic by Gail Borden.

For two years Ford waged a fierce crusade against liberal views. Unfortunately for his place in history, he had prejudices that placed him more and more outside the mainstream. Moreover, his volatile personality never allowed him to develop a philosophy.

He joined a splinter political party emerging in 1854. The American Party, familiarly called the Know-Nothing Party, was an extremist group that organized in the turbulent transition from agrarian to industrialist society. They were anti-Catholic, anti-Semitic, and above all anti-foreign. They were strict Unionists, who broke off from the Democratic Party when it began to talk of secession. Ironically, their votes as well as the votes of two other splinter groups so reduced the Democratic Party's numbers that Republican candidate Abraham Lincoln was elected in 1860.

Passionately, Ford leaped into the Know-Nothing ranks, following Sam Houston, a man he much admired. In their efforts to solidify Texas citizens, Ford and Houston were instrumental in organizing the Order of the Lone Star of the West, a white supremacist group. By 1856 Ford had realized his mistake. He disbanded the Order of the Lone Star. Unfortunately, the damage was done. The Knights of the Golden Circle, an extremist sectional movement, picked up the remnants. Together they helped push Texas out of the Union.

By 1858 the Comanches had regrouped. In a war of desperation, they were harassing the settlers on the Llano Estacado. The ring of forts the United States Army's 2nd Cavalry had built around *Comancheria* was proving less than effective. For the next seven years, more fighting occurred in Texas than at any time since 1836.

Governor Hardin R. Runnels promoted Ford to major and named him senior captain of a full Ranger company with jurisdiction over all the other companies. His orders were to seek out and attack the Comanche.

Ford leaped at the opportunity. He had recognized that his political sense had proved faulty. He thought his best efforts came from action. At forty-three, he considered himself to be in the prime of his life. He was somewhat slender and very lithe, with an erect military carriage. His curly, light-brown hair was just beginning to turn gray. His blue eyes were undimmed. Occasionally he resorted to profanity in the heat of battle, but he was mainly a model of correct behavior, a teetotaler who read a Bible passage every day even on campaign.

His men knew he would ask them to do nothing that he wouldn't do himself. Absolutely peerless with six-shooter, he could hit a small target consistently at 125 yards.

Former Rangers and other men who had heard of his deeds tumbled over themselves to enlist. His months as adjutant in Mexico City served him in good stead. Quickly, he assembled one hundred well-armed, well-mounted fighters. Each man carried a rifle, a shotgun, and two Walker Colts, enough weaponry to fire fifteen times without reloading. In other words, fifteen hundred rounds of lead would fly at any Comanche force they tracked down.

On a chilly February morning, Ford's Rangers left Austin in four parallel columns. They proceeded north through Brown County to the Brazos Indian Reservation. On April 26 they picked up Shapley P. Ross, Indian fighter and agent, whose son Lawrence Sullivan went on to be a ranger and later governor of Texas. One hundred friendly Indians joined them at Cottonwood Springs. Ford's plan was a new idea, one that no company had done before. He was riding deep into Comanche territory, taking the fight to the enemy rather than waiting inside a fort to give chase when an armed party came riding back from attacking settlers.

They rode 150 miles north into the Antelope Hills along the Canadian River in what is now Oklahoma. With them was Ford's seventy-three-year-old father, who had joined his son in the field. They crossed the Red, then rode north to the Washita.

Tonkawa scouts had located a large village. All day and night May 9 and 10, Ford led his men without rest so as not to lose the element of surprise. On May 11 Ford reconnoitered and planned his attack.

Then on May 12 the Tonkawas blundered upon a small camp of five tepees. They attacked, but two mounted Comanches got away to sound the alarm. Undaunted, Ford led his Rangers after them. Some three hundred fifty Comanches came out to meet them in magnificent savage display. They were resplendent in feather and horn headdresses. Their faces were painted black for war. They wheeled their horses like dervishes, screamed like maniacs, brandished all sorts of weapons, and made little threatening runs at the enemy. The Rangers, bearded and sweat-stained, clad in old clothing, sat their horses letting the adrenaline flow through their veins as they stared at Ford, who faced the Comanches. Both sides seemed to sense that this was a decisive battle. Cold as ice, Ford waited.

Pohebits Quasho, the war chief, had taken the name Iron Jacket. He galloped out in front of the screeching, prancing band, brandishing his lance, challenging the Rangers. He wore a chain shirt of overlapping plates of Spanish steel, once the property of some long-dead Spaniard, probably from Coronado's expedition. In Comanche and then in Spanish he yelled that his armor was powerful medicine. It made him invulnerable. He promised that the Tenawa Comanches would win victory that day.

"Kill the s.o.b.!" yelled Ranger lieutenant Billy Pitts.

Several shots rang out. The Spanish armor would turn arrows, but not a Sharps rifle ball. The Rangers shot Iron Jacket and his horse. Both went down in a heap, but the war chief rose and staggered toward them aiming his rifle.

They shot him again. He pitched over backwards and lay still.

His death threw the Comanches into confusion. While they milled their horses, looking for leadership, Ford yelled, "Charge!"

The Rangers spurred their horses forward into the thick of the Comanches, whom the forces of weaponry and superstition had rendered stunned. Knives, tomahawks, lances, and arrows were no match for carbines and six-shooters. Ford was everywhere, directing and controlling the movement of his men. The battle broke into a running fight of small charges, small retreats, hand-to-hand fighting with the dust and stench all around them.

The battle broke off at two o'clock. In the end seventy-six Comanche men had been killed, eighteen women and children had been captured, and three hundred of their horses had been taken. Indian losses were nearly unsustainable. The entire tribe had been soundly defeated. Yet enough escaped to carry the word to other tribes that the Texans would bring the war to them. It signaled an end to the majority of Comanche depredations. Two Rangers had been killed and two badly wounded.

Souvenir hunters among soldiers and Tonkawas stripped the scales off Iron Jacket's mail. They left his body lying naked in the dying afternoon. The Tonkawas cut the hands and feet off the Comanche bodies for their evening feast. Both desecrations were nearly devastating to the tribe who believed in somber rituals for their dead.

None bothered Ford as he turned his men back toward Texas. He had made a five-hundred-mile march across unfamiliar territory, fought a six-hour battle, sustained negligible losses, and led his striking force back safely. He had proved conclusively that Comanches could be beaten in their own territory with aggressive leadership. All Texas hailed him.

Another battle awaited him on the southern front.

Juan Nepomuceno Cortinas was born May 16, 1824, six or seven miles west of Brownsville at Santa Rita Ranch on the Texas side of the Rio Grande. He was the black sheep of his father's family who refused to learn to read and only learned to sign his name after he became governor of Tamaulipas.

In 1859 he was enjoying a wild life, stealing a few horses, rustling a few cattle, engaging in pursuits of the *vaquero* or working class rather than the *caballero* or nobility to which his birth entitled him. His appearance was a striking contrast to the men with whom he associated. Fair-complexioned, he had green eyes and red-brown hair and beard. He was spoiling for a fight. Stories of how he came to shoot the marshal of Brownsville in the shoulder are varied. The immutable fact is that Cheno, as he was called, shot a lawman. For sixty days he disappeared. Anti-American sentiment south of the border allowed him to raise a hundred men, enough to fight a good-sized war. His cousin Miguel Tijerina, commander of the Mexican cavalry in Matamoros, was unable to talk sense to him. He characterized Cheno as "a desperate contrary fellow."

On September 28 at three A.M., Cortinas and his hundred men attacked Brownsville. By dawn he had taken possession of it. His men killed the jailer who tried to keep them from releasing the prisoners. He killed three Americans and one Mexican for shielding one of them. He took possession of Fort Brown whose troops were in the field against some Indians. His men tried but failed to break open the powder magazine.

Tijerina and General Carbajal influenced Cortinas to move out of the city and back to his mother's ranch where he issued the statement that his act had been for the emancipation of the Mexicans and the restoration of their lands. Furthermore, his lieutenant, sixty-five-year-old Thomas Cabrera had been arrested. He had sounded exactly the right note for disgruntled Mexican-Americans who felt they had grievances. They flocked to his army.

When a troop of twenty men calling themselves the Brownsville Tigers came out to arrest him, his force was so intimidating that it sent them scuttling back to their homes in about forty minutes. Later a "lawless mob" broke into the Brownsville jail and hanged Cabrera. The death of the old man gave Cortinas a personal reason for continuing the fight.

He continued to make speeches in which he referred to the Texans and their laws as "flocks of vampires" sucking the lands of true Mexicans. He called on them to let him "break the chains of your slavery."

Meanwhile Cortinas raided ranches, rustled cattle, and killed Texans where he found them. Forty men joined him from Nuevo Leon. Sixty convicts broke prison at Victoria, armed themselves, and marched into his camp.

Major S. P. Heintzelman left Fort Brown with 285 men to fight Cortinas in his own camp. Unfortunately, when they arrived the camp was deserted, with signs indicating that it had not been occupied in a week. Though a skirmish eventually took place, it was largely ineffective.

Ford was in Austin nursing malaria when a call came for his Rangers to be reinstituted. He took eight lightly armed men on horseback to ride five hundred miles to Brownsville. Even though the governor had begged them to go, he could not appropriate one dollar. The Texas treasury was empty.

Along the way south, some of the old Rangers and a few new ones joined him. Fifty-three men arrived in Brownsville December 14. Cortinas meanwhile had been chased north to Rio Grande City. Heintzelman was pleased to see the reinforcements and more pleased to see the legendary Ford at their head. Ford led the charge into the center of Cortinas's line against two artillery pieces. A charge of grapeshot almost took off his head, but he managed to capture the cannons. The fighting was hand to hand when Heintzelman's troops appeared on the ridge above the town. Cortinas retreated precipitately.

Obviously, the regular troops never entered the battle. Rangers were wounded, Mexicans were killed, but not a single United States soldier was scratched. Ford had led the charge, but a Danish colonel wanted his command. By courting favor and making deals, he was elected commander. Ford withdrew from the organization and set out for Brownsville on his own.

Cheno Cortinas set up his headquarters in Mexico in January 1860. The local authorities were too weak to control him, particularly in the face of popular support. In need of money he fortified La Bolsa, a horseshoe bend of the Rio Grande thirty-five miles above Brownsville, and began to harass Texans again.

At about that time Don Savas Cavazos, Cheno's half brother, invited Ford and his Ranger patrol to Rancho Santa Rita. There Ford was introduced to Señora Maria Estefana Cortinas, Cheno's mother. The lady was seventy years old, tiny, white-haired, with a "pretty face, bright, black eyes, and very white skin." Ford was deeply affected by the meeting as he later wrote in his history. She took his hand and looked into his face for several minutes. Tears wet her cheeks. She did not beg for her son's life, but Ford read her message as if he had seen it written in fire. He gave orders that she was not to be molested. Till the end of her life, when danger seemed to threaten her, she would go to Brownsville and Ford would aid her.

Very soon, Cortinas's objective in fortifying the bend of the river became clear. The King-Kenedy steamboat *Ranchero*, carrying cargo valued at $200,000 including $60,000 in specie, was en route.

Army lieutenant Loomis Langdon, in command of a detachment, was aboard to guard *Ranchero* along with some of Ford's Rangers and a unit of U.S. Cavalry commanded by Captain George Stoneman. Langdon asked if Ford intended to ride into Mexico as other Rangers had done in the past.

Ford's reply was, "Certainly, sir."

When Cortinas opened fire, *Ranchero* ferried Ford and his fifty Rangers to the south side of the river where they attacked the Mexican position. With borrowed guns Ford led the charge against Cortinas's foot soldiers while a dozen Rangers with rifles kept the cavalrymen at bay. Cortinas's left flank collapsed beneath the deadly fire of Ranger six-shooters. The center panicked and the entire force of three hundred men ran for safety.

Daring death and Old Rip Ford, Cortinas was the last to leave the field, acting as a solitary rear guard until his men had disappeared into the brush. Despite Ford's reputation with a pistol, Cortinas miraculously rode away unscathed. No one will ever know what thoughts must have flashed through their heads as they faced each other across the field. Did Ford take aim at his enemy and then withhold his fire because of Doña Estefana? Did Cortinas salute his nemesis' courtesy before he galloped away?

La Bolsa was one of Ford's greatest victories. It established his reputation with the U.S. Army. Thereafter, Ford's Rangers, supplemented by Captain George Stoneman's Cavalry, patrolled the river. Word came that Cortinas was preparing to lead another attack. They crossed over and surprised the Mexicans at La Mesa. The attack was a victory where all but a handful of Cortinas's men surrendered. Cortinas fled deep into Mexico. The pursuit finally ran out of food and fodder for their horses. In March they returned without him.

Old Rip Ford became a western hero in Samuel Stone Hall's dime novels, published by Beadle's New York Library. He is reported to have laughed when he read of his colorful exploits. Hall had embroidered his adventures out of all reason, but the public read and to some extent believed. The stories added to Ford's name and therefore to his importance.

The Cortinas war was a short and certainly a minor war, but its consequences were severe. Fifteen Americans and eighty friendly Mexicans were killed. One hundred fifty of Cortinas's troops lost their lives. The delta of the Rio Grande and the land below it was laid waste. Damage claims of Americans alone totaled $336,826.21. At the final accounting, there are no minor wars.

In mid-May Ford was mustered out. He was forty-five years old, a considerable age for a man who had ridden as far and dared death as often as he had. He thought his career was over and was resigned to settle down to his writing and perhaps politics in Brownsville, which became his new home. Sam Houston was governor of Texas and struggling to keep Texas in the Union. Texans, particularly those favoring secession, were demanding Ranger companies of larger sizes while the U.S. Army was demanding their dismissal.

Sam Houston had no intention of dismissing a single man of them. He had the idea and the hope that he could keep Texas in the Union with large Ranger companies headed by himself that would obey his orders and control dissidents. He rightly recognized the precarious position Texas would be in if they seceded.

Before he could put his plans into action, Abraham Lincoln, whom many Southerners cursed for a "Black Republican President," won the election of 1860. In January 28, 1861, a special convention assembled in Austin to vote on secession. Houston pleaded for reason and for the Union. Ford, a delegate for Cameron County, declared for states' rights against his old friend. He was one of the major voices on the committee that drew up the Ordinance of Secession.

Sam Houston was voted out of office. His spirit must have broken along with his heart at the sight of old friends and comrades-in-arms turning against him. Immediately upon hearing the news, Lincoln offered Houston an officer's appointment in the Federal army, but the man who had saved Texas refused to fight against her. He retired to his home in Huntsville, a tragic figure, who did not live out the war.

On March 3, 1861, Old Rip Ford, Henry E. McCulloch, and his brother Ben were commissioned colonels in the newly organized Cavalry of Texas by the Committee of Public Safety. Their orders were to seize U.S. military posts and their all-important weapons and ammunition.

Ford was ordered back to the Rio Grande Valley. He landed with his force at Brazos de Santiago and persuaded the commander of Fort Brown to surrender the entire river, which he promptly did.

In the end between ten and fifteen percent of the total U.S. Army under Major General D. E. Twiggs were stationed in Texas. Twiggs, a Georgian by birth, was headquartered in San Antonio. He was later to maintain that he considered his position indefensible, so he surrendered the entire state to Texas and the Confederacy. He surrendered twenty-one Federal installations, giving the Confederacy and Texas between two and three million dollars' worth of military stores and supplies.

Ford stepped easily into command of the Texas Mounted Rifles, the old Second Texas Cavalry Regiment, stationed along the Rio Grande. Its mission was to prevent Federal invasion of Brownsville and to guard the border against Mexican raids. Using his considerable influence in Matamoros, the capital of the state of Tamaulipas, he negotiated an important trade agreement between the Confederacy and Mexico that kept border raids to a minimum. In June 1862 General Hamilton Prioleau Bee was appointed Confederate commander of the Military Sub-District of the Rio Grande. As so many before him, he could not deal with Ford's methods or his fame. Bee sent Rip back to Austin to be in charge of bringing new men into the army.

The Confederate Conscription Act of April 16, 1862, was the first draft law enacted in the U.S. All white male citizens between the ages of eighteen and thirty-five had to enroll for the draft. It was the end of volunteer armies, which Ford had always commanded with great success. He could not carry out his duties. He resigned in November 1862.

When General "Prince John" Bankhead Magruder assumed command of the District of Texas, New Mexico, and Arizona in the newly organized Confederate Department of the Trans-Mississippi, he called Ford back to work. It was a job Ford hated because he believed military service should be volunteer, but more because the draft law was discriminatory. Exemptions were not just for medicine and frontier defense, but for office holders, those with considerable wealth, holders of large acreages. Quotas were assigned and men too old, too young, and too ill were to be conscripted.

Relief for Ford came in 1863, when Magruder designated him commander of all state and Confederate troops assigned south and west of San Antonio. Supremely qualified for the job, Ford was given the authority to raise as many companies as he could among men exempt from conscription. That meant they had to recruit from thinly populated, manpower-drained West Texas. The nucleus of the force was small militia and paramilitary units. These men attracted by short terms of enlistment provided the largest contingent of Ford's force. He named his new command the Cavalry of the West. It was to be the largest and most important command of his career.

He donned a black cavalry fedora with the CSA emblem on its crown. No one disputed his right to call himself colonel. Over his headquarters in San Antonio he raised the Stars and Bars of the Confederacy and the Lone Star. At about the same time, word swept through Texas that Brownsville had been seized by an invading force of federal troops under Gen. Nathaniel P. Banks, the XIII Army Corps. Besides the Nineteenth Iowa, the Federal XIII had two black regiments.

And the Texans began to come. Old men, young men, farmers and dairymen with strong German accents came from Fredericksburg, men who feared what would happen to them if Union regiments of Negroes were placed among them. Boys stole horses and guns and made for San Antonio. One of Ford's officers reported, "Fifty-seven children have joined my battalion."

In thirty days Ford's call, backed by his reputation, had recruited thirteen hundred men and boys. On March 17, 1864, the Cavalry of the West mounted and rode through the plaza in front of the Alamo. Ford wore his black hat, parts of his old uniforms, and a sword sash. Behind him came his volunteers singing "The Yellow Rose of Texas." They might have been singing with different accents. Perhaps some voices were cracked sopranos. But with him at their head they were dangerous.

In April 1864 the greater part of his command reached Laredo. Meeting with Santos Benavides, they moved out, driving south along the river. By the end of July, the Confederates had driven federal forces from the Rio Grande Valley to Brazos de Santiago. The ladies of Brownsville hailed him as a conquering hero and presented him with a silk flag.

In March 1865 the ranking Union and Confederate officers still on the Rio Grande declared a truce between gentlemen. They met at Brazos de Santiago at the mouth of the river. Since the war was all but over, they reasoned that more bloodshed would not serve any purpose. Between them they effected an uneasy peace.

As they had predicted, on April 9, 1865, Robert E. Lee surrendered at Appomattox Court House hundreds of miles from Texas and its nebulous peace. The terrible war was officially over.

In May 1865 Ford led his troop down to Brownsville, his eye on the Union soldiers for any sign that the truce would be violated. On the twelfth he dined with his superior, Brigadier General James Slaughter, the man who had signed the truce in the first place. Slaughter had received a dispatch that sixteen hundred Union troops were moving on Brownsville.

Ford reasoned that the reprisals were about to begin. The plan was to impose black troops on the town and put the whole of South Texas under martial law and a cruel reconstruction. Too many Union generals had lost men to the ammunition bought with gold paid for by cotton run through the blockade on King and Kenedy steamboats flying a Mexican flag.

"General," Ford asked, "what are you going to do?"

"Retreat," Slaughter replied.

"You can retreat and go to Hell if you wish. These men are mine, and I am going to fight!" Ford declared.

The next day, May 13, he led his men out into a thick clump of brush that curved along the edge of Palo Alto plain where the Indiana and New York regiments rested, dead tired from the oppressive heat and humidity.

Mounted on a nervous, prancing horse, Ford shouted at his Texans. "Men, we have whipped the enemy in all previous fights. We can do it again."

His troops cheered.

The Union soldiers heard the noise and fired into the thicket.

Over their salvo Ford yelled, "Charge!"

Three hundred horsemen yelled so loudly their shrieking could be heard above the guns three miles over the prairie. Like a tidal wave they burst out of the palmettos and mesquites and struck the Union flank. Nothing on earth could have stopped them.

The veteran Union troops broke and ran. Those who tried to stand and fight were run down to the last man as the cavalry thundered onward. For seven miles Ford's men chased the fleeing troops. They did not stop until their horses were knee-deep in the waves at Brazos de Santiago.

When Ford withdrew and took his count, he had not lost a single man. The Thirty-fourth Indiana had lost more than two-thirds of its troops. One hundred eleven enlisted men and four officers had been taken prisoner. The last battle of the Civil War had been fought at a terrible cost.

Many will say it should never have happened, but who can know the cost had the Union not had a strong lesson in what *los diablos Tejanos* could do if they were not treated fairly?

General Slaughter tried to seize the opportunity for himself. He sold the Confederate artillery, which had been Union artillery four years before, to General Mejia, the Imperialist officer in Matamoros, for twenty thousand silver pesos. He planned to accompany the artillery to Mexico and keep the money for himself.

Ford arrested Slaughter at pistol point and forced him to sign over his command and dismiss his men. Ford then used the silver to pay his own men and ordered them to disband and return quietly to their homes. He kept four thousand for himself, but he was still deeply in debt. On May 26 Ford took his family across the river and placed them under Mejia's protection. Then he went back to face the oncoming Union troops.

When a Union force of twenty-five thousand under the command of Major General Philip Henry Sheridan arrived, they could find no one to surrender to them. Ford had never received a Confederate commission. Sheridan was furious. The rebels had stolen what had originally been U.S. Army weapons. He sent representatives to Mejia demanding the return of the supplies. The general did not even acknowledge them.

On July 18, 1865, Ford took a parole and settled down in Brownsville. Just a couple of months after his fiftieth birthday, he was resigned to the fact that his days of soldiering were over forever. He had had a good long time, more glorious, exciting days than most men see in a lifetime. He put away his arms and his campaign uniforms with the merest of sighs.

He went back into the newspaper business. All in all, he worked for three Brownsville newspapers including the *Sentinel*, which he helped establish.

Cameron County could not forget him. He was a delegate to the 1872 Democratic National Convention. For four years Texas government had been under the control of E. J. Davis, the most unpopular governor the state ever had. Coke, the Democratic nominee won the election, but E. J. Davis would not surrender his office. An angry crowd gathered in front of the capitol. Their antipathy for Davis's Negro troops was about to cause a riot. Threats and curses were in the air. The Texans threatened to loot the armory.

Ford mounted his horse. As if by magic, men from his Texas Rifles and his Cavalry of the West appeared behind him. Up to the capitol they rode as they sang "The Yellow Rose of Texas."

Once there Ford stepped up to the podium, chastising the crowd in his most picturesque language. He persuaded the leaders of the mob to desist. He warned them that aggressive action would play into Davis's hands. The state would be placed under a military government with the governor at its head for years.

Volunteers from among the Rifles stepped forward to assist Coke to take his office in an orderly manner. The crowd melted away under Ford's stern gaze. W. P. Hardeman later told Ford that stopping the mob in 1874 was the greatest contribution Ford had made to the state. Hardeman ventured that had the mob carried out its aims "not less than 20,000 people would have been killed in two weeks—and Texas would not have recovered from it for fifty years."

Ford's military career ended with a glowing tribute to peace.

In 1874 he was elected mayor of Brownsville. He represented Cameron County at the Constitutional Convention in 1875. Now sixty years old, he was experiencing economic hardship. He had no benefits or pension because so much of his soldiering had been done without Confederate or United States commissions.

An agent came to Ford's landlord and said no rent was to be collected for Ford's home. Days later a banker came with the news that at the beginning of every month $250 would be paid into Ford's account.

Ford never knew who paid it, but his daughter found out after his death. The benevolence had come from the King Ranch rebel Richard King.

From then on he lived in modest but comfortable circumstances. In 1876 he served as state senator. He was superintendent of the Deaf and Dumb Institute in Austin from 1879 to 1883. In January 1884 he was stricken again with malaria, which left him physically debilitated. He moved his family to San Antonio where he spent thirteen years writing articles and contributing to works of others. He began writing his memoirs, which was essentially fifty years of Texas history from 1836 when Ford arrived to 1885. He came to be recognized as one of the outstanding historians of the state. He was one of the founding fathers of the Texas State Historical Association when it was organized in February 1897. Ford wrote one of the first articles to appear in the *Quarterly*.

He was never able to find a publisher for his memoirs. The original manuscript, thirteen hundred handwritten pages, collected dust in the Archives Division of the University of Texas Library until J. Frank Dobie selected it for editing in his *Personal Narratives of the West Collection*. Stephen B. Oates took the job, and it was published by University of Texas Press in 1963.

In October 1897 John Salmon Ford suffered a severe stroke. He died on November 3 at eighty-two. His passion, his intelligence, and his rugged individualism worked sometimes for his benefit, sometimes for his detriment. He never became a great general or a famous legislator or a great writer or a great pioneer. Yet he remains one of the most talented Texans of the nineteenth century and surely one of Texas's greatest heroes.

*   *   *   *   *

The Texas Ranger Museum at Waco has many interesting artifacts of Ford's life and times.

His fascinating personal memoir, *Rip Ford's Texas*, is available at any library in Texas or through interlibrary loan.

The Artilleryman

Dick Dowling

From the Bank of Bacchus, Houston's busiest saloon, to the bank of the Sabine River under fire from Yankee gunboats is a step that stretches the bonds of credibility. It smacks of a tall Texas tale, certainly exaggerated, probably containing only a kernel of truth according to modern ways of thinking. Yet Texas's dynasty of courage was such that the leap seemed almost a natural step to a twenty-five-year-old Irishman born in Galway County, Ireland, in July of 1838.

Richard William Dowling, known to his many friends and few enemies as Dick, was such a character. Larger than life, he strode onto center stage for his brief moment in the pageant of Texas. Like a perfectly cast actor for a melodrama, he laughed and cursed and fought his way into history—part hero, part lover, part rogue.

In 1846 when the potato famine was ravaging Ireland, Dowling came with his family to New Orleans. Unlike so many cities along the eastern seaboard of the United States of America, it welcomed Catholics. The largest Irish colony in the South had settled there.

Unfortunately, the port proved terribly inhospitable in another way. In 1853 his parents William and Mary Dowling died in the yellow fever epidemic. As so many did, Dick and his brothers and sisters fled the disease by sailing for Galveston, Texas. In 1855 they moved on to Houston.

The young, brash state of Texas had for nine turbulent years been a sovereign nation. It became his home. He liked the feeling of independence. Quickly, he adopted its heritage—the Texas of the Alamo and San Jacinto. At seventeen he recognized no limitations on what he might achieve. This was the state of the filibusters, the *empresarios*, the cotton kings, and the cattle barons.

Dick was a good lad, a practicing Catholic, looking out for a good Catholic girl with whom to marry and raise a family. At mass he met the Odlums, the brothers Benjamin and Frederick and Benjamin's pretty daughter, Elizabeth Ann.

When Dick was only nineteen, Benjamin staked his future son-in-law to open a saloon in a two-story building on Main Street.

The Shades had a taproom on the ground floor and a pool hall and meeting place on the second. The likable Irishman often tended bar and was the originator of several drinks famous throughout the city. The most popular of his concoctions was "Kiss Me Quick and Go." Unfortunately, the exact ingredients existed only in their maker's memory. No one today has any idea how to make the drink that "lingered on the palate like the memory of a dream of paradise."

Shortly thereafter, Dick married Annie Odlum, whose name comes down through history because he named his guns after her. How he must have laughed and chucked her under the chin when he told her how she was with him in every battle!

Benjamin Odlum's initial financing provided all the impetus Dick needed. He worked hard and prospered. Comfort and conviviality, then as now, were the keys to a successful barroom. He installed gaslights and invited all sorts of fraternal and political clubs to meet upstairs.

The Shades was a success as much because of Dick as any of the amenities. What was not to like about this charming family man with the big smile and the shock of blazing red hair? He was as happy as only an Irishman could be.

His fortunes grew as he sold one business and bought two. The *Houston Telegraph* recorded one of them: The Bank of Bacchus on the corner of Main and Congress Streets. The enterprise was a combination to leave modern bankers white-lipped and

trembling. Dick cashed drafts, lent money, and operated a pawn shop for his customers. Either before or after that business was concluded, he sold them brandy, rum, whiskey, and champagne.

By today's standards he sounds unsavory. By rough-and-tumble nineteenth-century-Texas standards, he was a respected member of the community. The men who made the state had

150 · *The Artilleryman*

little time for measuring their peers by who their families were or whether their fortune was stable.

Every man was a newcomer and the more daring the better. If a man tried and failed, he could start all over again. Texas seemed like a boundless country with boundless opportunities. Results not means were what counted.

As a consequence Dowling's customers included many of the most admired men in Houston and certainly their most up-and-coming. Among them was Edward Hopkins Cushing, the editor-owner of the newspaper the *Houston Telegraph*.

Doubtless, Dick liked Cushing. Dick liked everybody. As a courtesy he furnished the editor as well as the paper's pressmen complimentary drinks. Cushing's paper, one of the influential papers in Texas at that time, carried advertisements for Dowling's enterprises, probably free of charge. The *Houston Telegraph* was one of the few newspapers in the entire South that published uninterrupted throughout the war.

As regional differences mounted in intensity and threatened to split the Union, southern cities were organizing local military units. Houston had several. One of its most famous was the Houston Light Artillery. In 1859 Dowling joined the unit because his wife's uncle, Frederick H. Odlum, was a ranking member.

The *Houston Telegraph* spread the company's fame. Cushing always carried glowing reports about them. The unit's ranks were filled entirely with Irishmen, all in their twenties or younger, brave and determined fighters, survivors whose sense of brotherhood made them formidable.

In the early days of Texas *empresarios*, two colonies had been settled by Irishmen McMullen and McGloin. The Irish fit well into the desperate plans the Spanish made to keep Texas a part of Mexico. They were generally Catholic. Therefore, they were not readily accepted in the heavily Protestant United States. They were tradesmen who carried the tools of their trade with them. They were good family men. Most important, they were willing to swear allegiance to the King of Spain, an oath most Anglo-Americans were not prepared to take.

In 1860 when the Houston Light Artillery all but disbanded, Dick and his Uncle Fred reorganized them into the Davis Guards, named in honor of Jefferson Davis, the leader of the states' rights faction in the United States Senate.

Odlum, who had some scant military training, became their captain, and Dowling became his first lieutenant and company paymaster. Other members of the Odlum and Dowling families held similar high positions. The rest of the company were dock-walloper, roustabouts, bartenders, and buckoes whose common ground was Ireland.

In 1861 they moved to Galveston where they came under the command of Colonel John Salmon "Rip" Ford, Texas Ranger and Mexican War officer.

A genuine war hero, Ford, whom Governor Hardin R. Runnels had appointed to the rank of major and senior captain of the Rangers, had fought and won a decisive battle against the Tenawa Comanches on the Canadian River.

Now in command of an expedition to the Rio Grande to force the Union army to withdraw from Fort Brown near Brownsville and Fort Ringgold Barracks near Rio Grande City, Ford needed men.

In fact, he had come to Houston for the Davis Guards.

Unfortunately, his men didn't mix well with the Irishmen. A great deal of prejudice existed between the families brought in by the *empresarios*, the original Anglo inhabitants of Texas, and the new settlers who had come into Texas in two waves.

The first wave, a gentle lapping at the shore, had come after Sam Houston's defeat of Santa Anna in 1836. The second wave, a tidal wave of adventurers and fortune-seekers, had come in 1845 when the United States annexed Texas.

Still, a fight was what the Davis Guards were organized for. Under Ford's command they sailed to the mouth of the Rio Grande where no battle ensued. The Union garrisons on the border surrendered and withdrew without a shot. With no common enemy, the enmity between the Davis Guards and the former army of the Republic of Texas was at the point of mutiny.

Odlum cried religious prejudice and discrimination. His entire unit was in danger of being court-martialed, but Ford managed to soothe their outraged feelings and reinstate them. The Irish received a sympathetic editorial and a great deal of favorable publicity from Cushing's *Houston Telegraph*, which sent the story statewide.

The Davis Guards returned to Houston as quickly as Ford could get rid of them in March 1861. No doubt that would have seen the end of them because no regimental commander wanted them assigned to him.

But at dawn on April 12, 1861, the South leveled her guns at Fort Sumter in the middle of Charleston Harbor. Their thunder, which killed no one but ushered in the bloodiest war this nation would ever fight, changed the fortunes of the Davis Guards forever.

The North blockaded the southern ports almost from the beginning of the war. The plan was always to starve the South rather than risk Northern lives. But as a year rolled by and the taxpayer expense mounted, the strategists grew desperate. In an attempt to end it quickly, they decided to splinter the Confederacy as well as starve her.

In April 1862, almost a year to the day after the South had fired on Fort Sumter, Rear Admiral David F. Farragut blasted through Forts Jackson and St. Philip, at the mouth of the Mississippi River, and steamed upriver.

Although the forts poured cannonade like "all the earthquakes in the world, and all the thunder and lightnings . . . going off at once," Farragut steamed ahead to New Orleans. The city surrendered; Baton Rouge and Natchez followed. The South had only one stronghold left to hold it together—Vicksburg.

So long as the town on the bluffs held, the cotton wagons could go through, carrying their vital cargo overland to Houston, Galveston, and eventually to Brownsville and Rio Grande City. There Texas riverboats flying Mexican flags would carry the precious cargo out into the Gulf of Mexico. The ships of Holland, England, and France awaited them to pay bright gold for the raw materials to keep their looms operating.

So long as Vicksburg held.

So long as Galveston held.

In Houston the Davis Guards were first assigned to the Third Texas Artillery Battalion as Company F. They helped to install the guns in and around Galveston. Dick Dowling had his first experience in actually handling the artillery he was supposed to be firing.

The battalion became a full regiment, retaining their Company F designation. In October 1862 they became part of Joseph J. Cook's First Texas Heavy Artillery Regiment. Cook had been assigned the defense of the Texas coast from Sabine Pass, the easternmost boundary, to Velasco, south of Galveston. He was a Methodist and a graduate of the U.S. Naval Academy at Annapolis, but he recognized excellent raw material in the Irish Texans. He began personally to train and drill the unit in gunnery techniques.

And drill them he did.

Legend has it that they had nothing but whiskey barrels from Dowling's saloons to make targets from. Of course, full barrels would not float, so many of the Irishmen "volunteered" to drink the barrels down to a reasonable weight so they could be used for target practice. When the barrels were deemed appropriate, the artillerymen would string them out at hundred-yard intervals in the bay and shoot at them. It was recorded that every Saturday night the Davis Guards worked diligently to provide the targets so that practice could make perfect.

In October 1862 Commander William B. Renshaw, commanding a Union naval squadron of eight vessels, moved into Galveston Bay to capture the city and neutralize the port.

Cook chose not to fight. Instead, he pulled his guns back, retreating to Virginia Point but keeping a manned battery at the south end of the railroad bridge that crossed from the island to the mainland. In this way he hoped to keep Renshaw on the island, leaving the waterway open to ocean-going traffic to Houston.

Renshaw dug in. Cook waited. For three months nothing happened. The Davis Guards grumbled as they cooled their heels at Virginia Point.

On Christmas Eve, Renshaw ordered Burrell to make the first move to take Houston. His objective was Kuhn's wharf, a particularly strong dock at the end of Twentieth Street. Partially made of brick, it would make an excellent bastion.

The Southern effort at repulse was led by a group of incompetents headed by General John B. Magruder, called "Prince John" because of his love of fancy military uniforms. He was a recent reject from Eastern Seaboard operations.

The commander of the naval force was Leon Smith, said to be the brother of Lincoln's Secretary of the Interior. The Confederate infantry force was under the command of General "Dirty Neck Bill" Scurry.

Only Colonel Cook's regiment, including the Davis Guards, was ready to fight.

The battle commenced with the signal shot from an artillery piece fired by Magruder himself on the morning of January 1, 1863. It was the first and only shot Prince John fired. From there the battle disintegrated into a comedy of errors.

No one seemed to know how to utilize Scurry's infantry.

The Davis Guards were given scaling ladders and ordered to plunge into the bay off Twentieth Street. Though they protested they were an artillery unit, they obeyed. Under fire they waded out to Kuhn's wharf and attempted to scale the pier where the Union occupying force had torn up the planking.

Once in the shadow of the warehouse, Odlum, Dowling, and the rest of the Irishmen discovered the scaling ladders they'd been issued were too short. Ignominiously, they retreated, cursing and sustaining casualties. Four men were wounded and one was killed.

In the end Leon Smith arrived late with his ragtag navy. With a lucky shot he succeeded in putting one of the Union gunboats out of action. The rest of the Union navy turned tail. Commander Renshaw asked for a truce and withdrew his vessels from Galveston. Burrell surrendered.

Galveston was restored to the Confederacy almost through no fault of her own.

The *Houston Telegraph* carried the account of the Davis Guards' action, heaping glory on them, although they really did nothing significant. The account was probably written by Dowling himself, who eloquently praised "the sons of old Erin."

The inaccurate account incurred resentment among the Confederate officers who had actually engaged in battle. Magruder, in particular, wanted favorable press for himself in the hopes of effecting a transfer back to "the action." Forthwith, Dick Dowling and his men were assigned to Fort Griffin on the Texas side of Sabine Pass, a half mile south of Sabine City and more than a hundred miles from Houston.

The assignment was probably a punishment. Magruder could see no strategic importance in Fort Griffin. Let the Houston Light Artillery make heroes of themselves over there. He was chagrined when almost immediately they did

Within days after arriving at Fort Griffin, on January 21, 1863, the Houston Company was ordered aboard two Sabine River steamers, *Uncle Ben* and *Josiah H. Bell*, officially designated as the Second Squadron of Magruder's navy.

They were a pitiful pair of "cotton-clads." That is, in place of armor plate they had bales of cotton strapped to their railings to protect the crew from shot and shell. Cotton actually did as fair a job as anything else. In nineteenth-century sea fights, the deadliest damage to personnel was done by splintering decks and superstructures. The thick bales absorbed the sharp oak spikes better than iron. Unfortunately, between the two boats were seven guns, only one of which was really serviceable.

Dowling boarded *Bell* where Frederick Odlum was given the title chief of ordnance. Dick immediately manned the eight-inch Columbiad rifle mounted on the deck. In keeping with the artillery tradition, he named it "Annie" in honor of his wife. Also on board were a battalion of cavalry (without their horses) and infantry. They were to serve as sharpshooters to take out the enemy's crew at close range and to board the enemy vessels when the fight was joined.

Bell and *Uncle Ben* set out at daylight, crossed the bar an hour later, and steamed toward their objectives. Two Union sailing ships, *Morning Light* with nine guns and *Velocity* with two, had been standing off Sabine Pass blockading shipping.

Thanks to Colonel Cook's target practice, Lieutenant Dowling directed "Annie's" fire with deadly accuracy. Shot after shot fell on the open deck of *Morning Light*, wounding and killing wherever they struck. They struck often and from all sides because the windjammers could not outmaneuver the steamboats.

The range closed to a thousand yards. From there the sharpshooters opened up to drive the unarmed crewmen below decks. Cheering and laughing, Dick and his men cut the sails to rags, splintered the spars, and riddled the deck. With a couple of well-placed shells below the water line, the hold of *Morning Light* began to fill.

She struck her colors and hoisted the white flag. *Velocity* followed her lead. Lieutenant Dick Dowling commanded the party that went aboard *Morning Light*, which he saved from sinking. Eventually, *Morning Light* had to be burned because she was too heavy to negotiate the bar, but *Velocity* became a member of the Confederate navy. Besides the small ship, the expedition captured $100,000 worth of stores and eleven artillery pieces, each one better than the ones on *Bell* and *Uncle Ben*. For the sharpshooters they obtained one hundred fifty stands of small arms.

When "Junius," a.k.a. Dick Dowling, wrote the story for the *Houston Telegraph*, Cushing read it aloud outside the newspaper office. The crowd cheered, bells pealed, all Houston celebrated. Of course, "Junius's" account featured the exploits of Company F. Captain Odlum, Lieutenant Dowling, and the Davis Guards were covered in glory. Dick's exploits with "Annie" were touted far and wide, to the disgust of Prince John Magruder and the rest of his staff, who had hoped to hear nothing more of the Irishman for the duration of the war.

Dick wrote that although he and his gun crew "occupied the most dangerous position during the entire engagement, not a man flinched, and the enemy gave him credit for making the prettiest shots they ever saw." His boyish delight in his accomplishment sings in the lines. He was making the "prettiest shots" and loving every minute of it.

A Texas hero was in the making.

Magruder gritted his teeth and left them where they were. Surely. Surely, nothing else would happen to add to the glory he so craved.

Josiah H. Bell and *Uncle Ben* steamed back up the Sabine. The Davis Guards went back to Fort Griffin, undoubtedly groaning and cursing at the ingratitude and short-sightedness of the men in power. For the rest of the winter, the spring, and the summer, they worked to strengthen the fort.

The whole encirclement was made of mud and shored up with timbers. Three bastioned walls were twelve feet thick and eight feet high facing east, south, and west toward the river. The likelihood that the walls were high enough to stop incoming cannonade from gunboats was remote. Consequently, the artillerists dug bombproof shelters for their own protection. Likewise, they dug magazines to store their powder and shot, mindful that a lucky shot could turn their fort into a boiling cauldron.

Still the unit knew they couldn't do much but hug the walls, as they stood to their weapons, if enemy shells came whistling over and exploded inside.

Across the north side at their rear was an earthen redoubt only about four feet high. If the enemy managed to land a force to outflank the Guards, they would have no defense. Their fort would turn into a barrel. And they would be the fish.

The half-mile road between Sabine City and the fort was repaired. Most of the men spent their nights there, so no barracks were ever built inside its walls.

Probably because of Magruder's jealousy, the Guards were not allowed to keep the armaments they had captured from *Morning Light* and *Velocity*.

As it stood, Fort Griffin's armament consisted of two thirty-two-pounder smoothbores, two thirty-two-pounder howitzers, and two twenty-four-pounder smoothbores—salvage pieces from an abandoned fort and from another ship. Everyone knew they were in such bad shape that they were really unsafe for sustained firing.

Their maximum range was not much over one mile. These were faced south and east in order to engage an enemy force soon after it had crossed the bar and entered the channel.

The better of the thirty-two-pounders Dick named "Annie." It was his weapon, the one he served whenever they practiced firing.

And practice they did.

With precious little to do, they drove stakes painted various colors into both the Louisiana and Texas channels of the pass. Between them they strung a few buoys and the legendary whiskey barrels.

In this manner they constructed accurate gun-sighting tables all across the pass. Their fire was deadly accurate within a distance of about two thousand yards. If an enemy ship steamed within the staked area, it wouldn't stand a chance.

With nothing else to do, they watched and waited.

In September 1863 the strategy of the Northern Congress and Abraham Lincoln's generals turned to attack. The Northern constituency wanted victory and an end to the increasingly bloody and costly Civil War. No longer could the Union be content with standing off the harbors and blockading. They had to win as the war grew increasingly unpopular.

"Divide and conquer" became their literal motto. Send boats up the Mississippi, down the Tennessee, and up the Sabine. Isolate the parts from each other, blockade the ports from foreign trade and supplies, let the South run out of ammunition, not to mention all kinds of manufactured goods.

In those days the Sabine was open to riverboats as far north as Jefferson, in effect the entire eastern border. Domination of the Sabine would have cut Texas off from the rest of the South. Likewise, scores of young men who would have left the farms and ranches to ride east to swell the numbers of the Confederacy would have been contained in Texas.

Lincoln's generals were right. The loss of the Sabine River would probably have shortened the war by months, perhaps years.

With New Orleans in Union hands, the two objectives of highest priority became Mobile, Alabama, and the Gulf Coast of the Lone Star State. The choice of where to attack the Texas Gulf Coast was left to General N. P. Banks, commander of the Department of the Gulf. Although he was nominally a general, he was actually a political appointee, nicknamed derogatorily "Commissary Banks" and "Hero of Boston Common."

Banks chose Sabine Pass not because he would cut off the entire state but because it would be easy to take. Another inducement was some forty thousand bales of cotton reported to be stored in Sabine City. The sale of those bales would put money in the pocket of the North—directly after he drew a percentage for himself.

A glance at the map and a quick reading of his reports revealed nothing to prevent him. Indeed, he would be an instant success. He could claim his victory and watch while others fought the hard battle at Mobile.

Banks selected as his tactical commander General William Buel Franklin, who had fought with the Army of the Potomac until he'd been court-martialed by General Ambrose Burnside for insubordination and lack of activity. Although Franklin was later exonerated, his career was compromised. Like Magruder, he'd been transferred to a less important post where he could do less harm.

Banks's plan was that after the surrender and capture of Fort Griffin, an army of some fifteen thousand men would commandeer the Beaumont-to-Houston railroad to carry them overland to Houston. Banks probably pictured a train bristling with Union guns—chugging through the town. Such an attack coming from within Houston's very heart would meet with little or no resistance. With the town secure, nearly five hundred miles of Texas railroad—easy access to the rest of Texas—would be obtained in one fell swoop.

Nothing stood between them and the completion of their plan but a mud fort and a handful of Irishmen.

The Neches and the Sabine Rivers flow into Lake Sabine, ten miles wide and twenty-five miles long. At its southern end, the lake becomes Sabine Pass, a relatively narrow channel between one and two thousand feet wide and approximately two miles long. Fort Griffin sat at the mouth of the pass with its guns toward the Gulf. Thirty miles from the Gulf at the northwest corner of the lake, Beaumont sat undefended with its all-important railroad.

Banks's first problem occurred when the fifteen thousand troops were reduced to five thousand. Still the plan seemed doable. The Western Gulf Squadron assigned four gunboats to the operation—*Clifton, Sachem, Arizona,* and *Granite City*. All except *Clifton* were poorly equipped and lightly armored. Acting lieutenant Frederick E. Crocker was placed in charge.

Though resentful, Banks was unconcerned. He was certain that he would meet with no resistance. The fewer men and arms he had, the more he would cover himself with glory. With visions of reinstatement and return to the Army of the Potomac, perhaps in command over Burnside, he ordered his task force into the pass.

According to his best intelligence, the enemy would meet him with four cotton-clads, the ever-ready *Uncle Ben* and *Josiah H. Bell* along with *Florida* and *Roebuck,* neither of which had any weapons at all. Behind the mud walls of Fort Griffin were approximately fifty men, a baby-faced lieutenant named Dick Dowling in command.

How Banks must have grinned and rubbed his hands in satisfaction at the prospect of the easy victory!

On the first of September the expedition sailed from New Orleans. The four gunboats of the Western Squadron steamed ahead to protect the fleet while it cut its way through the Gulf. Once inside the pass their orders would be to reduce Fort Griffin to rubble.

Behind them came eighteen transports containing over five thousand troops, fifty wagons and ambulances, and hundreds of horses and mules. It was an army of occupation. Six of the heavily laden ships were designated for attack.

Did Lieutenant Dick Dowling know they were coming?

Captain Odlum at Sabine City received a dispatch from Magruder on September 6. Immediately, he placed the fort under twenty-four-hour alert and tried to reach the seventeen men on leave. At that time only forty-seven men with Dowling as their commander were in the fort.

On September 7 Magruder received a telegram informing him of the size of the flotilla. He sent word to Odlum that it would be useless for the handful of Davis Guards to offer battle. His orders were to blow up the fort and fall back to Beaumont.

Magruder was no coward, but he was a prudent man who knew very well that he had only a handful of Confederate troops in the area to support the men in the fort. At this point he thought to save every man for the bigger battle he foresaw—the defense of Houston.

Odlum sent the word on to Dowling. He did not actually order his lieutenant to obey. Instead, he left the decision to him. Spike the guns and retreat—or stay and fight to the last man.

The dock-walloper and bartenders led by their twenty-five-year-old lieutenant came to a unanimous decision to fight. The overwhelming odds only fortified their decision.

Like for the men of the Alamo, Sabine Pass was their moment in history. The Alamo with under two hundred men had held out for thirteen days against more than two thousand crack Mexican troops. Sabine Pass could do no less than make a stand. They saw their destiny clear before them. They embraced it with lusty cheers.

The pass itself presented a difficult route for the gunboats to sail into. A massive oyster bed half a mile wide and a mile and a half long split it into two distinct channels. The depth of the water over the bed was only about two feet. It severely limited their maneuverability as well as created a tricky barrier for the heavily laden attack transports.

The western channel, called the Texas Channel, was less than five hundred yards from Fort Griffin's guns, not a pleasant prospect for any captain. The eastern channel, the Louisiana Channel, although wider, was within the one-mile range of the "Annie" as well as the other smoothbores and the howitzers. Dowling and his men must have grinned as they sighted across the Louisiana Channel between the painted stakes they had used for target practice for so many months. They were primed and ready. They would probably not have retreated if they had been ordered to.

On September 6 *Granite City*, commanded by Massachusetts whaling Captain Charles W. Lansom, dropped anchor at the bar of Sabine Pass. The designated point vessel was supposed to wait and observe. What he thought he observed sent him into a panic. Nervously sweeping the Gulf through his spyglass, he was sure he had sighted the dreaded "ghost ship of the Confederacy" *Alabama* steaming past him.

Lansom lost his nerve completely; weighing anchor in record time, he deserted his post and left the area. Heading east he hid in the Calcasieu River, thirty-five miles from Sabine Pass. When he was found, he stuck to his story of the Confederate raider. What he had really seen was the Union warship *Ossipee* taking the new commander of the Texas Coast Blockading Fleet to his duty station off Galveston.

Searching for *Granite City*, the Union flotilla missed the pass and steamed on to Galveston before discovering their mistake. With their plans in disarray, they turned around and sailed back only to miss the pass again. On the morning scheduled for the attack, General Godfrey Weitzel found himself and the First Division of five thousand infantry, more than half of whom were seasick, off the Louisiana coast. There he had found *Granite City* cowering in the river mouth.

The entire flotilla then sailed back to Sabine Pass where they anchored, two days late. The attack was then replanned for the morning of September 8. Of course, by this time the Union forces had lost the element of surprise. Everyone on both the Louisiana and Texas coasts knew where they were and what they were there for.

In an effort to offset the mistakes and the sheer incompetence, General Franklin abandoned his plan for an artillery-supported infantry landing on the sandy beaches west of Fort Griffin. Instead he ordered the gunboats to shell the fort into submission. This tactic had worked well in the past. Several times when Confederate forts had been fired upon, the occupying force had withdrawn without a shot.

Franklin was counting heavily on their retreat. The obvious incompetence and probable cowardice of *Granite City's* captain bothered him. He wanted a quick victory to get the men on the ground at Beaumont.

The only person with reservations about the new plan was Acting Lieutenant Crocker in command of the gunboat *Clifton*. His craft didn't have the guns necessary to inflict heavy damage. Since he had never seen the mud fort, he had only Lansom's word that it could be blown apart without much trouble.

He had to keep these doubts to himself. Since his gunboat was to move up the channel at daybreak of the eighth, he could say little without being thought a coward, which he most certainly was not.

Consequently, at dawn *Clifton* steamed over the bar and moved to within three-quarters of a mile of Fort Griffin. At that distance, they dropped anchor and opened fire with his long-range, nine-inch Parrott rifle. Twenty-six shells screamed toward the fort. Most were near misses, but two scored direct hits. They sent dirt and debris flying in all directions, but Crocker could see through his spyglass that he was doing little damage.

He was also suspicious of the lack of return fire. Through his glass he could see the dirt walls were intact. He could see the heavy caliber guns yawning in his direction. He knew he was well within their range. He retreated to the bar and pondered the situation.

Despite seeing a few men moving about and the bow of a miserable little "cotton-clad" sticking out around the north side of the fort, he could detect no possibility of serious opposition, should the Confederates decide to resist at the last minute.

He really had no choice.

He signaled the attack to begin.

Three more gunboats crossed the bar. Six attack transports moved up to anchor at the mouth of the pass, two miles below the fort. The plan was to let off twelve hundred infantry, twelve guns, and fifty wagons including ambulances. The infantry would close at the same time that the gunboats moved up the channel to bombard the fort.

A combined land and sea attack would level the fort and kill or capture its company in a matter of minutes.

Unfortunately, the army could not land. When a small boat carrying Lieutenant Crocker made a reconnaissance of the Texas shore, he reported that sailors sank to their knees in muck. Franklin reckoned that fully equipped infantrymen would sink past their belts.

The land attack was therefore moved to the site of old Fort Sabine on a low bluff where the boats could get in closer. The fact that it was well within the range of the guns of the Davis Guards was ignored.

More plans were discarded and made.

Inside the fort, Dick and his men played cards, cooked and ate their lunches, peered over their walls at the hustle and bustle going on so close to them, and in general, behaved as if nothing momentous was about to happen to them.

At three-thirty in the afternoon, he observed the gunboats at last moving up the channel. He advised his men to put their cards away and stand to their guns. In minutes they were ready. Manning the six guns required almost every man. Only three were assigned to run powder and two were spared to serve as couriers.

Dowling commanded the thirty-two-pounder smoothbores, including "Annie." Sergeant Tom Dougherty commanded the two twenty-four-pounder smoothbores. A recent addition from the Corps of Engineers, Lieutenant N. H. Smith commanded the thirty-two-pounder howitzers.

When everyone was as ready he would ever be, Lieutenant Dick Dowling stepped to center stage in history. In a motley uniform, a saber at his side, and a pistol stuck in his belt, he mounted the parapet. From there he gave his men a speech taken straight from William Barret Travis's letter from the Alamo—"Victory or Death."

He compared their position to the Alamo. He reminded them that the innocent Texas families fleeing from Santa Anna in the Runaway Scrape had been depending on the men at the San Antonio mission to fight to the last man. So it was with the men of Fort Griffin. They knew they were outnumbered. They knew they couldn't win. But, by heaven, Texas depended on them.

Every man among them must have swelled with pride and determination. Dick's last words were a caution to them. They were not to fire until the gunboats were well within range—that is, in the Louisiana and Texas Channels between the painted stakes where every shot would count.

Almost before he finished speaking, the battle was joined.

The gunboat *Sachem*, commanded by Acting Lieutenant Amos Johnson, steamed up the Louisiana Channel firing as she came. *Arizona* followed in her wake but made little headway. She was much heavier than *Sachem*. Her captain was an acting master pilot with neither a naval commission nor a pilot's license. Within minutes *Arizona* floundered and became stuck in the mud.

Undeterred or perhaps unaware that *Arizona* was aground, *Sachem* continued up the Louisiana Channel, firing even though her gun crews hadn't found the range. Meanwhile, *Clifton*, under the command of Acting Lieutenant Crocker, steamed cautiously up the narrower Texas Channel. The shells lobbed from her Parrott gun also were largely ineffective because her efforts to maneuver kept the crew busy resighting.

Inside the fort the Davis Guards waited, no doubt polishing their gunsights, as the vessels moved closer and closer to "stake range." At twelve hundred yards *Sachem* slipped among the painted markers. Dick sighted "Annie" and touched off the powder. The boom was the signal for the rest of the guns to speak.

The thunder from the fort was answered by the thunder from the channel. One of *Clifton's* nine-inch shells clipped off the sighting screw on "Annie" just seconds after Dowling fired the first shot. If battles are won by one brave deed, they are also lost by one tragic mischance. The outcome at Sabine Pass would surely have been different if Dowling had died on the first salvo.

Meanwhile, *Arizona* had managed to back off the mud and opened fire also, but her shells fell far short and actually whistled close enough to *Clifton's* wheelhouse to make her crew duck.

Sachem meanwhile was in trouble. She was now opposite the fort, among the painted stakes, broadside to the guns of Fort Griffin. The third salvo smashed into the railings and took away several lifeboats, a section of the cabin, and part of the smokestack. The devastation was horrible. The exploding wood sent a hailstorm of splinters into the crew. Men screamed in agony as wood and fiery shrapnel rained down on them.

To his credit, Johnson never faltered. Through it all, the gunboat steamed on, desperately trying to reach Lake Sabine and outflank the fort. The broadside destruction continued all along her length. Shells from "Annie" and her sisters holed *Sachem's* superstructure, disabled half her guns, and splintered her deck in several places. Whether her rudder was damaged or the wheelhouse disabled is not known. What happened was that she suddenly swung to starboard and stuck on the mud.

The gunners behind the walls cheered and clapped each other on the back, as they loaded up another round to finish her off.

Now a sitting target, she was struck amidships by the next shot. It drove completely through her armor, through her boiler, and landed in the mud beyond. Her crew as well as the sharpshooters on her upperdecks were enveloped in live steam. Men with their hair and clothing afire deserted their posts and jumped overboard to escape being burned and cooked alive.

Acting Lieutenant Johnson on board *Sachem* signaled frantically to *Arizona* for help, but the heavier gunboat's acting master pilot had no stomach for the fight. He reversed the engines and backed as rapidly as possible out of danger. In so doing, he deserted a fellow officer, left many badly wounded men to drown, and raised the white flag.

The Davis Guards fired a few more rounds into *Sachem* until Dick Dowling yelled a warning to watch out for *Clifton*. Guns thundering, she came at full speed straight up the narrow Texas Channel toward Fort Griffin.

The lieutenant directed all six of Fort Griffin's guns on the steaming gunboat. By now the gunners had been working their guns so fast that they were blistering their hands on the hot barrels. Concerned about their nearly hysterical glee at their unexpected success, Dick cautioned his men to make every shot count. The loss of one ironclad and the cowardice of another's captain was not the end of the battle.

They were mercilessly outgunned. Recoil had backed one of their thirty-two-pounder howitzers off its carriage, leaving them with only five serviceable weapons. Their protection was a mud wall. And most devastating, they were outmanned. They were only forty-eight men against more than five thousand. The odds were more than a hundred to one. Of course, Dick didn't tell his men that. Perhaps he didn't know the odds himself. He told them they had to keep fighting, make their guns wreak maximum destruction with their limited ammunition at the next most dangerous target.

At the same time Lieutenant Crocker, *Clifton's* commander, ordered his gunners to throw everything they had at the fort in the hope of disabling their guns or at least pulling their direction away from *Sachem*. Because of the oyster bed, he could not come to their aid. The ensuing rapid fire sent great chunks of earth geysering out of the fort's south wall. Whether he knew that he was attacking by himself is unknown. *Granite City*, with the cowardly Lansom still in charge, had not yet crossed the bar into the pass.

Clifton was still outside the staked target area and zigzagging as much as she could in the five-hundred-yard channel. The noise and the damage to the fort were incessant. Still, the Guards never faltered. They stood to their guns. When *Clifton* finally came into range, a lucky shot on the first salvo tore away her tiller.

Bad luck had her headed toward the bank, where she ran aground in the mud and reeds. Three hundred yards from the fort, the 210-foot vessel presented a target a blind man could have hit. Now every shot fired by Dowling's men was a direct hit. Her superstructure was torn to pieces; splinters rained over the crew and sharpshooters. Another shot breeched her steam drum, sending her screaming men into the water to escape the live steam and the flames.

Crocker's executive officer was killed. His doctor hid behind the rudder rather than remain on deck to tend the wounded. Yet in the face of sure defeat, Crocker was every bit as determined as Dick Dowling would have been under those circumstances. Turning his port side Parrott rifle inward, he blasted a hole through his own cabin to get a clear field to fire toward the enemy.

Inside the fort Dowling ordered his men to switch to grape shot and canister to sweep the decks clean. In the midst of the bombardment, Commodore Leon Smith, who had commanded the navy at Galveston the year before, and Captain Frederick Odlum entered the fort. They had come by road from Sabine City without opposition.

Dowling immediately saluted with the intention of relinquishing command, but they both refused to take it. Smith shook his hand and told him to carry on. The commodore declared he was merely taking the opportunity to observe a great victory in the offing. Morale flying high, the Davis Guards paused to give the visiting officers three hearty cheers.

Their voices rang out over the water undermining what little morale remained on the dying *Clifton*. Crocker gave an order to his second executive officer to collect a detail and attempt to put out the fire. The man refused to obey. Instead, within minutes he had hauled the ensign down.

Crocker could do no more. His ship was disabled. Only two guns were operational. Most of his officers were dying or in hiding. Most of his crew was in the water or too badly wounded to jump. Crocker raised the white flag.

In the meantime, Johnson, aboard the wreck of *Sachem*, ordered the thirty-pounder Parrott gun spiked, the magazine flooded, and the signal book destroyed. With his men already wading ashore in Louisiana, he hoisted the white flag in surrender.

In the eerie silence the Guards looked at each other. They couldn't believe they had destroyed two out of three gunboats. This must be a trap. They were supposed to fight to the death. They had made up their minds to die.

Dick Dowling himself carried a white flag of truce tied to his saber. He didn't bother to don a shirt. Perhaps he couldn't find his in the confusion of mud, heat, and powder-smoke that prevailed in Fort Griffin. Stripped to the waist, his red hair singed and black with powder smoke, his sweat leaving white runnels through the grime on his skin, the lieutenant was rowed out to *Clifton*.

What Crocker thought of the man who accepted his surrender is unknown. He might have been amazed at his obvious youth. But he would have recognized his equal in the bright red powder burns on Dowling's chest and arms.

Two brave men stood face to face as Crocker yielded his sword. Then Dowling went below to inspect the magazines. His men had fired nearly one hundred fifty rounds from his six cannons without stopping to swab the guns. He was delighted at the Union ordnance still dry and very plentiful. He believed these moments to be only a brief respite before another fight. He was less pleased with the prospect of three hundred prisoners to march off to Sabine City and then to internment at Camp Groce for the duration of the war.

What was he going to do with them?

As for the men still on board *Sachem*, those who had not swum to the Louisiana shore were picked up by the cotton-clad *Uncle Ben* that they had made fun of two days before.

Dick reported that live action during the battle lasted only forty-five minutes. During that time he had in effect sunk two gunboats, killed twenty-eight Union soldiers and sailors, wounded seventy-five others seriously with many more sustaining minor wounds mostly from splinters. Thirty-six were missing and presumed drowned. Three hundred prisoners were taken.

No one inside the fort had any but the most superficial wounds, burns on the hands and powder burns to the body as Dick's were. Two of the guns had pieces sheered off, and the steel splinters had to be pulled out of two gunners, but they were inconsequential.

As a matter of fact, victory was theirs. Their courage covered them in glory without the sting of death. At the same time, cowardice and stupidity on the part of the Union forces contributed to their own defeat. The flotilla sailed back to New Orleans with such speed that it can only be called a rout.

Two of the attack transports that had crossed the bar behind the gunboats became so demoralized when first *Granite City*, then *Arizona* came churning by, that they jettisoned their cargoes in order to escape. One threw 200,000 pounds of rations onto a sandbar. The other dropped two hundred mules over the side with their forelegs tied to their halter ropes to be sure they drowned rather than fall into enemy hands.

Though Franklin made all sorts of excuses, his career was justly finished.

The importance of victory at Sabine Pass cannot be belittled. It rightly raised a great outcry about the efficiency of the Union navy and the choice of officers to command it. The battle raised morale all over the South and so thoroughly frightened the North that no effort was ever made in the area again.

Two weeks later Braxton Bragg whipped Rosecrans soundly at Chickamauga. The rout at Sabine Pass followed by the loss of 16,600 men in one battle gave the Union a severe psychological shock. U.S. credit declined abroad while the dollar lost five percent of its value against gold.

By order of Jefferson Davis, one of the two war decorations officially awarded by the Confederacy was struck for the Davis Guards.

Four days after the battle, General "Prince John" Magruder came to Fort Griffin to bring them gratitude, spiritual blessings, and a proclamation naming Sabine Pass "the most brilliant affair..." He distributed gifts and honors. The officers received sabers. The enlisted men received the right to wear the word "Sabine" embroidered in a wreath design on their hats.

The story was told by the *Houston Telegraph*. Cushing compared the battle to the Alamo and then later to Thermopylae where the three hundred Spartans held the pass against the Persians in ancient times. He compared his friend Dick Dowling to Leonidas. Newspapers all across the South told the story.

Jefferson Davis heaped praise on "his" Guards. Sabine Pass, he said, was more remarkable than Thermopylae because of the greater numbers and variety of forces arrayed against them.

The city of Houston struck forty-eight medals out of Mexican silver dollars. On one side was engraved "Battle of Sabine Pass, September 8, 1863." On the other were the initials "D. G." for Davis Guards. The medals were threaded through with shamrock green ribbons. A benefit was staged that collected $3,380 for Dowling and his men.

For the next year and a half, the Guards waited at Fort Griffin for the next attack—that never came. Dowling was promoted to captain and then to major. He was detailed to travel around Texas recruiting men for the South.

Six weeks after Appomattox, May 18, 1865, he was paroled by Federal authorities and returned to Houston. The Union flag was raised over the fort he had fought so well to defend.

After the war his popularity stood him in good stead. The Bank of Bacchus became a favorite meeting place for the men in gray. For the next two years he invested his profits in real estate, farms, ranches, a warehouse in Galveston, a construction company, a steamboat, and oil and gas leases.

In September the luck of the Irish ran out. Only twenty-nine years old, the husband of his beloved Annie and the father of a son and a daughter, Dowling died of yellow fever. Thousands of silent Texans stood with bared heads in the soft rain as the funeral cortège made its way to the cemetery of St. Vincents. In the words of the *Telegraph*, "The far-off echoes of the guns of Fort Griffin have served as the funeral salvos for the warm-hearted hero, Dick Dowling."

* * * * *

A memorial park has been built on the site of Fort Griffin to honor the men of the Davis Guards. An impressive bronze statue of Dick Dowling was erected in 1936, the year of the Texas Centennial. The strapping Irishman, stripped to the waist, defiant, resolute, and—above all—courageous looks down the channel where his courage never faltered.

The first weekend in September has been designated "Dick Dowling Days." Crowds gather in the park to celebrate his victory.

The Confederacy of the Rio Grande

Santos Benavides

"The cotton belongs to the Confederacy. If the day goes against us, fire it. Not a single bale of it shall pass into the hands of the Yankees."

Colonel Jose de los Santos Benavides gave the orders to his brother Cristobal just before he led his men into combat against a force that outnumbered them five to one.

This scion of the founding father of Laredo performed with utterly ruthless courage and endurance throughout the Civil War. His superiors were in awe of him. His enemies, both Yankee and *bandido*, feared him, for they quickly learned that he would not stop. If they turned tail and ran, he pursued. If they splashed across the Rio Grande into Mexico, he led his troops after them. Implacable as Nemesis, he ran them down.

He took no prisoners.

In the annals of Texas history, he joins a select company described by one of their number, Ranger Captain Leander McNelly. "Courage is a man who keeps on—coming on! The man who keeps coming on—is either going to get there himself—or he is going to make it possible for a later man to get there."

Such a man was Santos Benavides, an aristocrat who kept his part of Texas free and independent for over a decade.

He was born November 1, 1823, in Laredo, a small town north of the Rio Grande in the state of *Coahuila y Tejas*, one of the northernmost states in New Spain. He was the great-

great-grandson of Don Tomas Sanchez de la Barrera y Garza, who founded the town in 1755.

Don Tomas came north to find new land and make a home for himself and his family without favor from King Ferdinand VI or the government in Mexico City, which was little interested in anything so far north unless it came from the silver mines of Zacatecas.

When so many *grandees* were being awarded huge grants of land by the weak Bourbon king in an effort to buy their alliances, Don Tomas did not even sue for such a thing. He wanted to be a rancher beholden to no man. He had served in the army to fight Indians before he dared the desert and the fierce Lipan Apaches to establish a settlement on the northern side of the big river. On May 15 he officially established his headquarters at the crossing called Paso de Jacinto. It couldn't be called a town. It was *Rancho de Laredo* with three families living there.

The site was registered as sixty-six thousand acres to be used for the inhabitants of the settlement. Don Tomas named himself *capitan de guerra y justicia mayor*, captain of war and major justice, setting a precedent for governance by him and his family that lasted through the next century. A priest from Revilla, twenty-two leagues away, came for an annual communion. Otherwise, the Garzas were left to their own resources. Once in a while, a *visitador* would come from Mexico City or more often from Monclova, the capital of Coahuila. Over the decades, they noted that the *rancho* became a town. Its population and its wealth grew steadily.

Laredo had the advantage of a great river, the Rio Grande, whose water flowed from the snows of the Rocky Mountains through deep stone canyons. Even though the town itself was hot and dusty most of the time, the herds of cattle and horses, the flocks of sheep and goats had plenty of fresh water and unlimited acres to graze.

Because no Indian tribes lived in the vicinity, it had no mission. Therefore, the best land had not been claimed by the Church. For the most part they were outside the arms of God. The people who came to live there had to have a strong streak of

independence while leaders had to have a strong sense of responsibility.

While viceroys came and went in Mexico City and rebellion fomented, the Garza family and their direct heirs in the Benavides family remained the caretakers of Laredo and the land around it.

In 1821 Mexico won her independence, but ways of living changed very little on the border.

The flag changed from the castles and lions of Imperial Spain to the tri-color eagle and serpent of Mexico, but Laredo scarcely noticed. The town was growing slowly and steadily under a Benavides son who had married a Garza daughter.

In 1836, when Santos was thirteen years old, Texas, the state primarily inhabited by Anglo-Celts from the United States, won her independence from Mexico and became a sovercign nation. She took Laredo on the northern side of the Rio Grande with her, more in an accident of geography than political leanings. The flag changed again to the Lone Star. By that time the majority of the people in the state spoke English. Indeed, fifty thousand of the state's sixty-eight thousand inhabitants spoke it.

Rather than being discouraged or fearful, the Benavides family, direct descendants of Don Tomas, was quietly pleased. While the language of Laredo was Spanish, city governors were still strongly Federalist in favor of local rule with no interference from Mexico City. So long as the Texans did not tell them how to run their business, everyone was happy. In this way they continued the tradition started by the town's founder, who had never depended on the strong central government of kings and viceroys. As yet their politics had never been tested. When danger came from these political leanings, would the Benavides rise to defend their convictions?

Santos became a rancher on land his father set aside for him. With ranch profits he opened a small store and began to read for the law. In this way he became more attached to the town than the cattle ranch. In 1842 he married a worthy young woman, Agustina de Villareal. The next year, at twenty, he entered politics when he was selected Laredo's *procurador,* that is, the town's attorney. He saw himself as a settled family man.

He wanted comfort for all the people of Laredo. Politics, the art of human happiness, was also part of his heritage. He grew up at the side of his uncle Bacilio Benavides, who had been three times elected Laredo's *alcalde,* or mayor, while the town was still part of New Spain. Santos was sure that eventually his life would lead him there. An almost too lazy, comfortable future stretched ahead of him.

Rumblings from south of the Rio Grande soon dispelled the notion that the future would be too comfortable. Conflict tore the new Mexico apart soon after she won her independence. The Federalists fought the Centralists, who believed that a strong government in Mexico City collecting taxes and doling them back was the best for the people. With the idea of collecting more and more taxes, the Centralists looked northward. Texas belonged to them, not to herself.

General Antonio Lopez de Santa Anna had been defeated and captured at San Jacinto in 1836. But he had come back to Mexico City and staged a second rise to power. It had cost the government of Mexico dearly. Expelled in 1845, he still represented a threat to the Herrera government, which still had not recognized Texas as a separate nation.

In 1845 a new flag flew over Laredo—the Stars and Stripes. Texas was annexed to the United States. Mexico declared war. Her troops tried to cross the Rio Grande at Brownsville, El Paso, and several points in between. When Texas troops from Austin met them outside of Laredo, Bacilio Benavides joined them, taking his nephew Santos with him. At the young age of twenty-two, he had his first taste of fighting.

No record exists to tell whether he was afraid or whether he acquitted himself admirably. In the light of his later performance, he was probably no more or less afraid than any other raw young man. Those engagements must have tested his mettle and tempered it. No record tells whether his older brother Refugio, the one destined to inherit the bulk of the Garza *rancho*, was with him, but in all likelihood, no one could have kept him at home.

Still Santos was the leader. Refugio was probably more cautious from a sense of his own responsibility. Probably their six-year-old half-brother Cristobal would have given up his hope of Heaven to go with them. What exciting times the brothers Benavides must have had. Reared in the tradition of the *caballero*, they would have been magnificent horsemen. What a picture they must have made riding hell-bent-for-leather with their comrades, their white teeth bared in the sheer pleasure of drinking the wind. There they learned soldiering, learned to be a part of Texas and the Texans. Surely they bolstered and encouraged each other as brothers will. They formed a bond as strong as steel that lasted for the rest of their lives and undoubtedly affected the history of their new state and nation.

Three years later in 1848, Webb County was created. Laredo was incorporated and became its county seat. Bacilio Benavides became its state representative.

At twenty-five Santos Benavides, now a veteran of a border campaign, was ready to assume his uncle's mantle at home. In every way this was his town and these were his people.

They elected him mayor of Laredo in 1856 and chief justice of newly formed Webb County in 1859. Far from sitting in the courthouse, he organized a company of Rangers and led several campaigns against the Lipan Apaches and Comanches, tribes that were growing more and more hostile toward Texans as they saw their lands encroached upon and their food supply endangered. By this time, more mature and more experienced with the respect and admiration of his men, Santos's troop must have presented a formidable force. Again the experience of leading men and planning battle strategies would stand the Benavides' brothers in good stead. Across the southern part of the United States a movement for states' rights began. As the central government of the United States tried to strengthen its position, it was resisted bitterly. Talk of secession from the young union, less than a hundred years old, was rising.

In Austin, Texas, on January 28, 1861, the Texas Secession Convention came to order. Not one of the 176 delegates was of Mexican descent even though eleven counties along the Rio Grande including Webb, Zapata, Hidalgo, and Starr had few Anglo-Celts and very few slaves. In fact, in Webb County where the Benavides held sway not a single person owned a slave.

Texas secession was never about abolition of slavery although some of the large cotton plantations in East Texas depended on slaves for their harvests. It was about the hard-headed independence that characterized the people who populated the state. Washington, D.C., was farther away from Austin than Mexico City was. They truly believed that it had no knowledge of or interest in them. For that reason Webb County under the leadership of the Benavides family voted seventy to zero to take Texas out of the Union.

Fort McIntosh had been built outside the town as part of the ring of forts to protect citizens from the Comanches and Apaches. When Major Caleb Sibley, commanding two companies of the Third Infantry stationed there, pleaded for supplies and munitions from San Antonio, he was refused. Less than two months later, the federal commander of the Department of Texas, General David Twiggs from Georgia, surrendered all the military posts.

Sibley refused to turn the contents of Fort McIntosh over to the South. On March 12, 1861, he gathered every scrap of equipment and supplies he and his troops could carry, hauled down the Stars and Stripes, and headed due east for the coast. He led his troops as far as Matagorda Bay. His valiant march had been in vain. He found he could not book transport. He was forced to surrender everything.

All over Texas fort commanders were faced with two choices, surrender or treason. All over Texas forts were abandoned or taken over by vastly less experienced citizen's militias who in most cases maintained no discipline and offered little protection. The people on the Rio Grande and on the edge of *Comancheria* were virtually unprotected.

One of the few forts to maintain a real garrison and offer protection for its citizens was Fort McIntosh. By April, Santos Benavides had recruited sixty-eight men into a company of rangers of which he was elected captain. He set up headquarters in the fort. Within two weeks, Refugio and Cristobal had joined him. The younger half-brother was twenty-three and no doubt delighted at the prospects of serving with his brothers. Ironically, though all the brothers were ready to fight for the Confederacy, in past years Santos had acted as a slave catcher, pursuing escaped Negroes across the Rio Grande and bringing them back.

The governor of Texas as well as officials and officers in the Texas army breathed a little easier to know that the Benavides family was with them. John Salmon Ford, one of the most versatile and intelligent men to appear in the pages of Texas history, wrote that "the Benavides family broke ground in favor of secession" and "did the Confederacy an immense favor by declaring for her."

The Stars and Bars rose above Fort McIntosh where Santos Benavides prepared to fight for his fifth flag. Although elected captain by the Texas Rangers he had recruited, he carried a commission as captain in the Thirty-third Texas Cavalry, which quickly became known as the Benavides Regiment. They were to patrol and defend the Rio Grande Military District.

Texas was extremely lucky to have such a regiment. The fight came sooner than Benavides expected and from a different direction. Besides the Comanches and Apaches, Mexican opportunists and bandits could read the signs of confusion across the Rio Grande. The Army was gone, vast underpopulated acreages lay open for the taking. Now was the time to resume the territorial border feud.

Did the Rio Grande really form the border? St. Denis had instructed Cadillac to extend French territorial claims to it. In 1836 the Texas Constitutional Convention had claimed it, but Mexico had maintained her border was the Nueces, a hundred miles north. Was the time right to create a new state from northern Mexico and southern Texas? Revolution against the revolution broke out.

In Zapata County, Antonio Ochoa challenged the authority of elected Confederate county officials. Though he led only forty men, he expected and received aid from Brownsville, in the form of one of the most amazing villains in the history of the Rio Grande Valley.

Juan Nepomuceno Cortinas had red hair and blue eyes. They seemed to be the only thing about him that was Spanish. Everything else was Mexican—and Cheno, as he was called, hated

Texans. Trying to find her feet before the Civil War began in earnest, the entire state was in turmoil. One in four Texans did not want to secede. Many of them were doing all in their power to hinder and cause problems for those who did. One of the rumors perhaps started by Cheno himself was that these Unionists were furnishing money to his own Cortinistas.

Cheno styled himself the "Robin Hood of Mexico." The newspapers reporting his exploits called him the "Rogue of the Rio Grande." He had earlier engaged the Texas Rangers when he and his Cortinistas had raided ranches and small villages.

Sure enough, Cortinas came north to aid Ochoa. Neither of them had counted on the brothers Benavides.

Ochoa, backed by Cortinas, marched into Carrizo, the county seat of Zapata. His intention was to seize the treasury and take over the government. The county judge, Henry Redmond, sent for Santos Benavides, who rode immediately downriver with a small troop of his Rangers. Arriving at Redmond's ranch, they found themselves trapped by one hundred of Cortinas's heavily armed men.

Santos knew he could not have picked a better place to defend. The largest buildings were made of stone. Used at one time as a U.S. Army fort, it still had a six-pounder cannon with plenty of ammunition. Enough food and water were available to last several days.

Under a state of siege, Santos observed that Cortinas's men fired frequent volleys but missed everything they shot at. Furthermore, rather than settling down for a siege, they seemed to be riding around through the sagebrush. Satisfied that he wasn't ordering anyone on a suicide mission, Santos sent a rider through Cortinas's line to Laredo. His brother Refugio rode sixty miles down the Mexican side of the river to join his brother. A few hours later sixty-one-year-old Don Bacilio Benavides led thirty-three Laredo Confederates to relieve his nephews.

The siege was broken with vicious thoroughness. Within hours Santos led his combined forces into Carrizo to stop Cortinas's men, many of whom were bandits recruited to swell the army's numbers. The undisciplined force had ceased to obey Ochoa and were pillaging the town.

Santos struck like a thunderbolt. Acting under orders from a leader they respected, the Confederates and Rangers killed seven Cortinistas in a running gun battle and wounded or captured eleven more while two were drowned trying to cross the river. Judge Redmond passed summary sentence, and the survivors were executed.

Stopped that day at the river, he made sure he would never be stopped again. With his family's connections in Mexico, he persuaded Mexican General Guadalupe Garciato to give him and his Thirty-third Cavalry permission to cross in hot pursuit. He reasoned that the Confederacy was no longer hampered by United States treaties with Mexico.

As Santos wrote later to Ford, "I particularly ordered my men not to arrest any of the bandits, but to kill all that fell into their hands."

The word spread along the southern side of the Rio Grande. *Santos Benavides takes no prisoners*. When he sent his report of the victory on May 21, 1861, to Austin, the government was so cheered they immediately passed the news on to Richmond. Coming just thirty-eight days after Fort Sumter's surrender, the news bolstered the spirits of those who might have come to doubt the prospects of the Confederacy.

Santos Benavides had praise heaped upon his shoulders. He was commended by the state legislature and promoted to the rank of major. Newspapers wrote glowing reports of "The Confederacy Along the Rio Grande."

John Salmon Ford, the commander of the Texas Rangers, wrote a personal letter of praise: "Whenever our enemies have appeared on our soil, you and your brave men have been present and driven them back, with great honor to yourselves and the gratification of your state."

Governor Edward Clark sent one of his personal friends on a special mission to carry a handsome engraved pistol to Benavides. He commissioned the man to read these complimentary words: "I am happy to believe that in your hands it will always be used in the defense of your country and prove an instrument of terror and destruction to her enemies."

More telling was the reaction of the Union high command. Many people in the United States did not like Abraham Lincoln, who had been elected by a minority of the people. Fifteen days after Fort Sumter, he had ordered a blockade of all the southern ports. Important trade was cut off, for the South supplied the raw materials—particularly cotton—for the North's mills. Many people began to lose their jobs. Others did not see the reason for going to war over slavery when none of them had any contact with it whatsoever. They also were not sure that states did not have the right to secede if a majority of their population wanted to. The besieged commander in chief and his staff were desperate to counteract the victory. They moved immediately to offer Benavides the rank of general in the U.S. Army.

Austin as well as the South probably held its breath. What if he had taken the commission and used his Rangers to wage war in the West against Texas? The results would have had far-reaching and grave consequences. Luckily for them, he refused their offer and remained loyal to the Confederacy throughout the war. How long the war was prolonged because of his loyalty will always be open to speculation. Certainly by months, possibly by years.

Money, as always, was a prime mover in the affairs of both sides. If the blockade of southern ports damaged the North's economy, it sent the South's into a tailspin. King Cotton was worth thousands of dollars to the northern mills, but those were not the only markets. England and France imported it too, but how to get it there?

At this point Santos Benavides met Captains Richard King and Mifflin Kenedy, who owned a fleet of steamboats that carried goods up and down the Rio Grande from Boca del Rio east of Brownsville to Rio Grande City, 240 miles into Texas.

The captains had already been enlisted by John Salmon Ford. U.S. troops were being forced to abandon all manner of equipment as they left Texas. Kenedy and King boats were now carrying guns, ammunition, and supplies back into the interior to the forts that desperately needed them for defense against the Indians.

By this time the mills of Europe were standing idle. Weavers, dyers, haberdashers, everyone in the garment trade, was out of work. If gold was what the Confederacy wanted, gold they could have. The world was for the first time feeling the ramifications of a global economy.

The captains saw a way to get the cotton out of Texas and perhaps Arkansas and Louisiana as well. They registered their boats with the Mexican government in order to fly Mexican flags. Cotton wagons from East Texas came to the King Ranch 125 miles north of the river. King guided them south to Rio Grande City where Santos Benavides defended the docks.

Thousands of bales of cotton passed over those docks, steamed down the river, through the port of Matamoros out into the Gulf of Mexico, where Yankee blockaders watched in acute frustration as it was loaded onto European ships. They knew gold was being exchanged, but they were helpless. They were not at war with Mexico. The Matamoros cotton market became the richest in the world. The fabled wealth of the cotton merchants, *Los Algodones*, began at that time. And Santos Benavides was one of the men who made it all happen.

At the same time the cotton was sold, millions of dollars' worth of ammunition and supplies for the South were loaded onto the steamboats for the trip back upriver. The South could hold out indefinitely.

Abraham Lincoln did not have an indefinite amount of time. When his blockade was not immediately successful, he was forced to call out the might of the U.S. Army.

If the Benavides family had not been loyal, exactly the reverse might have happened. The United States would have been able to move supplies, guns and ammunition, and even troops up the Rio Grande. The entire southwestern flank of the Confederacy might have been exposed. Texas, which of all the Rebel states saw the least amount of destruction from Northern troops, would have turned into a battleground.

In March 1862 Santos Benavides struck again. When one of his men was killed, he and a troop of forty crossed the river into Nuevo Laredo and spent three days searching the town before they were convinced that the murderers had fled. The politics had changed in Matamoros. This time Albino Lopez, the governor of Tamaulipas, formally protested Benavides's actions. Mexico herself was in danger at this time. The Civil War meant that America could no longer enforce the Monroe Doctrine of European noninterference. In 1862 the soldiers of Napoleon III landed at Veracruz ostensibly to collect debts the rebel president Benito Juarez had ceased to pay.

The emperor was taking advantage of the civil wars and revolutions occurring simultaneously. He did not really want Mexico. His ultimate plan was to re-enter the United States through the Confederacy and reclaim French land sold for pennies by Napoleon I.

Abraham Lincoln and his generals had more than one reason to secure Brownsville and bottle up the Rio Grande. Invasion was a necessity before the French could form an alliance with the Confederacy and put troops in Texas.

Small guerilla armies began to operate along the border, raiding and looting where they could. One of their leaders, Octaviano Zapata, rode into troubled Zapata County at the head of such an army. They hanged county judge Isidro Vela in front of his wife and children and posted a sign warning that they would kill any person who dared to bury the body.

No one was there to pay any attention to this lawlessness except Santos Benavides. He and his men patrolled every inch of the river where they kept the law. At his command Confederate captain Refugio Benavides, with fifty-four of his men, trailed the Zapatistas across the Rio Grande to a *ranchito* near Camargo. Falling upon the camp, they killed eighteen revolutionaries and wounded fourteen others. Those captured were later said to have "escaped."

The protests from Mexico were bitter, especially since in the meantime the political climate in Matamoros had become decidedly anti-Texan. Cheno Cortinas had suddenly gotten himself named second in command to the military governor of Tamaulipas.

The Confederate general at Brownsville, General Hamilton P. Bee, a nervous and ill-trained man, panicked. Things were getting too dangerous. The position was untenable. Rather than risk the enforced surrender of his troops, he determined to retreat.

On November 1, 1863, twenty-six transports with seven thousand Union troops steamed up the river between Brazos de Santiago and Padre Island. Bee ordered a retreat. He dumped his siege guns in the river and set fire to the installations and the cotton. When his men lost control of the blaze, which spread along the riverfront, eight thousand pounds of gunpowder exploded. Firebrands shot high in the air, setting small fires all over town. Two blocks of the riverfront were destroyed, as well as Fort Brown.

As Bee pulled his troops back from the disaster he had created, the city was left undefended, and Cheno Cortinas managed to get himself named acting governor of Tamaulipas. The way was clear for the Union to move in without ever firing a shot. The South could forget about moving cotton onto ships in the Gulf.

Except that Santos Benavides still held the river north of Rio Grande City. As never before his position at Laredo became crucial to Texas and the Confederacy. The word arrived from Austin that he was to assume the rank of colonel. He became the highest ranking Mexican American to serve on either side during the Civil War.

Meanwhile, the Union army, designated the Federal Rio Grande Expedition, occupied Brownsville. Since the fort had been destroyed, they quartered their troops in the town. With them was Edmund J. Davis, a renegade Texan with a military background. He had a spurious position as colonel of the Union First Texas Cavalry by virtue of the fact that he had spent the first two years of the war in Mexico. There he had organized a small band of guerillas, whom he claimed he had recruited into the U.S. Army.

Perhaps the officers above him allowed him his position because they realized he understood the situation along the river better than they. Certainly, he understood the importance of Santos Benavides, whose name was becoming legendary. If Benavides could be made to see the futility of the struggle, if the intrepid colonel could be lured into the Union army, the war in Texas—indeed in the entire South—might be changed.

With that end in mind, Davis offered Santos a brigadiership. Along with it went food, clothing, and medical supplies for his men. Most tempting was a payroll, something they had not seen in six months. It Santos would accept, it would be dispatched immediately. A lesser man would have accepted, especially since the news was bad from east of the Mississippi, but Benavides had stronger convictions. Loyal as ever to the South and contemptuous of Davis, Santos refused.

Few others were as resolute.

With Brownsville, Rio Grande City, and Roma in Union hands, Davis had been able to recruit more than nine hundred Texans from among the citizens of the Lower Rio Grande Valley. By late 1863 Benavides's command was all that remained of the once proud Confederate Army of the Rio Grande. Davis saw a chance to secure the entire river.

In the meantime, Santos had ordered all the cotton in Rio Grande City—some twenty-six hundred bales—moved. The task was a formidable one for every bale weighed an average of five hundred pounds. The effort required on his part and on the parts of his men was stupendous. A great many bales he had hidden in Mexico, but some had been moved north to Laredo. As a matter of fact, nearly five thousand bales were stacked in San Agustin Plaza, the main square at Laredo, awaiting shipment into Mexico.

Since Bee had fired the cotton in Brownsville and, in so doing, blown up the town, Davis and his men were determined to have the bales in Benavides's possession. Already the Union regarded them as spoils of war. Davis's hands undoubtedly itched for the gold they would bring. From his location in Texas, only three hundred miles from Austin, he could move to the capital in a two weeks. The possibilities for self-aggrandizement were there for a man with ambition. He could control Texas. Hell! He could be governor. Only one man stood between him and total control.

The Confederacy also knew Benavides's value to them. General John Magruder, commander of the District of Texas, Trans-Mississippi Department, was made aware of the state of Benavides's men. Without gold to pay his own men, he authorized Santos to impress 250 bales of cotton, sell them, and place the money in a credit account in Monterrey. With this Benavides was to pay his men and refit them. In the same order Magruder promised to make Benavides a brigadier general.

By this time Santos Benavides was completely exhausted, both psychologically and physically. For three years he had been almost constantly in the field, sometimes riding twenty miles a day, then sleeping on the ground without a tent. Sometimes he and his men had to lie down without blankets, pillowing their heads on their forearms.

Colonel John Salmon Ford had called on his old friend from Laredo to be his eyes and ears while he outfitted a private army in San Antonio. He wrote to Santos, "I am confident you and myself can drive the enemy from the valley of the lower Rio Grande." Ford's plan was to travel overland through the Wild Horse Desert south of the Nueces by way of El Sal del Rey. In this way he hoped to surprise the troops stationed at Brownsville.

Benavides knew from experience that Ford's plan would be a strain on men and animals. The winter of 1863-64 had been the driest in memory. Without proper food, without water except the Rio Grande, his own men had ridden up and down the river, escorting cotton wagons and answering the calls for help from everywhere—from *ranchitos* to townships—when bandits would attack. Many a night their mounts had had to forage for stems of dead grasses where there was little but dust.

In March of 1864 Santos Benavides was forty years old. His brother Refugio was forty-two. They had both pushed their bodies too far. When the word came that an expedition had marched north to Rio Grande City and was coming overland to Laredo to take the town from him, Santos had been in bed for several days, too ill to rise.

His troops were equally tired as well as short on supplies. Attrition had diminished their numbers. Still morale was high because of their colonel's spirit.

When out of the rolling dust rode his cousin County Judge Cayetano de la Garza, excited, a little frightened, his report was the worst possible news. A large Union cavalry force—as many as a thousand—was approaching from downriver. Though Santos doubted that a force of that size could have gotten so far without his scouts bringing in word, almost any number would be too many. Whatever the odds, he was determined to fight.

"This would not have happened had I not been confined to bed…" he told a friend. "I would have known all about their advance and would have gone below and attacked them. As it is I have to fight to the last; though hardly able to stand I shall die fighting. I won't retreat, no matter what force the Yankees have—I know I can depend on my boys."

Rising from his sickbed, he organized men from his brothers' companies and from a unit of irregulars who happened to be in Laredo. He might not have received the rank of general, but with his finest hour upon him, he behaved like one. While the small bells rang from the tower of San Agustin Church, he gave his orders.

He sent a cavalry force, hardly more than a scouting party in fact, along the river road with ominous instructions. Delay the Yankees.

He sent a rider at top speed to more than one hundred men grazing their horses at a camp twenty-five miles north of town. They were to come on the double.

An express rider was sent upriver to Eagle Pass, which had a small garrison. They were to come as quickly as possible. However, with over a hundred miles for the rider to cover and then a hundred miles for the reinforcements to return, Santos did not hold much hope that they would arrive in time.

He sent out a call for civilian volunteers to bring their rifles. He stationed them on the tops of the adobe buildings looking down into the plaza. Their job was to snipe at the enemy as they rode in. Other townspeople were put to work moving some of the bales to barricade the streets leading into the plaza.

Then he gathered his brothers' forty-two men and his company of thirty Texas militia in the square in front of and surrounded by cotton bales. The sight must have been impressive—huge jute-wrapped blocks of compressed white lint each belted with six or eight flexible black metal bands an inch wide. They would stop the best shot the Yankees could throw at them. The finest jumping horse could not clear one. The wealth of the Confederacy protected them as they were protecting it.

He gave final orders to Cristobal. "There are five thousand bales of cotton in the plaza. It belongs to the Confederacy. If the day goes against us, fire it. Be sure to do the work properly so that not a bale of it shall fall into the hands of the Yankees.

"Then you will set my new house on fire, so that nothing of mine shall pass to the enemy. Let their victory be a barren one."

No man who heard him speak that day nor those who read his words today could doubt his courage. His brothers and his men were not surprised. He was the man who would not stop.

He managed to climb into the saddle with some dignity. Then at the head of his men, he rode east out of his town. On the way to the banks of Zacate Creek, he almost fell from his horse several times. At last he positioned his men near an old corral. Here they would have cover and a clear field of fire at the advancing forces.

The trip up-country had been harder than Colonel E. J. Davis had told Major Alfred E. Holt. The terrible drought had dried up the watering holes and left little trail grass. The supply column had not been able to keep up. The cavalry had to dismount more often and lead their horses and mules now on half rations. Much valuable stock had been left to die beside the trail.

Benavides ordered a bugler to ride up and down the creek bank blowing the call to arms. In this way he hoped to confuse the attackers to make them think that they were engaging a much stronger force.

The ruse worked if only psychologically. Holt was uncertain about many things. He didn't know how many men he faced. Instead of leading his cavalry in a swift charge against the corral, he dismounted them and ordered them to advance on foot—at a much slower pace. Concerned about the "hidden" army, Holt dared not throw all two hundred of his men against the enemy. If he had done so, particularly on horseback, his numbers would have overpowered them in a few minutes.

In the face of repeated charges of equal numbers, Benavides's men held for three hours. From time to time, a single bravo would gallop out on horseback and charge at the Yankees, emptying a pistol into their ranks and destroying morale with his daring. Through the dry blaze of noon, the Rebels at Zacate Creek held.

For the Yankees the battle was a disaster. So ashamed were they of it and of what happened, that they left no written record. Whether Holt never put his blunders in writing, or whether Davis destroyed them rather than take the blame for putting a timid fool in charge, no one will ever know.

In the end despite outnumbering their enemies five to one, they retreated into the chaparral, carrying their wounded and dead with them. Rebel scouts followed them. Sharpshooters sniped at them. The retreat turned into a race to get away. Three miles south of Laredo, they halted more from exhaustion than from an order from their timorous commander.

Benavides held his position until he was satisfied that the retreat had been real. Then he pulled back behind his cotton bales. At two A.M. pickets north of town reported a cavalry coming fast. In the darkness the brothers Benavides waited in the San Agustin Plaza.

Within minutes the church bells began to ring. Cheers resounded as the delighted citizens dashed out into the streets to welcome a group of reinforcements from north of town. Santos encouraged the celebration no matter how premature it might be.

Undoubtedly, it was heard by Holt's men, or their scouts brought back the word of it.

At dawn Santos sent his brother Refugio out at the head of sixty men to find the enemy. In the dry bed of Zacate Creek, he found bloody trails in the sand and a grisly track of blood-soaked rags. Three miles downriver, he discovered Holt's camp, now abandoned.

They must have pulled back in desperate haste because they abandoned five horses with U.S. branded on their flanks.

On the twenty-first of March, Refugio went out again. This time he reported that the force's retreat had turned into a rout. Evidently, they had broken into squads and retreated every man for himself with no semblance of order or command.

Three days after the battle, a large force of Union cavalry was reported advancing toward the town. Benavides mounted again, though he had to be helped to do so. Galloping at the head of his men, he lost consciousness and fell from the saddle, sustaining a head wound. W. W. Camp, the regimental surgeon, reported that Benavides was suffering from fatigue and exposure and forbade him to ride again at the risk of his life.

Fortunately, he had no need to. The Union cavalry never came. The Battle of Laredo had been fought in the best possible manner—with no damage done to the town and few lives lost. It had been one of the most decisive battles fought in Texas throughout the entire war.

Colonel John Ford wrote to Santos, "You have added to the reputation you and your command have already acquired." He reached Laredo April 15 to find everything under control.

Don Santos Benavides's poor health kept him from taking part in the rest of the war. Ford faulted him for that and for staying in Laredo, even though he was under doctor's orders to do so. Captain Refugio Benavides took over the command and led them south, but the men immediately had problems. Used to operating more in the manner of guerillas or rangers, they did not drill or appear in dress uniforms. Indeed, they had none. They lacked the "spit and polish" Ford's adjutants wanted to see.

Within days both Refugio and Cristobal were in trouble and their men were simply heading back to Laredo. When Santos came down to try to straighten out the dispute and reconcile the hot tempers, Ford accused him of falsifying records. Although Santos had been promised a brigadiership, Ford later blocked it.

The two were never friends again. Nor did Santos's health allow him to serve at the head of his regiment for the rest of the war.

However, the Texas Legislature, meeting in joint session, commended Benavides and his men for the vigilance, energy, and gallantry displayed in "pursuing and chastising the banditti infesting the Rio Grande." They appointed him a brigadier general of Texas state troops.

Santos returned to Laredo while the Benavides Regiment that remained in Brownsville took part in the battle of Palo Alto on May 13, 1865, five weeks after Lee's surrender at Appomattox Court House. Refugio was commended by Ford for gallantry.

A surprising friend to Santos Benavides came in the form of Edmund J. Davis, who succeeded in getting himself elected Reconstruction Governor of Texas. While he was the most hated governor Texas ever had, he had a great deal of respect for his old enemy, and the two even became friends.

During Reconstruction Santos returned to work his ranch and his store in partnership with his brother Cristobal. The cotton trade and the military activities brought money into Laredo. Immigrants flocked into Laredo because of her prosperity.

Refugio and Santos were the *de facto* heads of the town government, but Santos was the one everyone looked to for guidance. He instructed his brother Refugio to hire extra policemen to protect the citizens from the newcomers as well as the bandits now rife along the border. The extra policemen and the reputation of the Benavides brothers, who had never taken prisoners during the war, spared Laredo much trouble.

So effective was Benavides's regime that he and his brothers were invited to Washington to testify before Congress about their successful peacekeeping operations.

All the money was not spent on policemen. A dozen teachers were hired and public schools were created including a school to teach the children English. In 1868 the Ursuline Academy was established supported by the Catholic Church.

By 1870 Reconstruction was over. Santos was elected almost unanimously to serve two terms as alderman for Laredo. In 1875 he and Refugio were called to Austin to explain how they kept the Laredo area in a peaceful condition. He served in the Texas Legislature from 1879 to 1885.

In 1884 he was Texas's representative to the World Cotton Exposition in New Orleans, a fitting position for the man who kept the cotton wagons moving for nearly four years and defended the bales in San Agustin Plaza with his life and the lives of his men.

He retired from political life in 1886 at age sixty-three. After a life of dynamic heroism, he died quietly in his home on November 9, 1891.

Texas mourned the passing of a hero of unquestioned loyalty. Because he would not stop, he was never once defeated in battle. And more important—because he would not stop, he made a place for the men who have come after him.

* * * * *

The downtown area of Laredo is called Villa de San Agustin where many of its older buildings stand around a plaza. Visitors may take a walking tour of historic Laredo in just a few blocks. The Museum of the Republic of the Rio Grande, constructed in two stages in 1830 and 1840, faces the plaza with artifacts of life in the nineteenth century. Santos Benavides participated in this ill-fated rebellion. San Agustin Church where he was married stands on the spot of the original church built in 1767.

At 202 Flores stands the Benavides-Vidaurri House, built in 1874 by Colonel Santos Benavides. Next door is the house built for Maria Benavides, sister of Santos.

Farther south between the plaza and the Rio Grande is old Fort McIntosh established in 1849. Santos Benavides took command of the fort at the beginning of the Civil War and from here fought the battle of Laredo, driving off Union soldiers that had come to take the hundreds of bales of cotton stored in San Agustin Plaza.

The Free Man

Milton M. Holland

The first African-American to be awarded the Congressional Medal of Honor was also the first Texan to receive it. Milton M. Holland fought gallantly and beyond the call of duty at the battle of New Market Heights near Chaffin's (or Chapin's) Farms, Virginia, September 29, 1864. Although he was barely twenty, he took command of Company "C" of the Fifth United States Colored Troops and led them to victory.

With fighting spirit and fierce determination, Holland took command of his men. For over a year they had come to depend on him, to trust his judgement. When he called upon them, they followed him. They stepped over the bodies of their dead and wounded commanders and followed him. They looked to their leader rather than fear the barrels of some thousand Confederate sharpshooters spitting death to stop them. Though wounded himself, he never stopped until he reached the heights.

Holland was born either in Carthage or Austin, Texas, in 1844. In all likelihood he and his two brothers, James and William H., were the sons of Bird Holland, a planter from East Texas, who moved to Austin where he served the Republic and then the State of Texas as secretary of state. Rather than have these three boys live the lives of uneducated slaves, Holland sent them to Albany Enterprise Academy, a school in Ohio operated by free African Americans.

Thanks to his assumption of responsibility, they lived most of their young lives as free men in and around Athens, Ohio. Though it was the custom for all slaves to take the last name of the master, the fact that Bird Holland spent so much money and provided so liberally for them certainly seems to indicate that he was their father. Whether he ever confirmed that relationship with them, whether he loved them and visited them, whether he influenced their adult lives beyond educating them is unknown. He must have provided handsomely for them in his will because they were able to leave their ranks after the war and move into the mainstream of society.

After his tour of duty, William attended Oberlin College, one of the finest and most expensive in the state. He then returned to Texas where he taught school. As one might expect, he entered politics as a Republican (not a pleasant thing to be in Texas during and after Reconstruction). From a seat in the Texas Legislature, he helped establish Prairie View Normal School which became Prairie View A&M. He also established the Texas Institute for Deaf, Dumb, and Blind Youth, which he ran for fourteen years.

Milton went from the Fifth Regiment, U.S. Colored Troops to Washington, D.C., where he established an insurance company and worked for the government. He seems never to have known poverty as thousands of American veterans of both races did when the war ended and they returned to neglected or often destroyed farms and businesses.

Shortly after Fort Sumter in 1861, when the first call came for volunteers, Milton tried to enlist. Only seventeen at the time, he was told he was too young. Perhaps he was passing for white at this time because neither the North nor the South was actually mustering blacks into their armies. Rather than return to school, he got a job as a civilian servant to a colonel in the Quartermaster Corps. The job allowed him to work in close proximity to soldiers and to learn soldiering.

During 1862 as Lincoln developed the abolition of slavery issue as the reason for his unpopular war, more and more people in the North demanded that Negro troops be trained and used. There seemed to be no shortage of them. Indeed there were too many. Blacks were defecting to the North in record numbers. Northern armies making their first sorties into Southern states

were stretched to the limit of their supplies by the dozens and dozens of slaves who followed them wherever they went. An inadequate solution was refugee camps, which had to be paid for with taxpayer money. The voters began to complain that so long as the war was for the benefit of black people, they should fight in it.

In January 1863, when Lincoln issued his Emancipation Proclamation, he called for the mustering of Negro regiments. Bird Holland's son stood ready to join. He was mustered into the Fifth United States Colored Troops, a segregated regiment where blacks fought in their own units, commanded by General Benjamin F. Butler and his white staff. As circumstances later proved, Milton was destined to be a fighter as Bird Holland was before him.

The first black troops were used to build roads and fortifications and to stand guard duty. They were outfitted with castoff uniforms and issued damaged and defective weapons—but they were in. The white troops at first objected viciously, displaying race prejudice so malign that people witnessing it today would think the perpetrators insane. However, as the war heated and the casualty lists grew, the idea very quickly took hold that a black soldier could stop a Rebel bullet just as well as a white soldier. When he did so, some white soldier who would otherwise have died would go on living.

In just six months time, the North was raising Negro regiments and putting them on the same field of battle with whites, sending them charging together into the teeth of the guns, and exchanging fire with the enemy. The result was that the Union put more than one hundred fifty thousand blacks into battle, and the white soldiers adjusted to the idea "just fine."

All modern historians concur that if the war had been fought by officers with a competency in military strategy, the end would have come much sooner and the terrible loss of life and property reduced significantly. General Benjamin Butler and General Nathaniel P. Banks were two who were largely incompetent. They had received their commissions as a matter of political expediency. Abraham Lincoln needed them because of their staunch abolitionist positions. Neither knew how to plan a campaign or to lead men.

General Benjamin Butler was a blundering amateur among a host of lesser amateurs. He caused problems for Grant throughout the battles against Lee's Army of Northern Virginia, but as a friend of Lincoln he was virtually untouchable. Moreover, he was one of the few white officers actually to prefer using black troops in battle. Unfortunately, his reasons did not stem from any philosophical recognition of their equality with whites or intellectual observation of their proficiency as soldiers.

"I knew that they would fight more desperately than any white troops in order to prevent capture," he said, "because they knew...if captured they would be returned to slavery."

Butler's men spent time in the swamps of North Carolina in the winter of 1863. They raided Confederate supply trains and freed slaves. They took part in the Yorktown, Virginia raid that liberated Union soldiers from the infamous Libby Prison. Though the tour hadn't enough glory to Butler's liking, his men were learning to soldier rather than plunge into battle untried.

By the dawn of 1864 Milton Holland had been promoted to the rank of sergeant.

Butler's troops were ready in the spring of 1864. He was placed in charge of 33,000 men on the south side of the James River when Grant tried to rout Lee's army and capture the Confederate capital Richmond.

Ironically, while Milton Holland was moving into position for his first major engagement at the Bermuda Hundred and winning the attention of General Butler himself, the man who had in all likelihood fathered him and paid for his education was killed in action.

General Nathaniel Banks, another Lincoln supporter, conceived the idea of a flotilla of gunboats sailing up the Red River and taking control of the area between the Red and the Sabine. His object was to stop the flow of Southern cotton through Texas to the Rio Grande and thence to foreign ships. His plan failed at a considerable loss of life and equipment on both sides. On April 8, 1864, they met an army half their size—and lost. The Confederate attack was "as sudden as though a thunder bolt had fallen upon us and set the pines on fire—we found ourself—in a hissing, seething, bubbling whirlpool of agitated men."

Unfortunately, one loss was Bird Holland. In the defense of his state, he was killed that fine April day beating back the Union offensive just thirty-five miles from Carthage and the

200 · The Free Man

Holland home and plantation. The civil tragedies of the war when kin fought kin had hit home to the Holland family. When Nathaniel Banks tried to retreat down the Red, he found the river shallower than when he sailed up it. He would have lost the entire flotilla if not for a junior officer who suggested a detail be sent downstream to create a temporary log dam. The water backed up sufficiently behind it to allow Banks to get his gunboats out.

The North was losing badly at the beginning of March 1864. Ulysses Simpson Grant was given command of the North's armies. Lincoln had at last decided that it took a soldier to do a soldier's job. Immediately, Grant took the offensive. The key to the war was the capital at Richmond where Jefferson Davis's government sat. Three armies must converge on Richmond.

He put himself in the field with the Army of the Potomac, whose aim was to engage General Robert E. Lee, commander of the Army of Northern Virginia, cut his supply lines, and defeat him soundly or drive him back into Richmond to be starved out.

Grant had no choice but to put Ben Butler in charge of the Army of the James, a force of 33,000 men gathered from Butler's own black regiments as well as other regiments around Fort Monroe. They were to move north along the peninsula toward Richmond. Grant probably sighed and shook his head when he gave the orders. He knew Ben Butler's weaknesses probably better than most.

The Army of the James should have had an easy time. Instead, when they met the Southern soldiers, they retreated to Bermuda Hundred and dug in. Rather than engaging Butler further, the Confederates drew a fortified line across the base of the peninsula and put the general and his army of 33,000 out of action as if he had been "put in a tightly corked bottle." Grant probably had to have a stiff drink when he read the reports.

In charge of the Army of the Shenandoah was German-born Franz Sigel, also an abolitionist. His military skill may be judged by the report that, as his troops sought to move up the valley, they were decisively routed by Virginia Military Institute's corps of cadets.

Both Butler and Sigel had powerful numerical advantages over the forces that the South could summon. Their results should have been swift and relatively painless. With Grant they should have been able to besiege if not actually take Richmond and capture the Confederate government. The rest of the war would have been short and bloodless.

It was not.

Meanwhile, Grant's army was having more momentous problems. He had left it to himself to engage one of the premier military strategists of this or any other country. General Robert E. Lee never wanted to fight where his opponents wanted to fight. He always chose his own battlefields. In this case he chose to engage Grant's army as it tried to hack its way through a jungle-like growth filled with creepers, ravines, watercourses, and sloughs known as the Wilderness. Here with visibility no more than fifty yards in any direction, movement was impossible. Superior firepower meant nothing because the artillery never had clear targets.

Moreover, because Lee's army had a high percentage of men from country such as this, his troops were less handicapped than the men from the North. Still, the two-day battle between Grant and Lee was as vicious as any fought in the war. In the oppressive heat, the South hit the North from both sides, broke in the flanks, and fought them to a standstill.

Around the miserable troops, the Wilderness caught fire. Wounded men burned to death where they lay. The smoke mixed with the fog to reduce visibility to a few feet. One soldier reported that it was "simply bushwhacking on a grand scale." At the end of the battle, the North had lost 17,500 men and gained not an inch of ground. Lee had lost fewer than eight thousand.

Any other general would have retreated, but Grant made a crucial decision. He slipped sideways to a crossroad at Spotsylvania Court House on the road to Richmond. If he could capture it, he could march into his objective, leaving Lee behind.

In the end Lee had to beat him to the crossroad, fight when he did not want to fight, and expend troops that were irreplaceable. Every day he had to fight. The twelve-day battle at

Spotsylvania remains one of the bloodiest and bitterest that ever took place on the American continent.

Grant tried an offensive distraction, sending Phil Sheridan's cavalry galloping toward Richmond. His troops actually reached a suburb of the city before Jeb Stuart, sent by Lee, met him at Yellow Tavern. Sheridan had to retreat, but Jeb Stuart was killed. Lee spoke of him later, "I can scarcely think of him without weeping."

Lee countered with an offensive of his own. He sent Jubal Early dashing up the Shenandoah Valley to within a dozen miles of the Capitol building at Washington before an army corps sent by Grant drove them back. A very perturbed Abraham Lincoln witnessed that battle himself.

And still the battle for Spotsylvania Court House went on. No one was winning. No one was losing. But in the end Lee knew he would lose.

By that time Grant had lost sixty thousand troops. He had been fighting constantly for a month, never out of contact with Lee's army, yet neither army could win. An endless stream of wagons bearing wounded and dead moved north toward Fredericksburg and south toward Richmond. Lincoln's presidency was in jeopardy.

Grant met his nemesis again at Cold Harbor where the North lost seven thousand men in half an hour against Lee's entrenchments. After ten days Grant broke contact, marched across the Peninsula, crossed the James, and headed for Petersburg.

There he dug trenches to besiege Petersburg, a town of great strategic importance because most of the railroad lines to the South ran through it. If he could occupy it before Lee got there, Richmond would have to be abandoned. To this end he began trench warfare, a precursor of World War I's miserable battles. One soldier called it "hell itself...One half of the line would fire while the other worked on the pits [trenches] or tried to sleep." Artillery duels and sharpshooting were incessant. For six weeks they labored with no rain. Then there was too much rain and their feet rotted.

The end—however far away—could not be in doubt. Several of Lee's most valuable units had been decimated. He had lost a third of his general officers. He had few or no replacements for either.

Grant had lost sixty percent of the men who had marched into the Wilderness behind him. He had tens of thousands of replacements—virtually a new army.

September 28 and 29, General Butler's Army of the James crossed the river again to assault the defenses north of the river. When the order came to attack, Milton's men didn't even wait for their boat to land. They jumped from the guardrail of the boat and waded through waist-deep water to the point of attack. Taking full advantage of the element of surprise, they captured the Rebel flag, the signal station, and the officers at the station. This was the first blow at the Rebel stronghold at Petersburg.

All told during the night twenty thousand Union soldiers moved around Lee's left flank. For twelve hours from the Petersburg trenches to Deep Bottom Bridge, Butler's men marched. At his orders, they carried greatcoats, packs, haversacks, canteens, rifles, tent halves, sixty rounds of ammunition, and three days' cooked rations each. The troops must have resembled pack mules more than men.

At dawn the columns of black troops—Brigadier General Charles Paine's Third Division including Company "C" of the Fifth—faced a tiny force of two thousand Confederate soldiers, scattered along New Market Heights. Milton Holland was a sergeant major, the highest rank a black man could attain at that time. The division was made up mostly of freedmen rather than slaves. They were ready and eager to fight. They had fought together for over a year.

In this case experience must have told them what they were facing—many casualties and perhaps defeat.

Though they had superior numbers they had no information to that effect. A hundred thousand men might be facing them—in which case they would charging into a trap from which they could not hope to escape. Even if they surrendered, they might be murdered in violation of the rules of war.

Among them were those who had heard the reports of the massacre at Fort Pillow on the Mississippi River. After the fort surrendered, several dozen soldiers, mostly black, were murdered in cold blood. The story had been told that when a white Union soldier had protested the shootings, the Rebels asked him if he fought with "these goddamned niggers."

When he answered, "Yes," they shot him too.

From Milton's view, he could see that the ground they had to cover left them at serious disadvantage. The Confederate earthworks lay three hundred yards ahead across a rising plain. A stream flowed directly across the attack route. They would have to slog through it. On either side the ground was marshy. The most difficult problem was the abatis that had been thrown up across the middle of the plain. One hundred fifty yards from the earthworks was a barrier of fallen trees with sharpened limbs pointing down the slope. Fifty yards behind it was a network of sharpened stakes, or pales, set in the ground to stop any charging cavalry that managed to jump over the abatis.

The only way to attack was straight ahead into the teeth of deadly fire from one thousand Texans of John Gregg's Texas Brigade, strung out along New Market Road. Texan was going to meet Texan in this most uncivil of wars.

Posted six feet apart with plenty of ammunition, each of the Rebel Texans could fire four times in a minute. Four thousand well-placed shots per minute trained downhill at men, among them Milton Holland, coming uphill over rough terrain.

General Butler's order for the advance further supports the charge that he was an amateur with no business to be in uniform, much less to order men into battle. An experienced general would have realized that the only way to take the heights would be to send all the troops together in one long line, firing as they came to provide some cover for their "pioneers," the troops whose job was to set explosives to blow gaps through the abatis and chop down the pales.

Butler "feared" to risk so much. He ordered only one unit comprising Colonel Samuel Duncan's Fourth and Sixth Regiments to attack. He further ordered the troops to take the caps off their rifles, thereby essentially disarming them. His idea was that they wouldn't accidentally fire their pieces and kill some of their own. At 5:30 A.M. with the fog clearing, Butler ordered the black soldiers to shoulder their arms and advance in orderly manner against the Confederate trenches.

What the Texas troops on the Heights thought is unknown. They probably accepted the incredible stupidity as the fault of black soldiering. They might have grinned as they swiped their thumbs across the sights at the ends of their rifle barrels and drew a bead down on the men marching toward them. Having no reason to fire early, they waited until the targets were well within range.

As the regiment crossed the creek, their commanders, whom the Texans had already marked, ordered the NCOs to show the colors to keep the line steady. Some Texans took aim at the colorbearers.

When the "pioneers" began to hack away at the abatis, a solid sheet of lead mowed them down. All but one of the colorbearers fell dead. Duncan fell with four wounds. All the axemen went down. Their comrades behind them slung their rifles over their shoulders and picked up the bloody axes. As some of those fell, their comrades took their places. Behind them the survivors of the Fourth and Sixth recapped their rifles and crouched down behind the barricade. When it was finally breached, those still alive bravely climbed through and charged the Confederate parapet.

Unable to spread out into any kind of a battle formation, they were flanked on both sides by the Texas troops. Their officers were all killed. The smoke from exploding shells and small arms became so thick that their only hope was retreat. When the Fourth and Sixth fell back they left 365 of their original 683 on the field.

The second Union attack came a few minutes after six A.M. Not even a hint of the protecting fog remained. Clearly, the Texans could see the blue lines moving toward them. The Fifth, Thirty-sixth, and Thirty-eighth followed Duncan's path through the break in the abatis.

Sergeant Major Milton Holland saw his officers drop in quick succession. Their whiteness made them prime targets for the sharpshooters. Likewise, the colorbearers were all killed within the first thirty minutes of the advance. His troops faltered, he was wounded himself, but he scarcely felt it. The enemy was in front of him and his men were with him.

Leading the way through the abatis, they ran straight at the enemy, firing and reloading as they ran, the Yankee version of a battle cry pouring from their throats. Within thirty yards of the Confederate trenches, they dropped to the ground and stared.

Incredulously, they watched as the Rebels retired. With an easy victory in sight, John Gregg's Texas Brigade was being pulled back to support the defense of Fort Harrison at another point in the line. Incompetent generalship was not the exclusive property of the Union. With a savage howl, Holland led the men of the Fifth as well as the men of the Thirty-eighth over the main fortifications to take possession of the earthworks. By seven A.M. New Market Heights belonged to the Union.

When Butler followed the path of his victorious troops, he must have been properly appalled at the loss of life. He counted 543 bodies in just three hundred yards. Perhaps he cared. More than likely, he counted the cost in terms of battles won. Generals learn to deal with what they call acceptable losses.

He spoke to Milton Holland as well as several other men who had performed with equal gallantry. Of the seventeen African-American soldiers who were awarded the Medal of Honor during the Civil War, fourteen received the honor as a result of their actions at New Market Heights.

Buoyed by victory, Milton refused to give any attention to his wound. The battle for Fort Harrison was under way. White troops were pinned down by fire from the parapets. He led the men of Company "C" in a covering charge that allowed the white troops to get back to their lines.

He was recommended for the rank of captain by General Butler, but the promotion was denied. Milton always felt that he remained a sergeant major because of his race. However, by this time, the loss of white officers had reduced the ranks so that blacks were being promoted to command black troops. More than likely, his failure to be promoted was a reflection of Butler's lack of credibility.

This small dark cloud can never dim his accomplishment. Like the men he faced on New Market Heights, he was a fighter. Steadily and swiftly, he had risen through the ranks with each engagement. His officers who promoted him and his men who followed him recognized his quality. His courage was proved in battle as surely as Jack Hays's or Dick Dowling's. He was part of Texas's dynasty of courage.

Official records show a total of 178,985 enlisted men and 7,122 officers in black regiments during the Civil War. Nine percent of the Union army was black. They fought in 449 engagements of which 39 were major battles. Approximately 37,300 black men lost their lives. Besides seventeen black soldiers, four black sailors were awarded the Congressional Medal of Honor.

The psychological impact of their presence was probably greater than their actual physical numbers. They discouraged and frightened Southerners. They brought joy to the hearts of black slaves who saw them as the fulfillment of a promise. They were proof that the North really was freeing them, therefore, those still enslaved deserted as swiftly as possible, depriving the South of their labor and the essentials that it provided to the troops in the field. All this they did "despite unequal pay, unfair work duties, severely limited opportunities for advancement, inadequate equipment, and inferior medical care."

Finally, their bravery and devotion to duty brought honor to themselves and changed the way white men came to look at them.

Across America more than the Emancipation Proclamation, more than the destruction of the ante-bellum South, the uniform changed the black man's status forever. A man who wears his country's uniform and faces death in its service cannot be anything less than a full-fledged citizen. A significant number of men throughout the country recognized that fact even though they were still in the minority. The black man made great steps forward because he won what he wanted almost before he knew he wanted it. He won respect.

* * * * *

Milton M. Holland, Texas hero, died on May 15, 1910. He was buried in Section 23 of Arlington National Cemetery where his grave may be visited to this day.

On Route 171 four miles south of Mansfield, Louisiana, is Mansfield Battle Park, where Bird Holland was killed. The forty-four-acre site also has a museum exhibiting weapons, uniforms, and other artifacts of the Civil War.

In the Name of the Congress of the United States

The Medal of Honor is the highest military award for bravery that can be given to any individual in the United States of America. A Navy and Marine medal was first conceived and introduced into legislation by Senator James W. Grimes of Iowa in December of 1861. In February of 1862 Senator Henry Wilson of Massachusetts introduced a Senate resolution for an Army medal that included volunteer forces. President Abraham Lincoln signed both decorations into law in 1862 and made them retroactive to the beginning of the Civil War.

The provisions for the medal are as follows:

1. The deed of the person must by proved by incontestable evidence of at least two eyewitnesses.

2. It must be so outstanding that it clearly distinguishes his gallantry beyond the call of duty from lesser forms of bravery.

3. It must involve the risk of his life.

4. It must be the type of deed which, if he had not done it, would not subject him to any justified criticism.

The medal is always presented to its recipients by a high official or a superior officer "in the name of the Congress of the United States." Therefore, it is sometimes called the Congressional Medal of Honor.

Ten different forms of the medal have been awarded over the 137 years of its existence. The Navy medal has been seen in four different forms. The Army, in five. The Air Force, in one.

The original was designed by James Pollock, Director of the U.S. Mint in Philadelphia. From the first it has always been made of sterling silver heavily electroplated with gold. In bas-relief on the star, a figure representing the Union holds a shield in her right hand. At her left an attacker crouches holding forked-tongued serpents that strike at the shield. In her left hand Union holds the fasces, the ancient Roman symbol of unified authority, an ax bound in staves of wood. Thirty-four stars encircle these figures representing the number of states at that time—all thirty-four of which Abraham Lincoln was determined should remain within the Union. The Navy medal is attached to the red-and-white striped riband by an anchor. The Army medal is attached by the American eagle standing on crossed cannon and cannonballs. The reverse is blank to receive the name of the hero.

During the Civil War the Army medal was awarded 1,199 times; the Navy medal, 327 times. No other war has ever seen so many. In fact the Civil War numbers reflect only a bit under half of all the medals awarded to the present day. Perhaps so many were awarded because the idea of medals was new. No other medals existed except the Purple Heart, awarded originally by George Washington.

Why were there so many for that terrible war?

Perhaps the Civil War inspired more passion in the hearts and minds of the soldiers who fought for the Union. Perhaps the fact that it was fought on the soil of the Unites States spurred them to greater efforts. Perhaps because it was fought by amateur armies commanded by amateur officers, individual soldiers saw what needed to be done and acted without commands from their superiors.

In April 1890 the Medal of Honor Legion was organized in Washington, D.C. Its purpose was to protect the medal and to allow men who had earned it to come together to perpetuate the ideals of the medal. In August 1890 the Legion was made a national organization during the encampment of the Grand Army of the Republic in Boston. In 1955 the Legion was incorporated by Act of Congress. Today it is the Legion of Valor of the United States of America.

A Congressional Medal of Honor Society of the United States was chartered by legislative act of Congress in 1958 and signed by President Dwight D. Eisenhower, himself a Texan by birth.

Both societies have much the same purposes. Among them are the following:

1. To form a bond of friendship and comradeship among all holders of the Medal of Honor.

2. To provide appropriate aid to all persons to whom the medal has been awarded, their widows, or their children.

3. To serve our country in peace as we did in war.

4. To inspire and stimulate our youth to become worthy citizens of our country.

The philosophy behind the awarding of this medal or any other medal should be clear to every American. When a soldier does a brave deed defending our nation and her people, he cannot boast about it. He does not do it because he wants a medal or because he wants to perform an act that will attract attention to himself. He does it because he sees the terrible need and knows someone must do it. Therefore, he throws his body into harm's way. *Someone must do it.*

The medal is to pay honor to such people. To say to them, "We respect and honor and admire your courage. We can never reward you because we can neither create nor amass a just recompense for your deed. Therefore, please accept this symbol reserved strictly for you. Wear it proudly, so we may honor you as one above the many—a hero."

The Soldier's Soldier

Audie Murphy

"As long as there's a man in the lines, maybe I feel that my place is up there beside him."

In a quiet moment in a hospital behind the lines in Italy, Sergeant Audie Murphy answered the question that would be asked of him over and over for the next year of his life. Why did he keep returning to the front? Why didn't he take the rearguard positions offered him by officers who caught sight of his smooth boy's cheeks and stared into his baby-blue eyes and couldn't bring themselves to send him back to Hell.

Stricken with a recurring malaria contracted in North Africa, he had fainted while checking the company's machine gun emplacements on Anzio beachhead in March of 1944. His own men carried him back to the base hospital where he took less than a week to recuperate, so anxious was he to be back to do his part.

Five foot five and weighing slightly more than a hundred pounds, he was a natural leader. His men were older, taller, heavier, and better educated. Yet they followed him, obeyed his orders, and looked to him to keep them safe. From the afternoon in Sicily when he killed his first men, he was recognized as an extremely valuable soldier. He proved to be among the smallest percentage of all soldiers—the fighter who understood from the very beginning that war was "the business of killing." Among his superiors, he was also deemed one who might not live long.

As few as twenty-five or thirty percent of men carrying weapons in an infantry company ever fired them. Of that small number, Audie was the quintessential soldier, the man who would take and hold the ground. He was always the first to pull the trigger, to toss a grenade, to set a satchel charge, or to lead a sortie. Tommy gun or Garand rifle spitting death from his hip, he would be counted on to lead the attack.

On Anzio still three months short of his twentieth birthday, he had already been promoted twice as he was promoted consistently throughout the war until he reached the rank of first lieutenant. The more responsibility he was given, the more he stoically assumed.

He accepted his job, broadened his shoulders, and lengthened his step. His naturally cocky attitude infected his men and strengthened their morale. He loved them, respected them, and lived to memorialize them with grace and honor. The men from Texas that he served with were Dowdy, Black, Robertson, and Corliss Rowe. His autobiography *To Hell and Back* is dedicated to Private Joe Sieja, killed in action on the Anzio beachhead, January 1944, and Private Lattie Tipton, killed in action near Ramatuelle, France, August 1944. A decade later when he wrote it with the help of David "Spec" McClure, he changed the names of his comrades to spare their families.

The little Irishman they called Murph, with the big clever hands and the hair-raising courage, was born in northwestern Hunt County, Texas, June 20, 1924, He had eleven brothers and sisters. His father was Emmett Berry "Pat" Murphy, one of thirteen children. His mother was Josie Bell Killian, also one of thirteen.

Three of Audie's great half-uncles fought in the Texas Revolution. Five of his uncles fought in World War I. At the numerous Berry and Killian family reunions, he naturally gravitated to his uncles. They reminisced about the war fought less than a quarter of a century before in France, a strange country whose location he had no idea of.

All Audie knew was that he was surrounded by brave men, all survivors who had done their duty and lived to tell the tales.

From one of those Audie remembered the story, a tale which surely reverberated in his ears as he worked his way across Europe.

In *To Hell and Back*, Audie recalled a pair of hands. Calloused and streaked with dirt, they looked more like claws as they cupped around the match flame at the end of the cigarette.

"You knowed where they were?" the little farm boy asked the man with the gnarled hands.

"Course I knowed where they was. Any ijiot would have. It was still early mornin'; and when they crawled through the field, they shook the dew off the wheat. So every blessed one of 'em left a dark streak behind."

"So what did you do?"

"I lined up my sights on the machine gun and waited."

"A machine gun?"

"Yeah. It's the devil's own weapon. When they got to the edge of the patch, I could see 'em plain. There was nothing to it. I just pulled the trigger and let 'em have it."

"You killed 'em?"

"I didn't do 'em any good."

"Did they shoot at you?"

"Now what do you think? This was war."

"What was they like?"

"The Germans? I never took time to ast 'em. They was shootin' at us; so we shot at them."

"But you whipped 'em."

"We whopped 'em all right, but it wasn't easy. They was hard fighters. Don't ever kid yourself about that."

"Some day I aim to be a soldier."

Audie's father deserted his family in 1940. In 1941 his mother died. His older brother and sisters were poor as their parents had been before them. They could not take responsibility for the younger ones. Since Audie was too old to go with his younger brothers and sisters to an orphanage, he lived with generous families in the town of Celeste, Texas, paying for his mother's hundred dollar funeral a little at a time until the Japanese bombed Pearl Harbor December 7, 1941.

He told a friend that he planned to enlist in the Marines. He wanted to train as a sniper. When the friend, who was two years older, enlisted in the Navy, Audie went with him to join up. Eager, underage boys all over Texas were doing the same thing. Since most had no birth certificates, some actually were able to convince desperate recruiters that they were old enough.

Imbued with the tales of Rip Ford's Cavalry of the West, whose lower enlistment age was fifteen, those who were turned down couldn't understand why such a thing as a birthday could keep them home a minute longer.

Audie was, of course, turned down not just because he was seventeen and lying about his age, but because he looked somewhere between thirteen and fourteen. The blow to his pride was hard to swallow.

A few days short of his eighteenth birthday, he went again. The Marine recruiter rejected him because of his weight. He was sent home to eat more bananas and drink more milk. So much for his coveted sniper training. The Paratroopers, whose uniforms included such handsome boots, laughed at him for the same reason. So much for the admired boots. The humiliation merely strengthened his resolve.

Nothing was left but the Army. On June 20, 1942, his eighteenth birthday, he enlisted. He had never shaved. His education was finished in the fourth grade. He did not know even the basic rules for the all-American game of baseball. In all likelihood he was still a virgin as were a great many young men who entered World War II.

They put their entire lives aside along with the hope of their posterity to answer their country's call.

As Hitler's Panzers chugged and clanked into France and Russia and his Luftwaffe thundered through the skies above Great Britain, the Army found a fertile recruiting ground in Texas. The state had only five percent of the total population of the United States. Its boys made up seven percent of the total armed forces. They expected to fight. They longed for it. Courage was their chief virtue. And at the end of the war when the losses were added up, Texas's war dead *exceeded* seven percent of the total killed in action.

Audie Murphy with his fourth grade education wrote letters home to his sister Corinne Burns. "... in Dallas when I was taking my phisical [sic]. Came through with flying colors, eyes checked 20-20, ears and teeth 100 percent. (body! Oh, wouldn't you like to know)."

Despite his happy letter, he was homesick. In contrast to the men he trained with, he was skinny and pale. He looked as if he suffered from malnutrition (a possibility given his precarious existence back in Celeste). He still owed some on his mother's funeral, but the mortuary excused it since he was now a soldier. He took out an insurance policy for his sister but was worried about it because of the price—$3.40 a month.

He might have looked like a sad sack, but with a rifle and fixed bayonet in his big, long-fingered hands, he was a different person. He moved like a rattlesnake with a smooth, gliding step that flowed over the ground. Throughout his movie career, the elegantly coordinated movement across the screen was one of the reasons for his success.

Early in his training, various officers pitied the "little boy" and tried to move him into easier duties. Someone tried to send him to Cook and Baker's School, but Audie protested until the idea was dropped. Because of his phenomenal skill with weapons and his spit-and-polish attitude, his company commander wanted him to become an advanced trainer at Fort Meade. He thanked the man kindly, but he wanted to go overseas. A captain secured him a job in a post exchange. Audie protested again. He'd trained to fight, not to sell shoes and socks.

In October 1942, after thirteen weeks of basic training, he visited his sister in Farmersville. Over his left pocket he wore the first two of the thirty-two awards, citations, and decorations he would receive in his military career—the Marksmanship Badge with the Rifle Bar and the Expert Badge with Bayonet Bar.

Corinne recalled that he had taken to the Army "like he was born in it. The crease in his trousers was so sharp that it looked like a person could cut their hand on it." All his career, except at the front covered with mud and blood, he took pride in his uniform. The habits learned in the Army carried over into civilian life. He was an immaculate dresser with never a wrinkle or a hair out of place.

When he left to be shipped overseas, Corinne would not see her brother until his return stateside in mid-June of 1945. On February 20, 1943, having been promoted to acting corporal, an unofficial rank that nevertheless carried two stripes, he landed in Casablanca, North Africa, with the 3rd Division of the 7th Infantry.

On July 10, 1943, the 1st Battalion landed in Sicily. On July 21 outside Palermo, Sicily, Audie was promoted to full corporal. On patrol duty outside the town of San Cataldo, Audie killed his first men. As the patrol moved up the road, two Italian officers fled an observation post. Instead of surrendering, they mounted horses and attempted to ride away. Without hesitation and without command, Audie, who was in the lead element, dropped to one knee and fired two quick shots from his M-1 rifle.

Men who knew him or who saw him in combat all agreed that the Texan was a much better shot when he fired instinctively. In this case he killed them both instantly.

The lieutenant in command acted outraged. He reprimanded the youngster in front of the others. He demanded to know why Audie had fired.

Audie's reply was, "That's our job, isn't it? They would have killed us if they'd had the chance. Or have I been wrongly informed?"

The lieutenant looked sheepish as if he'd forgotten for the minute what their job was—to deal out death. He looked everywhere but at Audie. "To hell with it," he said. "I guess you did the right thing."

For himself Audie recalled that he felt no qualms, but neither did he feel pride or remorse. His only feeling was exhaustion. The swift rush of adrenalin that had enabled him to do his job left him very tired and slightly nauseated. It was always the same. Once the job was done, he was exhausted.

Sicily fell in only thirty-eight days. On September 21 Audie, seasick but not so scared, landed at Battipaglia south of Salerno beachhead, which they were ordered to help secure. For nearly a year he would be in Italy waging the Boot Campaign, some of the hardest, most heartbreaking fighting of World War II.

The war in Italy was called the Boot Campaign because Italy is a peninsula extending between the Mediterranean and the Adriatic and shaped like a high-heeled boot kicking the island of

Sicily. It is less than two hundred miles at its widest point, crowned by the rugged Apennines whose chain boasted three active volcanoes. It was hell on men and equipment.

Audie's unique qualities of aggressiveness plus battle sense stood out from the beginning. He was promoted twice in the course of the campaign, to sergeant on December 13 and to staff sergeant a month later. The division won three battle stars for Naples-Foggia, Anzio, and Rome-Arno. All three were earned by Audie Murphy.

During the winter his health became a precarious thing. Malaria he'd picked up in Africa and influenza kept knocking him back in hospital. He always returned as fast as he could stagger to the front, but he kept losing weight, which he couldn't afford. He had a fanatical sense of responsibility that brought him back again and again, sneaking out of his hospital bed in the night and moving up through the lines to join his unit.

In all likelihood he had attached himself to them as if they were part of his family. Certainly, his men cared for him. At this time they took to carrying his extra weapons for him. Besides his M-1 which he always carried, one of his heftier friends usually slung a Garand (semiautomatic) over his shoulder while another would carry a .30 caliber Browning automatic rifle (the highly touted BAR).

Likewise, when his unit came under fire, someone always passed Audie his favorite weapon, the .45 caliber Thompson submachine gun, the famous tommy gun. It and the ammunition required to shoot it effectively weighed twenty pounds. Sergeant Murphy weighed only about a hundred. Two-hundred-pound privates and corporals were happy to be his gun bearers in exchange for his taking care of them.

He was a soldier's soldier. A fourth promotion was "pigeon-holed" because he refused a direct order to drill his men when they'd been pulled back from the front lines for a brief rest.

He could scarcely have cared less.

With every encounter he became more skillful. He was able to spot camouflaged enemy faster than anyone else in his unit just by the slight difference in the color of the foliage, not necessarily because it had begun to die. His perfect vision could notice where a tank hid beneath concealing netting with a different type of leaf from the ones in the surrounding orchard or woods. Likewise, he could find snipers who had exposed the lighter green undersides of leaves when they stuck branches in their camouflage capes.

His reflexes were phenomenal. Shooting from the hip was his favorite position for fire. His patriotism coupled with good judgment was unquestioned. At the Volturno River, his patrol took out a sizable machine gun nest. His men hurled hand grenades into it, and Audie dropped to one knee, squeezed the trigger, and took out the survivors with his tommy gun.

Sadly, at the Volturno, the little group of friends lost one of their number. Avery Dowdy was hit as he tried to cross a stream. Enemy machine gun fire almost sawed his legs off below the knees. Although quick medical attention saved his legs, his days in the Army were over.

On the San Pietro Road, Sergeant Milton Robertson was badly wounded. Taken to a German hospital, he was repatriated to the United States with his right arm crippled for the rest of his life. The wounding of Audie's friends is mirrored in the woundings and deaths of his companions in *To Hell and Back*. His sorrow and anger are also poignantly reported.

Felled by influenza and malaria just before the Anzio beachhead landing, Audie came in among a boatload of replacements to return to his outfit. Five German planes buzzed the landing, but no one was injured. As he hiked inland, he passed jeeps drawing trailer-loads of corpses. The bodies, stacked like wood, were covered with shelter-halves, but arms and legs dangled and wobbled along the sides.

He didn't reel to the side of the road and vomit. He didn't turn white and slow his steps. Instead he increased his pace. His unit needed him. He had to get back to them as quickly as possible. He had to protect them. He had to keep them out of trouble. When a regular army sergeant tried to stop him, he told him to go to hell and marched away up the road marked with an arrow and a blue diamond, the code symbol of his regiment.

As he walked, he studied the terrain. The months in combat had taught him invaluable lessons that made him more and more difficult to kill. Now every roll, depression, rock, or tree was significant to him. His mind was already solving the German strategy. Before him rose a chain of wooded hills, up and up toward Rome.

"The enemy and his eternal hills must be taken with blood, guts, and steel."

When he reached his unit, he learned that one of his friends, Private Joe Sieja, the man named Novak in his book, had been killed. Two other friends had been wounded, one so badly that he would not be back, the Cherokee Indian Jim Fife, whom he named Swope.

The war had gone from not having enough water in North Africa to having too much. A chilling wind blew in from the sea. His men were covered with mud and knee-deep in icy water in their foxholes. Everyone had trenchfoot in varying degrees of severity. Everyone was trigger-happy because the Germans were sneaking down out of the hills at night and killing exhausted soldiers as they slept.

On three successive days the enemy attacked, but Audie and his men held. Gradually, on his orders they began to move forward, killing Germans as they went, leaving their own dead to lie beside them. The weather that had been such a problem for them became a problem for the enemy too.

A column of heavy German Tiger tanks came down the road. Audie called down an artillery barrage that disabled the first Tiger. The others retreated because the shoulders of the road and the ditches beside them were too soft to bear their weight.

Because the disabled Tiger sat like a roadblock to the German counterattack, it was too important to abandon. A crew would most certainly be out after dark to repair it. Audie had to destroy it beyond repair, thus blocking the road. He picked his men. Armed with Molotov cocktails, guns, hand grenades, and a grenade launcher, they headed for it just at dusk.

Ordering his men to cover him, Audie crept two hundred yards down the ditch from where he threw two Molotovs, but the bottles filled with gasoline failed to ignite and worse they rang like bells in the darkness. Crawling closer, he tossed a grenade into the tank's open hatch.

The exploding grenade stirred up the rest of the Germans not already alerted to the failed Molotov cocktails. They came to save their machinery and more important their road. Using the grenade launcher, Audie blew the treads off the tank and raced like the devil as far as the ditch went. His men covered him with a hail of fire until he caught up to them. Then they all ran like hell. He had destroyed the tank without putting them in danger. No one who ever fought beside him could forget him. No Germans thereafter tried to retrieve the Tiger and the road was effectively closed for their counteroffensive. On this campaign, Audie, still nineteen, won the Bronze Star with the V device for valor.

At this time headquarters began to suggest that he accept a battlefield commission to second lieutenant. He refused because to do so would have meant a transfer to another unit. He could not leave his men to someone who might not be experienced enough to save them.

On the other hand, another type of patrol Audie led wasn't so popular with his men. It was reconnaissance and intelligence to capture prisoners. On these patrols he would go out with Fredericks from North Dakota, a man of German descent who had lived in a German community and spoke the language fluently.

The technique was to infiltrate the German lines, let Fredericks lure a soldier, preferably a sentry or one from an outpost, into the open. Then Audie would capture him and hustle him back. Their missions were more dangerous coming back than going in, particularly if the German was discovered to be missing.

About that time Audie was called back to testify in a court-martial of one of his men. The man had deserted under fire and was found three days later cowering in a hut.

"His nerves gave way; and he could not force himself to face the enemy guns again. [He] wasn't a coward, but from the army point of view his offense is a serious matter indeed."

"Had he been a good soldier?"

"Yessir."

"Then to what do I attribute his act? To nerves. To fright. Do you think Thompson has a corner on fright?"

"Nosir."

"But you do not desert?"

"Nosir."

"It is natural to be afraid. We all are. But no soldier can let his fear govern his conduct to such a degree. Is that understood?"

"Yessir."

The man was sentenced to twenty years in prison, but he wasn't concerned. He told Audie he considered himself lucky to get to stay in jail and get out when he was thirty-nine. Audie would have to attack again and again, until finally he'd be killed. The coward's attitude was, "What's twenty years compared to a corpse?"

Unfortunately, his estimate of the situation with the Third Division proved too tragically true. Seasoned infantrymen joked with the new recruits that they had the best chance to be decorated of any branch of the services: more chances for Purple Hearts, more Distinguished Wooden Crosses, and more Royal Orders of the Mattress Covers (the tarpaulins used to wrap soldiers' corpses to carry them back from the front).

In April, with Italy as far north as Rome in American hands, the Third Division was pulled back for service as corps reserve. They received renewed training and a chance to rest. Audie had several furloughs to Rome but found the place dirty and disappointing. In fact all of Italy by that time looked like exactly what it was, a country that had been fought over. Abandoned industrial areas, houses in ruins or tired and disused looking, gates and hedges broken, rusting skeletons of vehicles in ditches, windows broken, human excreta in broken drains.

In August 1944 Operation Anvil began in France. D-Day had seen the Allies landed at Normandy. The hammer of the American army advancing from the north was ready to strike the anvil of an American army advancing from the south. On August 15, in a landing that took only forty minutes, Audie's regiment headed inland.

What he did in France was simply incredible, unbelievable, yet every exploit is documented by many witnesses, both American and German.

The legend began on the day of the landing. In *To Hell and Back* he wrote of moving to take out a machine gun nest. He was out of carbine ammo when his friend Private Lattie Tipton (Brandon in his book) caught up to him.

"You shouldn't have come up," Audie said.

"Why not? This is not a private war, is it?"

As they moved up the ditch, a German bullet clipped off part of Brandon's right ear. They continued until they were forced to dive into a German foxhole.

"Have you got any idea of how to get out of this spot?" Brandon joked.

"No, I'm open to suggestion."

"We should have looked it up in the field manual."

They heaved hand grenades into the gun emplacement.

The Germans yelled, "Kamerad!"

Brandon rose to accept their surrender.

"Keep down," Audie warned. "You can't trust them."

And they shot his friend.

For the first and only time Audie Murphy went crazy. He threw a grenade into another machine gun on a position yards to his right and killed both the men manning it. Their gun was undamaged. Jerking it out of the emplacement, he started up the hill. Shooting from the hip, the gun's cartridge belt dangling, he sprayed everything in sight.

The rest of his men, pinned farther down the hill, heard him shouting pleas and curses. When he came to the gun crew that had killed Tipton, he shot them to pieces, raked them again and again until not one so much as quivered. Then Audie returned to

Tipton's side where he sat down and bawled like a baby. When he rose, he had become a man obsessed.

At this point he became the hero of ultimate reality. Not red with rage, not blind with emotion, but cold as ice and deadly. He was a man with the personal crusade to rid the world of German soldiers wherever he would find them. He had had enough of seeing his friends die—his friends who were closer to him than family, friends who had families to go back home to.

So he fought harder to get the war over with as quickly as possible. He said he couldn't see the point of risking thirty men when one—that one being himself—could do the job. His determination brought out his mean streak. Ten years later, he said, "People think I brood about those Germans I killed. I don't. If my own brother had been on the other side, I would have tried to kill him."

At a later time after the war was over, Audie evaluated his own performance. "There was a time when I got to be a pretty good soldier. That is, I learned to play the percentages; I learned to stay under cover whenever I could find it. I tried to stay alive, which is what the Army teaches you. But there are times you have to stick your neck out, naturally."

One of the most famous stories of his ability to be a good soldier occurred at Montelimar during house-to-house fighting. Audie, with a friend backing him up, was standing in an abandoned house when a door creaked open.

"Suddenly I find myself faced by a terrible-looking creature with a tommy gun. His face is black; his eyes are red and glaring. I give him a burst and see the flash of his own gun, which is followed by the sound of shattering glass."

Moments later his friend burst into laughter. "That's the first time I ever saw a Texan beat himself to the draw."

They were able to joke, but the elements of tragedy are there for anyone else to see. Audie Murphy had become something he literally did not recognize. He had seen his own face in the mirror. It was the face of a killer.

Ernie Pyle, the famous war correspondent who named the man in the trenches G. I. Joe, wrote, "When Murphy was in the front lines, we in the rear went to sleep. If we got word that he was falling back, we prepared to get the hell out. When Murphy started retreating, it was time to clear out fast."

On September 15 Audie was almost killed. A mortar shell came in almost soundlessly. He thought "This is it," before he was blasted into unconsciousness. When he came to, he was sitting beside a crater with his favorite carbine, the one with the hair trigger, broken in his hands.

He ran his hands over his body to find everything intact except the heel of his right boot was missing. His fingers came away sticky with blood. He was only slightly wounded. The men he had been talking to were all dead. The shell had landed at his feet. Since they were farther away, they got the worst of the blast. His luck placed him in the vacuum cone created by the fragments going upward and outward.

He was distressed that his wound might require him to remain at the hospital for a few days.

Hospitals were anathema to him. He never really rested in one. Nor did he lose his combat edge as so many men did. Nurses would find him prowling in the kitchen at night—sneaking extra food like a child. He never developed a case of nerves, never had to undergo a difficult reentry period.

In the case of this incident, Audie got a new shoe, wrapped a piece of wire around the stock of his favorite carbine, and went back to the front.

In September he refused another promotion to second lieutenant saying that he wasn't qualified. He had no formal education. He spoke ungrammatically constructed sentences with a nasal Texas twang, which he never lost even after he went to Hollywood and received some of the best speech training the studio could pay for.

The Army didn't care. He couldn't stave off promotion much longer. He was simply too good a leader, and as the war drove closer to Germany, they were experiencing a growing shortage of junior officers.

Driving hard through the Vosges, the last two of Audie's friends from Sicily and Italy were wounded. At this point, he began to feel burnt out. He became emotionally detached from his men, many of whom were recruits so new and ill-trained that they didn't really know how to handle their weapons. He became a man who needed constant action, thrills, and danger to keep from thinking about the grief, pain, and love that he had felt for the friends gone from his side either from wounds or from death.

Within a few days Murphy was wounded for the last time. He got his "ass shot off" as one of his last friends in the line had warned him he would if he became an officer. Back at the aid station with a deep wound in his hip, he heard that practically his entire platoon had been wiped out.

Three days later the wound developed gangrene. For nearly a month the doctors pumped him full of penicillin and whittled away at the dead and poisoned flesh. By some miracle they were able to get it all and he went back to the front.

From Strasbourg, the Third Division was ordered to move south to Colmar and clean up a pocket of heavy German resistance. With their backs to the Rhine, crack German troops could not be left to form a rearguard action just as the Allies tried to cross the river that barricaded Germany as effectively as a fortress.

January 20, 1945, Audie Murphy and his men were so cold that he reported his hair froze to the ground. When gunfire woke him with a jerk, he literally left a patch of his hair in the ice.

They thought they'd gain some protection by following three of their own armored tanks, but the tanks quickly ran into trouble. Two sustained direct hits and burst into flames. The crews bailed out blazing like torches. Screaming, they rolled in the snow. When the third tank's gun didn't work, the tank commander made the decision to move his tank forward. He turned its side to the enemy and used it as a shield for the wounded.

His men loaded them on top of it, and he headed back with his cargo. Audie and his men watched the crippled machine clank past them so close that he could smell the burned flesh and see the bones in what was left of one man's foot. So much for armored support.

At daybreak fresh support had not arrived. It was their time to attack or be attacked. Audie called battalion headquarters for orders and he was told to hold the position. The attack was going to be delayed.

On one side of the road lay an open field stretching all the way to a distant village. All the brush had been cleared away and the surface was grease slick with ice. A drainage ditch ran down one side.

Two tank destroyers had moved up during the night and now deployed like sitting ducks on the road. Audie woke the lieutenant in charge and warned him to get under cover. The officer refused, saying he'd get his machine stuck.

At two o'clock in the afternoon, the German attack began with six tanks rolling out of the village and splitting into three groups.

At three Audie's commanding officer was killed, and Lieutenant Murphy assumed command of the company he had joined as a private in North Africa less than two years before.

As Audie yelled to his men to find cover, wave after wave of German infantry in "spook" suits (white camouflage capes) started moving across the snowy fields.

One of the tank destroyers started its engine, moved to get into position, and promptly slid into the ditch at an angle that left its turret guns completely useless. The driver revved the engine and spun the wheels but only succeeded in getting the heavy vehicle in deeper. The crew bailed out and ran for the rear.

Audie grabbed the map, estimated the enemy's position, and called battalion headquarters. "This is Murphy. We're being attacked. Get me the artillery."

"Coming up."

"I want a round of smoke at co-ordinates 30.5-60; and tell those joes to shake the lead out."

"How many krauts?"

"Six tanks that I can see, and maybe a couple hundred foot soldiers supporting."

"Good god! How close?"

"Close enough. Give me that artillery."

He hung up the receiver and grabbed his carbine just as the enemy's preliminary barrage began. His machine gun squad was killed in the first burst. The second tank destroyer was hit flush. Three of its crew were killed including the lieutenant who refused to move the vehicle off the road. The others climbed out of the smoking turret and sprinted down the road to the rear.

At that moment Audie believed his entire command would be lost.

But, miraculously, their barrage came in right on target as he called it. "200 right; 200 over. And fire for effect." A line of enemy infantrymen disappeared in a cloud of smoke and snow.

His telephone rang. "How close are they?"

"50 over and keep firing for effect," he yelled above the hellish explosions of the guns.

With those directions he called the barrage closer to his position, effectively keeping it on the German infantrymen at the same time his men were covered as they retreated.

The enemy tanks closed in, raking the company's position with machine gun fire. Nearly two-thirds of them were killed. Audie was the last of seven lieutenants. He yelled for his men to pull out at the same time he determined to stay with the phone as long as he could. Taking cover beside the fender of the tank destroyer, he aimed his carbine and started sniping.

The telephone rang. "How close are they?"

"50 over and keep blasting," he ordered again, bringing the barrage in closer.

The enemy were getting too close. He waved his own men back. "Get the hell out of here." He himself returned fire with his carbine, coldly calculating, making every shot count.

When his men hesitated, he yelled, "That's an order!"

The telephone rang. "How close are they?"

"50 over. Keep it coming."

His carbine ran out of ammunition. As he turned to run, he noticed the burning tank destroyer had a perfectly good machine gun on its turret and several cases of ammunition.

The German tanks suddenly veered to the left, to get away from the blaze, guessing rightly that the tank destroyer had a full tank of gasoline and a full complement of ammunition and explosives.

Audie dragged the telephone to the top of the vehicle. With regret tinged with contempt, he dumped the body of the know-it-all lieutenant into the snow. He had warned the man. He had no time to waste mourning him. The telephone rang. "How close are they to your position?"

"Just hold the phone and I'll let you talk to one of the bastards." With that he pressed the trigger of the machine gun. Three Germans staggered and crumpled.

The telephone rang. "This is Sergeant Bowes. Are you still alive, lieutenant?"

"Momentarily." Audie spread the map on his left palm. "Correct fire:—"

The tank destroyer received a direct hit that almost threw him off the top of it, but he managed to hang onto the telephone and the map.

"Lieutenant. Lieutenant. Can you hear me? Are you still alive, lieutenant?"

"I think so. Correct fire: 50 over, and keep the line open."

He brought the barrage in closer, clapped another magazine of cartridges into the machine gun, and locked his hands around the hot firing mechanism again. The smoke was so thick that he couldn't see except when the wind blew it away. In those intervals he mowed down anything that moved.

The Germans couldn't locate him because they were giving the tank destroyer a wide berth. They couldn't conceive of a man crazy enough to use it for cover.

Once when the wind blew the smoke away, he discovered a dozen German soldiers had taken cover in the ditch where his men had been only minutes before. He guessed they were searching for him.

Methodically, he pressed the trigger and raked them with a slow traverse of the barrel. They slumped forward, but he raked them again to make sure as he picked up the phone.

"Correct fire, battalion. 50 over."

"Are you all right, lieutenant?"

He knew he would be dead in a few minutes, but the job remained. Why was the sergeant wasting his breath? "I'm all right, sergeant. What are *your* postwar plans?"

The barrage he had called down landed within fifty yards of the tank destroyer. The Germans kept advancing, although not so many as before. A great many of them lay dead, their blood spreading in bright red patches over their white camouflage capes and the surrounding snow.

Audie had no hope of escape. He knew he would not escape. He couldn't possibly. Although the half-dozen tanks had started a retreat across the field, he was alone with no idea of how many enemy soldiers. Living didn't matter to him. Only the job of war. Like Jack Hays and Dick Dowling, like William Barret Travis and Milton Holland, he had a job to do. It was his overpowering concern. He was a soldier.

And besides his feet were warm for the first time in three days. Time to finish the job.

He snatched the telephone receiver. "Sergeant. Sergeant Bowes. Correct fire: 50 over; and keep firing for effect. This is my last change."

"Fifty over? That's your own position."

"I don't give a damn. 50 over."

A concussion from an enemy shell almost knocked him from the tank destroyer. He was stunned but managed to hold onto the telephone receiver. He spoke into it, but the line was dead.

He could do no more.

Carefully, he folded the field map and noticed that it and his legs had been riddled with shell fragments. His right trouser leg was quite bloody.

He felt nothing. Only the deep exhaustion that habitually followed his kills. He slid off the tank destroyer. He had nothing left to give. If the Germans wanted to shoot him, he wasn't going to try to stop them. He was too weak to care. Without looking back, he walked away down the center of the road through the forest.

He walked as he always did, the same gliding step, the same straight-backed carriage, head held high. Lieutenant Audie Murphy had done all the soldiering he could for the moment.

Within hours, however, he had found his men as well as some replacements and led them back to the front. He did not report to a field hospital about his wounded legs.

His ghostwriter, Spec McClure, recalled that Audie would sit with him, dictating, reading, telling the story. Sometimes he'd scratch an itch on one of his legs. It would be a piece of that shrapnel working its way through the skin. Spec said, "Audie never did get the war out of his system."

The Colmar Pocket was surrendered on February 7, finishing effective German resistance west of the Rhine. By that time the decision had been made to award Audie the Congressional Medal of Honor for almost single-handedly stopping the German counteroffensive.

On February 10 he was furloughed to Paris where he bought some perfume for his sister Corinne. On February 16 he was promoted to first lieutenant as the Third Division was pulled back to Nancy to rest and recuperate.

He couldn't rest. He became more moody and morose. His thoughts were with his lost friends who weren't there to rest and recuperate. He was heard to say, "The only real heroes are the dead ones."

On March 5 he received two medals—the Distinguished Service Cross for action at Ramatuelle where Lattie Tipton was killed, and the Silver Star for action at Cleurie Quarry. He wrote to his sister that he was soon getting the Medal of Honor. "Boy if I get that I will soon be comeing [sic] home."

With those three medals, he would have earned enough points (five per medal) to be sent stateside. He said years later that the only thing the medals ever meant to him were the points toward coming home.

On March 12 and 13 his regiment moved out to cross the Siegfried Line, but Audie was left behind to serve as liaison officer. He was given a Jeep, a driver, and an interpreter. It was an assignment designed to keep him out of combat. The Army had lost a Medal of Honor winner a few months before when the man was killed before he could receive his decoration. They did not want that happening to the legendary Audie Murphy.

Although Audie was behind the lines, he knew how quickly lines could change. Besides the .50-caliber machine gun customarily mounted on the Jeep, Audie loaded the vehicle with "a few rifles, two German machine guns, and a case of grenades."

In that position, he heard that his company captain had been killed, plus the senior lieutenant. His company had been pinned in a trench for two days. His men needed him. Not for the first time, he violated the regulations.

His communications sergeant guessed his intention. "If you don't come back, what kind of spot will it put me in?"

In his mind Audie had fixed the coordinates where his men were pinned. "I'll be back."

"But if you don't make it?"

"Just consider it none of your business."

When he spotted the famed Dragon Teeth, he climbed out of the Jeep and slung his carbine over his shoulder. The Jeep driver thought he should take more, but he refused.

Upright he walked toward the line, thinking that he would draw fire from far away. The Germans would be more likely to miss that way.

No one fired. The line was eerily silent.

Reaching his men, he started insulting them and pleading with them. Finally, he got a response from them and their only surviving officer, a shell-shocked second lieutenant, who twenty-year-old Audie reported looked very young. He would have liked to lead his men back for a rest, but he knew they had to go forward to a safer place.

The barrage was believed to have driven the Germans back, but nobody knew that for sure. Audie and his men found out for themselves. Upright and shaky, with the living legend at their head, they found better cover where they could wait in comparative safety for the rest of the army to catch up with them.

Audie rejoined his Jeep driver and returned to his base, where he discovered he had not been missed. It was his last time in combat. Like a lone Ranger, the Texan came in and stopped the rout. He took command as only he could do.

At the same time he had bared his chest for the bullet that had his name on it. No bullet ever came. May 8 was V-E Day. Germany surrendered. The war in Europe was over.

But for him there was no peace. His mind was like a horror film run backwards, images of the war flickering through his brain. Of the original company of 235 men of Company B, only 2 remained, a supply sergeant and Audie Murphy. All the rest had been wounded or killed; only a few had been transferred.

The Congressional Medal of Honor and the French Legion of Merit were awarded to him near Salzburg on a sunny day in June, less than a month shy of his twenty-first birthday. Nine U.S. senators were on hand to witness and shake the hand of the kid from Texas as he became the most decorated soldier in American history.

In the end he received thirty-seven medals, eleven of them for valor.

We shall not see his like again.

Today no man is left so long in combat to face the bullets until the one comes with his name on it. No man is expected to serve as Audie did for 400 days. From July 10, 1943, to January 27, 1945, Audie Murphy was away from the front only for short periods of time. Many of those times he was in the hospital with illness or wounds.

He returned to Texas shortly after he received the Medal of Honor. He had little to return to. Only his oldest sister and her husband were close to him. He barely knew his younger siblings. He would have nothing to do with his father, who tentatively tried to make amends.

The hometown welcomed him and entertained him. Texas to a lesser extent did the same. All the hoopla was probably less than satisfying. Audie wore his public mask to hide his true feelings and smiled. His smile never left him—still boyish, still looking like the smile of a fifteen-year-old. He appeared where people wanted him, took the money they offered, traded on his

236 · *The Soldier's Soldier*

persona while he tried to decide what to do with the rest of his life. He was still not old enough to vote.

He might have settled into obscurity as most of the Medal of Honor winners have done. He might have struggled with his sleeplessness and his night sweats in silence and alone. But other forces saw the "kid from Texas" as an opportunity to make a fortune for themselves.

And as he had lived those nightmarish 400 days, he fearlessly plunged into the rest of his life.

James Cagney saw his picture on the cover of *Life* July 16, 1945. He put Audie under contract for his own production company and brought him to Hollywood. Audie had the full treatment including a speech coach, who had little effect on his Texas twang. On the first day on the set, Audie told the director he was working under a handicap.

The director looked startled. Audie was hard and wiry as a coiled-steel spring, clear-eyed, fresh-faced, with a boy's smile and the sliding grace of movement that carried him throughout his life. He had a bone structure the cameras loved. The director blinked and shook his head. "What handicap?"

"No talent."

In 1949 he starred in his first movie *Bad Boy*. At the same time he worked to write his autobiography. Many pages he wrote himself, but mostly he dictated. McClure would type the material up at night. Audie would come back the next day and either change or approve it, or throw it all out with an angry "That's not the way it was."

Two years later he starred in *The Red Badge of Courage* for which he received an Oscar nomination. In 1955 he starred in *To Hell and Back*, his autobiography. It grossed Universal-International ten million dollars in real money when studios were pleased if movies made in the hundreds of thousands and ticket prices were less than a dollar. Audie earned a half million for himself.

It was his watershed. Though he would make thirty more motion pictures, he never had as good a roll or played anything with as much authority.

Still, he continued to work, continued to attack the life he had to live as he had attacked the terrain of Italy, France, and Germany. He worked from time to time for the Army and made countless personal appearances for charities in Texas and around the nation. He married twice, had two sons, formed his own production company, invested his money, was nobody's fool.

On a business trip that had nothing whatsoever to do with the Army or the movies, the private plane he was traveling in, a blue and white Aero-Commander, ran into "low clouds, fog and light rain." The civilian pilot, unqualified to fly under such conditions, crashed into the side of a mountain eighty miles north of Martinsville, Virginia.

Texas and the nation mourned.

To this day his grave is the most visited at Arlington National Cemetery. His courage is the measure for all men in war.

All Texas remembers him, and its young men set their eyes upon the peaks where he planted his battleflags.

* * * * *

The W. Walworth Harrison Library, Greenville, Texas, contains the research documents of Audie Murphy biographer Col. Harold B. Simpson. The library has an Audie L. Murphy Room with mementos, documents, and photographs. The ledger records hundreds of visitors every year filled with sentiments such as "God Bless America for giving us men like Audie Murphy."

The Texas Collection, Baylor University, Waco, Texas, contains unpublished materials about Murphy.

The Barker Texas History Center, University of Texas, Austin, maintains clippings and extensive materials in its research department.

Blockbuster Video has copies of many of his films including *The Red Badge of Courage* and *To Hell and Back*.

The Admiral

Chester W. Nimitz

"Tell Nimitz to get the hell out to Pearl Harbor and stay there till the war is won."

On December 9, 1941, two days after the bombing of Pearl Harbor by the carrier-based planes of the Japanese Empire, Secretary of the Navy Frank Knox left Washington, D.C., for a personal inspection of the military sites on Oahu. For ten days the Navy, the Army, and the world waited until he returned to report to President Franklin Delano Roosevelt.

On December 16, 1941, Knox called Admiral Chester W. Nimitz, ordering him to Hawaii in Roosevelt's exact words.

Nimitz sat stunned as Knox informed him that he had just been promoted and, in effect, been made commander in chief of the Pacific Fleet. While Nimitz was trying to digest this information, Knox gave him the barest details of the situation he would be stepping into at Pearl Harbor. The secretary promised more information would follow and hung up.

Nimitz took a deep breath, trying to make sense of what he had just learned. Like the entire armed services, he had been on alert waiting for orders, but this appointment was completely unexpected. Twenty-eight admirals had senior rank to him. His friend Admiral Husband E. Kimmel had been in command at Pearl Harbor for nearly a year.

But Knox had informed Nimitz that Kimmel was out, relieved of command after the Sunday morning attack that resulted in such staggering losses. Everyone on the islands including Japanese spies had known that the overwhelming majority of the fleet returned to port on weekends. Kimmel's policy of keeping the sailors happy and thereby keeping re-enlistments high had set seven battleships as well as eight other combat ships like ducks in a row around Ford Island.

The next in line for Kimmel's post was Vice Admiral William S. Pye, but he too had been passed over or forgotten. So Nimitz took command. As events proved, he was more than equal to the task, but on that cold December morning, he had no idea that he would wage a new kind of war, the first of its kind in world history.

Why was Nimitz selected? No one questioned Roosevelt, certainly not Frank Knox. But why was the Texan from the Hill Country the choice of the angry president? To this day no one knows.

Roosevelt died before the war ended. He was never able to write his memoirs, which would certainly have revealed why he made the decisions he did. The world will never know why he chose Chester Nimitz, a fourth-generation American of German descent. A hero for the time. A unique hero for Texas where heroism was unquestioned but where until that time almost all her wars had been fought on solid ground.

Chester William Nimitz was born February 24, 1885, in Fredericksburg, Texas, a German farming community west of San Antonio.

The undersized kid from Texas was the grandson of a fighting man. Around 1846 his grandfather Karl Heinrich Nimitz came from Charleston, South Carolina, with a naval background to join the *empresario* Baron Ottfried Hans von Meusebach. As an example to his colony, the baron dropped his title and changed his name to John O. Meusebach. They were going to be Texans and likely Americans. They must have American names. Karl Heinrich became Charles Henry.

Chester's father died before his son was born; the grandfather Charles moved his daughter-in-law and new grandson into his hotel. While Chester's mother, Anna, worked as a cook at the Steamboat Hotel in Fredericksburg, Chester grew up for a time

under the eye of his grandfather, his beloved *Opa*. When Charles Nimitz held a christening for his grandson, he is said to have toasted him, "To a future admiral in the United States Navy." Later Anna married Chester's uncle. He moved the family to Kerrville where he took a job as manager of the St. Charles Hotel, a glorified boardinghouse. Anna went to work also as a cook, and Chester went to school. During the summer he would go back to the Steamboat to be with his grandfather.

His stepfather always did little and consequently made little money. Even before Chester started high school, he was on the lookout for odd jobs to make money to help his mother out. He might have stayed there in central Texas if two young army lieutenants had not boarded at the St. Charles when Chester was fifteen. They were with the Third Field Artillery stationed at Fort Sam Houston in San Antonio and on training maneuvers in the Hill Country. From the moment he saw them, Chester admired the clean-cut young West Point graduates in their handsome uniforms.

He had never thought he could have a college education because of the family's financial situation, but suddenly he wanted it very much. The lieutenants told him they had gotten their education without cost to their parents and now were going to travel and see the world. The military academy was their ticket—all at government expense. Chester applied immediately.

"I want a college education," Nimitz wrote to Congressman James Slaydon of San Antonio.

He was fifteen years old with a year of high school still to finish. His grades were good. He earned fifteen dollars a month working at a hotel in Kerrville, Texas. With it he bought his clothes and schoolbooks and gave some to his mother to help with her needs. He believed West Point was his chance.

Slaydon dashed his hopes. "There is no opening now, and with so many career officers in the district whose sons get first priority, there is little likelihood one will ever come open for you." Even as he closed one door, Slaydon opened another. "I happen to have an opening in the United States Naval Academy. Are you interested?"

"I don't know anything about the Naval Academy," Nimitz replied, "but if it will give me what I want, then I'm for it. Perhaps it will be the best for me. My Grandfather Nimitz will think so and he is important to me."

With that correspondence began the career of one of America's greatest naval heroes—the warrior and strategist who stopped the Empire of Japan in her conquest of the Pacific Ocean and within the space of a few long months drove her back to her home islands where she remains today.

As the twentieth century dawned, better and faster ships were being built. The United States was becoming aware that isolation from Europe was no longer possible. The expansion of the U.S. Navy was inevitable and there was a shortage of officers to man the new ships. Nimitz was accepted at a time when the entire course of study was being accelerated.

On January 30, 1905, Nimitz and his classmates were graduated six months ahead of schedule. Chester was nineteen years old, one of the youngest midshipman ever to graduate from Annapolis. More important was that despite his less-than-sterling education from Kerrville schools, he ranked seventh in his class of 114. Fourth in rank was Royal E. Ingersall, who became commander in chief of the Atlantic Fleet the day after Nimitz was assigned to the Pacific.

Because of his more-than-ordinary capabilities and the need for officers, Nimitz moved up quickly. In 1907, while still an ensign, he was given command of the gunboat *Panay* at Manila Bay. Shortly thereafter when he was only twenty-two, he was given command of the destroyer *Decatur* with orders to sail her into drydock and hasten preparations to make her seaworthy.

Eager to make a good impression and prove that he should stay as her commander when she was readied, Nimitz worked night and day with the warrant officers in charge of her overhaul. He was able to have the ship refitted to top condition in less than the two-week period allowed.

As he had hoped, he remained her commander until an incident occurred that almost destroyed his career. In a moment of carelessness on July 7, 1908, he ran *Decatur* aground at Batangas Harbor in Manila Bay. Instead of taking readings, he estimated the destroyer's bearings and, furthermore, failed to check whether the tide was incoming or outgoing. The ship stayed on the sandbar overnight until Nimitz managed to flag a steamboat to pull her free.

He could probably have gotten away with the mistake. No harm had been done. No one would ever be the wiser. Certainly none of his crew would have reported him. He insisted on taking full responsibility. He reported himself.

According to protocol, any report required that a hearing be held. A court-martial had no choice but to find him guilty of "neglect of duty." Because of his spotless record, he was treated leniently. He received a public reprimand and was relieved of his command. He was sent home for two weeks, a punishment he rather enjoyed because he got to see his mother and grandfather. He fully expected that his career would be set back for a time.

Eighteen months after grounding *Decatur*, he received a promotion that indicated clearly that the Navy had recognized the court-martial as of no importance. He was promoted directly to lieutenant, skipping the rank of lieutenant, junior grade. In this way he remained on track with other men in his graduating class.

Through the next years he served on submarines, the newest branch of the Navy. Their uses and functions were still being developed. He had no rules to follow and no models to predict the results of maneuvers. He had to make up strategies as he went along. He was proving to his superiors and to the Navy as a whole what a valuable man he could be.

During that time he saved the life of one of his men. The Navy awarded him the Silver Lifesaving Medal. It was his first decoration and one he always considered very important because he had saved a life rather than taken one.

In April 1913 he fell in love with and married Catherine Freeman of Quincey, Massachusetts. Although he was then commander of the Atlantic submarine flotilla, the couple lived in rather ordinary circumstances. His pay was $213 a month, twenty-five of which he sent to his mother.

Over and over again, the details of his life show his devotion to duty, to family, to country, and to the Navy. He was the example of what a man should be. Without braggadocio, he let his deeds and the way he lived speak for him.

Three of his four children were born over the next five years and he and his wife were very happy. Then in 1919 he was sent to the Atlantic, where he chased German U-boats to keep the shipping lanes open for American ships carrying supplies and later troops to Europe.

In June 1920 he had his first assignment at Pearl Harbor, where he was to build a submarine base out of World War I salvage. Again he was given a demanding assignment with a nearly impossible task. Odds were good that he could not bring it in on time. His only authority was another stripe on his sleeve. At thirty-five he was promoted to lieutenant commander.

He worked as hard as he had ever worked, refitting the base on time and in good order. When it was ready, he became its commander.

In 1922 he was given orders to organize a Navy R.O.T.C. unit at University of California at Berkeley. He taught there for several years and learned more than he taught from his faculty associates. This experience was equivalent in time and course work to earning a Ph.D.

After teaching, he had several assignments at sea and ashore ending with the plum position of senior naval officer on the West Coast commanding Task Force Seven, which consisted of a large cruiser, several destroyers, auxiliary vessels, a tanker, and his flagship, the battleship *Arizona*.

The United States as well as the European powers were looking with wary eyes at the Japanese empire. She had increased her power and presence on the world stage by joining World War I on the side of the British. For her minimal help, she had acquired the German empire in the Pacific—the Marshall and Caroline Islands and all of the Marianas except Guam, which the United States, through the insistence of President Woodrow Wilson, had kept as a stepping stone from Hawaii to the Philippines, an American protectorate.

Wilson tried to continue the build-up of the United States fleet, which he saw as a deterrent to the Japanese in the event of war. Unfortunately, he was overruled on this point, so no new ships were added for over twenty years. The U.S. Army was in part responsible for this lack of readiness, for it jealously guarded its military superiority, maintaining that if an attack were necessary, it would be carried out from the Philippines using the Navy primarily as a vehicle.

To that end the Army increased their supplies and manpower to the point where they believed they could hold the island of Luzon for nine months. The thinking was that the Navy would need that much time to outfit and sail from California via Hawaii via Guam to pick up the Army and carry them to the defense of China where attack seemed most likely. They also counted on the aid of the British and Dutch, both of whom had excellent fleets and valuable interests in the Pacific.

The length of the lifeline, the division of forces, and the vulnerability of men and equipment did not trouble the majority among the Joint Chiefs of Staff and their strategists. They simply did not foresee that their enemy very well might be one unlike any the world had seen. An enemy with a land configuration like Japan's had never waged a war before. No one had any idea how to deal with them. Today's military strategists, who look at maps and study population and economics, always ask the question: How could the Army with such a small force expect to defend both the Philippines and the integrity of the Chinese mainland?

Moreover, Adolph Hitler had plunged Europe into war. All Dutch and British men and arms including their navies were dedicated to his defeat. Europeans had their eyes on their own countries in danger of being overrun. No immediate help would come from Europe. The Unites States would have to fight alone.

In 1940 the Japanese became more and more aggressive and continued to build ships and acquire supplies. The United States countered by placing an embargo on the oil and steel that were always in short supply in the island empire. To be on the safe side, the Pacific Fleet was moved from the coast of California to the Hawaiian Islands—specifically Pearl Harbor on the island of Oahu. This move placed them two thousand miles closer and many hours nearer to the Philippines.

The Navy like other branches of the armed services had recruitment problems. As the ships became more technical, training took longer and more money had to be invested in each man. The Navy needed career sailors. America was a strongly pacifist country whose sons were steered toward peacetime pursuits and the professions of their fathers.

The average young American could be induced to enlist and more importantly to re-enlist *only* if things were made pleasant for him—not too much work and lots of recreation. Pleasant and recreational involved free weekends on the beaches of the Paradise of the Pacific rather than gunnery practice on the high seas. To this end Admiral Husband E. Kimmel kept most of the fleet in port on the weekends. No effort was made to keep this information secret from spies or businessmen visiting the islands. Accusations were later leveled against the one hundred sixty thousand people of Japanese heritage living on the islands, but not a single disloyal act was ever proven against any of them.

Fleet Admiral Isoroku Yamamoto, commander in chief of the Japanese Combined Fleet had worked out a plan to neutralize the United States Navy.

1. Prior to the declaration of war, destruction of the United States Pacific Fleet and the British and American air forces on the Malay Peninsula and the island of Luzon.

2. Quick conquest of the Philippines, Guam, Wake, Hong Kong, Borneo, British Malaya, Singapore, and Sumatra.

3. Japanese amphibious invasion and conquest of Java and a mop-up of the rest of the Dutch East Indies.

4. Intensive development of the rubber and oil resources in Malaya and the Indies.

5. Invasion and subjugation of China, many of whose people could be counted on to provide political and economic support.

6. Development of a defensive perimeter stretching south from the Kuril Sea north of the Honshu through Wake and the Marshall Islands, then west through the Dutch East Indies to the Malay Peninsula, then north to Burma, a vast amount of ocean, but not impossible if Japan had the proper ships.

Yamamoto had looked at the Hitler model of *blitzkrieg*, or lightning war. He was confident that if his six goals could be accomplished within six months, communication among Australia, New Zealand, and Anglo-American powers would be cut and the English-speaking peoples would be forced to sue for peace.

Yamamoto's surety of success was based upon the fact that Japan had ten new battleships in its Pacific Fleet while the United States had nine, most of which were World War I vintage. For example, *Arizona*, Nimitz's former command, had been launched in 1913. Japan outnumbered the United States in heavy and light cruisers, destroyers, and submarines. Most important, Japan had ten aircraft carriers while the United States had three: *Yorktown*, *Lexington*, and *Enterprise*.

Even including the few British and Dutch warships remaining in the area, Japan still had a superior fleet. Victory would be theirs in one fell swoop if the fleet in port at Pearl Harbor were destroyed on a weekend.

Frank Knox called Chester Nimitz on December 16 with the news that Nimitz had seven days to get to Pearl Harbor and incidentally that he had been promoted to four star admiral. Nimitz literally grabbed his assistant, Randall Jacobs, as the young captain was running up the steps of the Navy Department building. In terse sentences, Nimitz handed his job as Chief of the Bureau of Navigation to Jacobs, shook hands, and walked home (the quickest possible way) to tell his wife what amounted to good-bye.

The next two days he met with President Roosevelt, Secretary Knox, and Admiral Ernest J. King, who had been appointed Chief of Naval Operation. Nimitz and one aide, Lieutenant (j.g.) Hal Arthur Lamar, were to travel cross-country by train. Lamar had been entrusted with a large canvas bag, which he was to give to Nimitz after the train pulled out of the station. Thereafter, he was to watch Nimitz for signs of strain and to do all he could to keep the new CinCPacFl physically and mentally in shape.

The reason behind those orders became apparent when Nimitz opened the canvas bag. It contained the official reports of the damage, the casualties, and the photographs of Pearl Harbor and Ford Island, Hickam and Wheeler Fields, the Navy Yard, and Kaneohe Naval Air Station.

He scarcely could keep back the tears at the sight of his former command *Arizona*, engulfed in smoke, her foremast broken and leaning. Over a thousand of her crew were dead. He recognized many names, foremost his friend Rear Admiral Isaac Kidd, who had taken command. Kidd, who received the Medal of Honor posthumously, had died on the bridge December 7. As the Super Chief rumbled across the three thousand miles stretching "from sea to shining sea," Nimitz grieved for his friend. He also sympathized with Admiral Kimmel, who he knew must be devastated.

He studied the damage and made plans for repair and refitting. He assessed the losses, staggering in terms of human life as well as equipment. Battleships *Arizona*, *California*, *Oklahoma*, and *West Virginia* sunk. *Nevada* heavily damaged and aground. *Pennsylvania*, *Maryland*, and *Tennessee* damaged. Even the ancient decommissioned *Utah* in use as an auxiliary ship during maneuvers had been capsized. More than half the United States battleships in the Pacific were out of commission, perhaps permanently.

He wrote to Catherine the first in a series of letters of hope and love. She was his touchstone as communication with her helped him to make sense of his tortured thoughts. "As I get more sleep and rest, I find myself less depressed about the situation," he told her. "Things are looking up . . . I only hope I can fulfill the expectations you and Mr. Roosevelt have in me. It is an awesome task and I need your prayers."

From Los Angeles Nimitz was driven to San Diego where he was delayed by abominable weather. When the rains and winds subsided, the Coronado took off on an overnight flight to Hawaii. As the navy flying ship, painted black for camouflage, descended, Chester remembered he was arriving on Christmas Day.

The gutted debris below made a mockery of "Joy to the World." Though the reality of the damage was much worse than the photographs and lists could ever show, Nimitz had much more to think about than Hawaii. His first question when he stepped off the plane was, "What do we hear from Wake?"

Vice Admiral W. S. Pye handed him the latest radio dispatch:

ENEMY ON ISLAND
ISSUE IN DOUBT
WE ARE STILL HERE
MERRY CHRISTMAS

Unfortunately, Wake Island, one of the key positions on the Japanese perimeter, was forced to surrender after the dispatch had been sent. Behind Pye stood Admiral Kimmel, wearing two stars on his collar rather than four. He had been demoted by Roosevelt, and subsequently he was eviscerated by the stateside press.

At his first staff meeting, Nimitz asked all the officers, Kimmel and Pye in particular, to stay on board. In doing so, he did much to restore their self-respect and availed himself of their experience and knowledge. Morale immediately improved among the rank and file as Nimitz came to be regarded as a man worthy of their loyalty. He was also acknowledged as someone who understood the challenge he was facing.

From the staff room, they went into the map room. The entire Pacific Ocean was his territory as he had never seen it before. Indirectly, he was in command of every ship in the water. As he looked at the huge map spread out before him he saw no names of ships but little numbers such as 46.13.4. Quickly, the system was explained to him. To the man who knew the codes, they were the exact locations of every ship. Nimitz was even more pleased that he had kept the staff. He didn't have the customary three months to build his own team and learn all he needed to know. Starting as he was from ground level, he depended upon the others. If he had sought glory for himself alone or assumed command determined to be an autocrat rather than part of the team, the war might have been lost there.

None of them knew that Admiral Yamamoto had given himself six months to gain control of the Pacific Ocean. He had been counting on Pearl Harbor being more demoralized than Nimitz allowed it to be. Rather than dismissing the team in disgrace, he kept them in place and worked through them. In this manner Nimitz shortened Yamamoto's time line.

Not surprisingly, the battleship commanders and the aircraft carrier commanders came down on opposite sides when planning strategy. Likewise, all planning had to be coordinated with General Douglas MacArthur, who had been driven from the Philippines after which the entire island system surrendered.

Yamamoto's strategy had made no mistake there. The Philippines had not been able to hold out for even one month, much less the projected nine. The defeat handed MacArthur was much worse than the loss at Pearl Harbor. Ready for attack at his air bases were thirty-five B-17s, the Flying Fortresses, the "greatest concentration of heavy bomber strength in the world." When the Japanese twin-engine bombers found them, the B-17s were lined up on the airstrips like the battleships at Pearl. Their losses and the losses of their support aircraft were devastating, and the islands were lost as well.

Fortunately for MacArthur, the American public did not perceive his defeat that way. Pearl Harbor was their own soil. The Philippines were foreign with the Americans merely occupying them.

Nimitz, almost as well as MacArthur, knew what was lost on Luzon. As a military man, he pitied the soldiers who were forced to make the Bataan death march. He wanted the Japanese leaders and the public to feel the same. Like the Texan he was, he wanted to hand them a dose of their own medicine. Attacking them immediately on their own islands using their own battle techniques was the way. Moreover, the Gilbert and Marshall Islands were strategically important. From them the Japanese fleet could intercept shipping between the United States and Australia thereby keeping the island continent from being used as a base.

Despite objections from those who wanted to exercise more caution, Nimitz ordered the raids. For this detail, he called on

Vice Admiral William F. "Bull" Halsey. Halsey seconded his strategy with the terse statement, "Whatever you do—do fast."

On January 11, just thirty-five days after Pearl Harbor, Halsey assumed command of *Enterprise* group—the carrier, three heavy cruisers, and six destroyers—on a search and destroy mission. Joined by carriers *Lexington* and *Yorktown*, he sent all their planes on raids on Wake and Eniwetok in the Marshalls. The double blow shocked the Japanese, who had expected little if any retaliation and none so soon.

At the same time a new dispatch indicated future problems for Nimitz. General Douglas MacArthur, ever the glory hunter, had garnered the press' sympathy with his dramatic vow to return to the Philippines. Roosevelt named him Supreme Commander, Allied Forces in the Southwest Pacific Area.

For January, February, and March, Nimitz's strategy seemed to be working. Navy carriers continued raiding the Japanese islands of their southeastern perimeter. Then in April came the raid that brought the war home to the Japanese people. Halsey's *Enterprise* group was joined by *Hornet*, newly arrived from the California coast with sixteen B-25 Mitchell bombers on her decks. With *Enterprise* providing fighter support, Lieutenant Colonel James H. Doolittle's squadron of bombers took off from *Hornet's* deck, knowing that they could not come back to land on it. They were to fly 688 miles to Tokyo, bomb the city, and fly 1,100 to friendly Chinese airfields.

The raid was successful. They bombed Tokyo at high noon, completely surprising and demoralizing the populace. The emperor was displeased. Moreover, Yamamoto believed that the bombers had come from the Aleutians—Kiska, Adak, and Attu. He was forced to plan an attack on them to appease the politicians.

Most important, Japan needed a victory. Yamamoto's six months were slipping away. Another six months would usher in 1943 when whatever advantage they had would be wiped out by American war production. The Japanese admiral presented two major goals. Air mastery of the Coral Sea could be achieved with the capture of Tulagi in the Solomons and Port Moresby on New

Guinea. In the north the capture of Midway Island and the Western Aleutians would complete the line. The U.S. Fleet would meet them at either or both places, and the war would be all but over. The Pacific Fleet would be destroyed.

Nimitz was aware of the same numbers with regard to American production. If he could hold out with his precious few, then the tide would turn. He needed intelligence, but he had no reason to believe that the Naval Combat Intelligence Unit at Pearl Harbor would provide it. If this was such a great operation, why did they let Kimmel down when he needed them most? To Nimitz's surprise, he got his intelligence from Lieutenant Commander Joseph J. Rocheford.

Details of Yamamoto's plans flashed between various Japanese commands. They were overheard by U.S. listening posts on islands in the areas. The messages in Japanese Code JN25 were passed on to Rocheford, who was able to decipher some of it. What they got were mere fragments, but from those fragments Pacific Fleet strategist Lieutenant Edwin Layton was able to deduce the Japanese intentions. Thus Nimitz knew by April 17 that three of Yamamoto's carriers would pass into the Coral Sea before May 3.

While *Enterprise* and *Hornet* were sending off Doolittle's bombers, *Yorktown* and newly refurbished *Lexington* steamed to challenge *Shokaku*, *Shoho*, and *Zuikaku*. Those who believed that Pearl Harbor ushered in a new era of warfare were wrong. The Coral Sea would be the beginning, and when the battle was over, it would have been a battle of ships that never saw or even found each other. Never again would huge battleships stand off each other's bows and fire countless rounds of ammunition until one was sunk. Now the battle belonged to the planes—the Nakajimas, the Aichis, and the Zeros—the Devastators, the Dauntlesses, and the Wildcats.

In the end *Shoho* was sunk by the Devastators and all her planes lost in thirty minutes. *Lexington* was badly damaged by bombers and torpedo planes and sank later, but her crew of 2,735 were rescued and nineteen aircraft were transferred to *Yorktown*, which was damaged but stayed afloat to fight another day. *Shokaku* headed home in flames. *Zuikaku* was never damaged because she was never even found. Ironically, her elusive tactics led to the loss of most of her pilots, who themselves couldn't find her and went down in the sea. At one time the remnants of one Japanese carrier's bombers and torpedo planes spotted *Yorktown* at dusk. Mistaking the ship for their own, half a dozen Japanese pilots lined up to land. *Yorktown's* gunnery officer yelled, "All hands, stand by to repel boarders," and the sailors opened fire, bringing them down.

In all, the American pilots, because of a new dogfight technique called the Thach weave, proved to be much more skillful fighters than the Japanese. Their new training and the element of surprise worked in their favor. Though the battle of the Coral Sea seemed a draw, in the end it was a victory for the United States. Japan lost *Shoho* forever and the use of *Shokaku* and *Zuikako* for the ferocious battle to come in Yamamoto's great plan.

Midway sits 1,136 miles west-northwest of Pearl Harbor. It is less than six miles in diameter. In 1935 Pan American Airways had used it as a base on its Trans-Pacific flights. The Naval Air Station had been added in August 1941. This worthless hunk of volcanic rock was crucial to the Japanese plan.

Yamamoto staked everything on the battle of Midway. He engaged a total of 162 vessels, including four huge carriers and three light ones, nine battleships, and all the accompanying support cruisers, destroyers, troop transports, submarines, and oilers.

By contrast Nimitz could manage to scrape up slightly fewer than fifty ships, among them just his three remaining aircraft carriers *Enterprise, Hornet,* and the venerable *Yorktown.* Their total complement was 230 planes. Midway Island had a total of 115 planes, which it would launch into the attack. The same two young men, Layton and Rocheford, had deduced that the main battle for the North Pacific would be at Midway. Yamamoto's attack on Dutch Harbor in the Aleutians would be a feigned attack. Because of their intelligence, no attempt would be made to defend there.

Just when nothing worse seemed possible, Nimitz lost Admiral Halsey to stress. *Enterprise* group was taken over by Rear Admiral Raymond A. Spruance, whom Halsey himself characterized as "a cold-blooded fighting fool."

May 28 Nimitz set his strategy in motion. To Spruance and Rear Admiral Frank Jack Fletcher in command of *Yorktown*, he issued these orders. "Inflict maximum damage on the enemy by employing strong attrition tactics. You will be governed by the principle of calculated risk which you will interpret to mean the avoidance of exposure of your force from attack by superior enemy forces without good prospect of inflicting greater damage on the enemy."

With fewer than 50 ships against 162, Midway was beginning to look a lot like the Alamo. Nimitz, as a Texan, would not have failed to draw the comparison nor failed to appreciate the possibilities. The Alamo took a sizable portion of Santa Anna's force out of commission. If Midway could do the same, San Jacinto could not help but come.

Somewhere around June 3 Rocheford's cryptoanalysts had been working night and day. Once Rocheford broke into the code, his team could swiftly decode the messages flying back and forth between their ships and send them immediately to Nimitz and his strategist Layton. The admiral called Layton in.

"As admiral of the Japanese fleet what are you going to do?" he asked abruptly.

Layton probably took a deep breath, knowing that what he said then would decide the course of the battle and possibly the war. "All right, here it is. The carriers commanded by Nagumo will attack Midway on the morning of the fourth. They will come from the northwest on a bearing 325 degrees and will be sighted about one hundred seventy-five miles from Midway about five o'clock in the morning."

Then it was Nimitz's turn to take a deep breath. Perhaps for the first time he could sense a favorable wind blowing after six months in a storm. For the first time he was in position to make the first strike. How much he longed to take Spruance's place on the *Enterprise's* deck will never be known. Instead, he stayed in Pearl and masterminded the entire battle.

Already he was coming to be regarded as a father figure to his men. His yellow hair was now nearly snow-white. His blue eyes could pierce to the quick when he wanted to, but he was all in all a quiet, thoughtful man, disciplined and totally military. He was a man who did his duty. His heroism was the kind that placed him in the rear, battling the demons of conscience and pity as he performed the hardest job of all—ordering men to go forth and die.

Heading to intercept the Japanese fleet was *Enterprise* group with *Hornet*, six cruisers, and nine destroyers. Behind her came the gallant old lady *Yorktown*, hastily patched at Pearl, with two cruisers and six destroyers. They sailed with purpose, knowing that the way to Tokyo led through Midway. More to the point, their commanders knew that the Japanese striking force was the carriers.

Shortly before dawn on June 4, a Midway search plane found Japanese minesweepers coming from the southwest. Other reported sightings followed. At five o'clock a patrol plane reported six ships coming from the same direction.

Suddenly, 108 Japanese planes of all three kinds came roaring out of the sun toward the island. Even as they appeared, a second flight of bombers was warming up on the carrier decks.

The Japanese carriers *Akagi*, *Kaga*, *Hiryu*, and *Soryu* were under the command of Vice Admiral Chuichi Nagumo, who was solely in charge. He had arranged them in a tight box formation in the center of a screen of two battleships, three cruisers, and eleven destroyers. At a crucial time, Nagumo's key officers had fallen ill, one with a fever, one with an emergency appendectomy. Aboard the flagship, Yamamoto had severe stomach cramps caused by a parasitical disease.

No one knew where the American carriers were, but Nagumo had been told that they would not reach Midway until June 7, by which time he was sure the island would be Japanese. Then and only then would he break his four carriers out of sight of each other.

At six o'clock *Yorktown* discovered that she could not immediately launch. Seven minutes later she ordered *Enterprise* to attack first. When Spruance objected, his chief of staff, Captain Miles Browning, insisted that if they hit the enemy at seven, they might catch the carriers in a vulnerable position when the aircraft would be returning from Midway for refueling.

Back in Pearl, Nimitz felt a thrill of elation. Layton's predictions were right on target. Within the hour planes from Midway and from the carriers were headed toward the fleet. The naval power of two mighty maritime nations was converging not as armor-plated battleships, but as tiny one- and two-man airplanes with thin aluminum skins.

Meanwhile, on Midway, resistance had been fierce. The airfields were still undamaged. Practically every kind of plane belonging to the Navy and Marines that Nimitz could lay his hands on was still taking off at will to defend the island's skies. At seven o'clock Lieutenant Tomonoga, commander of what was left of the 108-plane initial strike force, radioed that Midway needed another pounding.

Nagumo ordered the ninety-three planes below decks brought up and rearmed with incendiary and fragmentation bombs. Only fifteen minutes had elapsed before he received a report that "ten enemy ships" were heading toward them. He refused to believe it. No American ships were supposed to be there for three more days.

For another fifteen minutes Nagumo delayed. Then he canceled the change-bomb plans and ordered the ninety-three planes again rearmed to attack ships. The changeover took a great deal of time, particularly since the flight decks had to be kept clear to receive Japanese aircraft returning from Midway. Both types of ammunition were beside the planes on the deck.

Meanwhile, an all-out attack—twenty Wildcats, sixty-seven Dauntlesses, and twenty-nine Devastators—got airborne from Enterprise. By nine o'clock, *Yorktown's* six Wildcats, seventeen Dauntlesses, and twelve Devastators were launched. Their carriers steamed full speed behind them to make up the distance so their birds could make it back to land.

"What are they doing out there?" Nimitz fretted back at Pearl. The time to attack was now. His next incoming message, badly garbled and interspersed by static, received at ten o'clock sent shivers all through him.

TORPEDO 8 LOST EVERY PLANE—EVERY MAN
MIDWAY SUFFERS LOSS: FUEL TANKS,
HANGARS SEAPLANE RAMPS, BARRACKS,
MESS HALL, GALLEY ON MIDWAY
DESTROYED 33 TORPEDO PLANES DOWN

The Devastator torpedo bombers had attacked without fighter escort and had been devastatingly ineffective. Most had been shot down. At twenty-four minutes after ten, the Japanese thought they had won the battle of Midway.

Two minutes later the Dauntless dive-bombers brought about a complete reversal of fortune. Instead of coming head-on straight at their targets to launch their torpedos from their underbellies, the Dauntlesses climbed high into the clouds and the sun. Together, the two squadrons attacked *Kaga* and *Akagi*, Nagumo's flagship. At 14,000 feet the Dauntlesses tipped over and dived for the kill. Their coming in so soon after the ineffective Devastators caught the crews flat-footed. *Akagi* took a bomb in the hangar, detonating the torpedo storage, and another that exploded amid planes changing their loads on the flight deck. With his flagship on fire, Nagumo transferred to a cruiser. The carrier was abandoned and later sunk. Four bombs hit *Kaga*, killing everyone on the bridge and setting her afire from stem to stern. Abandoned, she was sunk by an internal explosion that evening. *Soryu* was turning into the wind when three half-ton bombs from *Yorktown's* Dauntlesses destroyed her flight deck. She was abandoned in twenty minutes. U.S. submarine *Nautilus* pumped three torpedoes into her, the gasoline storage exploded, and she broke in two.

Nagumo did not give up. He ordered *Hiryu's* planes to attack *Yorktown*. Though most of them were shot down, seven got through, three with bombs and two with torpedoes. All the carrier's power connections were severed and she began to list twenty-six degrees. Her watertight integrity had been impaired at Coral Sea and the hasty repairs left her vulnerable. She had to be abandoned.

Almost at the minute *Yorktown* was hit, her planes found her killer. The carrier received four hits that swiftly sank her, taking with her Rear Admiral Yamaguchi, who was slated to be Yamamoto's successor.

In the end the admiral lost his entire carrier group. Without them his only course seemed to be to regroup and retreat. On June 5 the battle was over with the loss of thirty-five hundred Japanese officers and men and 322 planes and their pilots, who were virtually irreplaceable.

The Alamo had become San Jacinto!

After the defeat, the first in the history of their navy, the Japanese warlords abandoned plans for Port Moresby, Fiji, New Caledonia, and Samoa. The name Midway was never mentioned again.

Nimitz received the following message:

THE ENEMY FLEET WHICH HAS BEEN
PRACTICALLY DESTROYED IS RETURNING
TO THE EAST. COMBINED FLEET UNITS IN
THE VICINITY ARE PREPARING TO PURSUE
THE REMNANTS AND AT THE SAME TIME
OCCUPY MIDWAY!

Nimitz celebrated the victory with the men he considered in large part responsible for it—his strategist and his crypto-analysist. He praised them for their work, in particular Rocheford. In a pensive mood he reflected that the battleship had limited usage thereafter. The airplane must be made faster and lighter with more power and maneuverability.

Here he showed his utter lack of bias that later characterized hardcore naval men. Nimitz was always searching for ways to win wars with the least loss of life and equipment.

The admiral later sent a message to a submarine commander, congratulating him for destroying three enemy ships on a given day. "When the subs hit them, they go down for the count," he radioed. When the commander relayed the message to the crew, their reaction was so jubilant that the commander said, "It was like God had spoken."

With the Navy squarely behind him, Nimitz made the decision to go on immediate offensive. The enemy should have no chance to regroup or to think about fresh attacks.

He saw three points crucial to carrying the offensive straight up the northeastern perimeter to the Japanese homeland:

1. Restructure the chain of command for coordinating air power in the Pacific.

2. Use all his influence as Fleet Admiral to procure men, arms, and supplies for the Pacific.

3. Participate in Washington's final decision to design the strategy for movement across the Pacific and the ultimate invasion of Japan.

His greatest single problem lay not with Yamamoto and his warlords, but with General Douglas MacArthur and his desire to make the Navy the transport for the Army.

MacArthur read the Midway reports and boasted that he could take Rabaul, in the center of the Dutch East Indies, with just one amphibiously trained division if the Navy would support him by aircraft carrier. Neither Nimitz nor Fleet Admiral King wanted to give him the carrier, for fear he would consider it expendable. They concurred that Guadalcanal and Tulagi at the southern tip of the Solomons was the place to begin the offensive to take the Bismarck Archipelago and the rest of Dutch East Indies, then onward to the Philippines.

MacArthur objected. If the Navy took Guadalcanal and Tulagi, he did not want to take the rest of the islands unless the Navy were under his command. Already, he was casting glances beyond the Pacific, which he thought could be wound up very quickly, to the possibility of a political future beginning with the 1944 elections.

In July when the Japanese began to construct an airfield on Guadalcanal, the decision was made. The island must be taken. Vice Admiral Robert L. Ghormley, a recent Washington appointee, became commander of the South Pacific. Ordered to

Melbourne, Australia, to confer with MacArthur, he came away discouraged and half convinced by the general's bombastic rhetoric. MacArthur had been arbitrary and demanding. Guadalcanal must be pushed back to August 7. To keep peace, Nimitz reluctantly agreed. Early on the morning of the seventh, the battle began. The Marines came ashore and secured the beachhead and the incompleted landing strip.

Yamamoto had committed a huge fleet including three carriers. *Enterprise*, accompanied by the newly commissioned *Saratoga*, and *Wasp* met his bombing raid and drove them back with minimal damage. Still Ghormley was pessimistic, even going so far as to suggest that the Marines be withdrawn. Nimitz insisted on flying to Guadalcanal to hear and see for himself. He was greeted there by a lively and gregarious Marine General A. A. Vandergrift.

"Are you going to hold this beachhead, General?" asked Nimitz.

"Hell, yes," Vandergrift replied. "Why not?"

Nimitz and King reported to President Roosevelt that the Marines could hold only with more men and supplies. Though North Africa was about to be invaded, Roosevelt ordered heavy reinforcements sent to the Pacific.

Next, Nimitz relieved the fearful Ghormley of command and replaced him with Admiral Bill Halsey, now somewhat recovered from his bout with stress. Guadalcanal deserved Halsey, who exhorted them, upon arrival, "Kill Japs, then kill more Japs."

For six months the battle raged for the Solomons, but the Marines were winning. By late December the Japanese forces were so decimated that the First Marine Division was withdrawn and replacement troops moved into place to mop up.

Back at Pearl on December 31, Nimitz counted the terrible cost in American lives. Sixteen hundred Marines and Army troops along with thousands of sailors. His only consolation was that fifteen thousand Japanese had died in the battle of Guadalcanal and nine thousand from the tropical diseases.

Nimitz himself had contracted malaria while ashore at Guadalcanal. Back on Pearl, he faced the new year weary and ill.

He could not know that for his Japanese counterpart the outlook was much, much worse.

Yamamoto's year was over. United States replacements and reinforcements had started to arrive.

Meanwhile MacArthur was making typhoon-high waves among the Joint Chiefs of Staff. The Trans-Pacific advance should be made through New Guinea and the Philippines. Being an Army maneuver, it should be commanded by an Army general—himself—with the Navy in their "proper" role as transportation for the real men to do the work.

Nimitz argued that MacArthur's way was expensive, roundabout, and time-consuming. The twenty-two new fleet carriers were coming out of the shipyards. These could be used in a direct attack across the Pacific, bypassing the heavily armed larger islands, knocking off a few small islands in the Gilberts, the Marianas, the Marshalls, taking back Guam and Wake and then Iwo Jima and Okinawa.

MacArthur protested vigorously. When the Joint Chiefs turned him down in favor of Nimitz's plan, the general took his arguments to the press. At home through press coverage, he had become the darling of the American public. The press was making him a national hero who must be allowed to return and free the Philippines as he had so dramatically vowed to do.

His own officers came to dislike MacArthur intensely for his grandstanding, while the Navy adored Nimitz. Every two months Nimitz met with Admiral King, usually in San Francisco. When King would start criticizing any of Nimitz's officers, Nimitz would say, "If something is wrong with him, you had better start looking at me."

Then on April 17 a Japanese dispatch was intercepted, decrypted, and translated. Commander Ed Layton took it directly to Nimitz. It was Yamamoto's flight plan for the next day. "Depart Rabaul in medium attack plane escorted by six fighters . . . 8 A.M. arrive in Ballale . . ."

Halsey was in the area. Nimitz hesitated only long enough to send a message to Roosevelt. Then he relayed the itinerary to Halsey with the personal note, "Good luck and good hunting."

At exactly the right time sixteen P-38 Lightnings took off from Henderson Field, the recently completed airstrip begun by the Japanese on Guadalcanal. They flew four hundred miles over open water before they spotted the two bombers and six Zeros.

Yamamoto's plane was shot down in the jungle. His staff in the second bomber was shot down at sea where a few survived. His death was a major defeat. He was a military genius who left no one to take his place.

In November Nimitz insisted on coming ashore only two days after the massive invasion of Tarawa in the Gilberts. Nimitz was aghast at the sight of bodies and parts of bodies everywhere. He remarked, "It's the first time I've smelled death."

As soon as Eniwetok on the western edge of the Marshalls fell in February 1944, Nimitz met personally with MacArthur. Though the general had been invited to Washington, D.C., to meet with Roosevelt and the Joint Chiefs, he had declined. Now he wanted a private meeting. Nimitz went warily. He knew the reason for the meeting. MacArthur was afraid that part of his command might be taken over by naval operations.

This change had actually been discussed by the Joint Chiefs, but they had decided to leave it, not certain what furor MacArthur could and would cause.

Nimitz acted very graciously, but he stood firm when MacArthur blew his composure and declared that the liberation of the Philippines was a sacred obligation whether the Joint Chiefs liked it or not. Logic, he maintained, did not matter. Nimitz declared that speed now was the important thing. The war needed to be over before more men lost their lives.

At last with MacArthur's cooperation the attacks of the Marianas began June 12. Saipan, Guam, and Tinian were attacked simultaneously one week after D-Day in Europe. The Japanese fought bravely, but Americans were now trained to combat their island defenses. Mortar emplacements, pillboxes, and machine gun nests could be taken with far greater efficiency. They had learned how at Guadalcanal, Tulagi, and Eniwetok.

The summer of 1944 saw the appearance of a Japanese phenomenon that showed more clearly than anything else how near they were to the end. The *kamikaze*, the "divine wind," appeared in the skies. All their well-trained pilots were gone. They had no time to train more. In six weeks they sent out sixteen- and seventeen-year-old boys on first flights from which they would never return. Carrying bombs, they were to crash their planes into the American ships, destroying the homeland's enemies with their deaths. The first attack was moderately successful. Five ships were hit, and the cruiser *St. Louis* was sunk. They were the first of many.

In the midst of all this Roosevelt insisted on visiting Pearl Harbor. Though he was very ill, he was making the trip for political reasons. He called for a meeting among himself, Nimitz, and MacArthur.

MacArthur tried to refuse, but General George Marshall ordered him to go. He arrived an hour before the president and refused to wait. Instead, he went directly to the home of Army General Richardson, with whom he was to stay.

To honor his president and friend, Nimitz donned his full uniform with all his staff in dress whites and waited on the dock. Security was at full maximum. The press were present and snapping pictures like mad. The presidential flag was hoisted, and the crew of every ship lined the rails to salute as the presidential cruiser docked.

The greetings had been made, the president accepted their applause when the proceedings were interrupted by sirens, whistles, cheering, and the roar of a motorcycle escort. Out stepped MacArthur dressed in a pair of khakis, a brown leather jacket, a Filipino field marshal's cap, and smoking a corncob pipe. MacArthur acknowledged the cheering crowd before walking up the gangplank to greet his superior.

The president of the United States regarded him with a silky smile. "Douglas," he asked, "why don't you wear the right kind of clothes when you come to see us?"

The contrast between Nimitz and MacArthur was marked and remarked upon. Later the pictures appeared stateside where

MacArthur had allowed his name to be entered in the Republican presidential primaries opposing Wendell Wilkie and Thomas E. Dewey.

In the end MacArthur went home sure that he had convinced the president that his plans would bring about victory. In actuality the Joint Chiefs had decided to use MacArthur's bombast to deflect the real point of attack. The plan was to land him in the central Philippines, close enough to let him spend the rest of the war fighting. The island of Samar in Leyte Gulf was the target. It could be used to launch the invasion of the Japanese mainland, already in the works. Thanks to MacArthur's posturing, the Japanese expected Luzon, so Samar was invaded virtually undefended. From its capital MacArthur made his famous October 20 broadcast, "People of the Philippines! I have returned."

Nimitz took the news with mixed emotions. He didn't have long to spend on MacArthur. Now that the war was winding down in Europe, the British wanted to enter it. Churchill proposed sending part of the fleet to serve under American command. In this case, under Nimitz.

Admiral King resented their presence bitterly, but Nimitz reacted with aplomb. He suggested that they wage their war in the Southwestern Pacific, retaking Sumatra and Malaysia, but they refused, guessing rightly that the homeland of Japan was the real objective. At that point Nimitz turned them over to Spruance, who put them protecting the fleet at Okinawa from attacks from the Chinese mainland. The British acquitted themselves gallantly.

At the end of 1944 Congress established a new level of military commission for generals and admirals to be denoted by five stars. On December 19 four generals—Marshall, MacArthur, Eisenhower, and Arnold—and three admirals—Leahy, King, and Nimitz—received the new rank. So far they are the only ones who have worn it.

On the day Nimitz received his commission, his sailor metalsmiths had a new collar insignia ready for the occasion.

The first of 1945 Nimitz moved his headquarters to Guam, where he could focus more clearly on Iwo Jima and Okinawa.

While MacArthur slogged through the Philippine jungles, the fleet moved ever closer to the Japanese homeland. After Iwo Jima, the bloodiest prize in the Pacific, fell within three weeks, the P-51 Mustangs left to escort B-29s on daylight attacks on Tokyo. From then on their bombardment was continuous.

The death toll on Iwo was hideous. More than twenty-two thousand Japanese died either by American guns or by suicide because they had been told the Americans would torture them. Six thousand eight hundred twenty-one Marines and sailors lost their lives. MacArthur contacted the *San Francisco Examiner*, which printed his story that lack of leadership was the reason so many American lives had been lost. The Navy and the Marines should be placed under his command. Nimitz was burning mad, and a group of Marines stormed the newspaper building demanding an apology. None was ever issued.

After Iwo Jima was secure, Nimitz returned to Washington to meet with Roosevelt, who he knew was dying. During the course of their meeting, Nimitz realized he would never see his friend again. He returned to the Pacific determined to end the war in 1945 while Roosevelt was still alive to see it.

Before Okinawa, thanks to MacArthur's bitter undermining, Nimitz received daily letters from mothers of sailors and Marines accusing him of killing their sons or begging him not to send them into battle where so many would be killed. Many cursed him as a poor leader and begged him to turn his command over to MacArthur, who would save them.

As always he wrote daily to Catherine, telling her how disturbed he was and yet how he could not stop. His duty was to end the war, not prolong it for a politician's dream.

Okinawa was a repeat of Iwo Jima except it took much longer and resistance was much heavier. *Kamikazes* accounted for a ship and a half a day. The death toll was much heavier than on Iwo Jima, but the bombs continued to fall on the Japanese mainland. The "Rising Sun" was setting.

Angry that he was being excluded, MacArthur announced that he was taking command of all the forces in the Pacific and breaking up Nimitz's unity of Navy and Marines, which he called unworkable. Before anything of that kind could be done, Roosevelt died.

A healthy, vigorous Harry Truman became president. In July he approved Operation *Olympic* and Operation *Coronet*. Meanwhile, Nimitz was to continue his raids on the Japanese mainland and the Navy was to push the Japanese farther and farther back to their home islands.

Nimitz hoped with all his heart that the Japanese would surrender before either of the operations could be put into effect, but Layton felt the *samurai* were too strong. The Japanese psychology would not allow them to surrender. Nimitz hated the terrible cost of human life, but he could not ask his men to invade the Japanese homeland without trying everything.

On August 6 Operation *Olympic* was put into action. The B-29 *Enola Gay* accompanied by two other bombers set out from Tinian in the Marianas. She circled above Hiroshima and dropped the first atomic bomb. Within moments eighty percent of the buildings in the city were reduced to rubble.

The Japanese still refused to surrender. Denying their own information, they concluded that a massive air raid had been carried out rather than just three planes and one bomb.

On August 9 another plane, Operation *Coronet*, dropped a second bomb on Nagasaki. By this time the burns and illnesses from the first were beginning to be diagnosed by Japanese doctors. The warlords had no choice but surrender.

On the fourteenth President Truman addressed the American people, announcing that the Japanese had unconditionally surrendered. Ironically, General Douglas MacArthur was called to preside over the signing of the armistice on the deck of the battleship *Missouri*, Truman's home state. Truman, an Army man himself, appointed MacArthur Supreme Commander of the Allied Forces and directed him to arrange the ceremonies.

Those who had fought the war realized the inappropriateness of the ceremony by an Army general on a battleship that had seen very little action in the Pacific. It should have been Nimitz aboard *Enterprise*, a ship that had taken part in almost every major engagement of the entire war, but MacArthur had grabbed the limelight for himself. MacArthur closed the elaborate ceremony with a brief prayer. "Let us pray that peace be restored to the world and that God will preserve it always."

The aircraft carriers had their say in the end. At 9:25, just as the sun broke through the clouds, a flight of 450 carrier aircraft flew over. Beneath their thunder came the stirring words of the "Navy Hymn."

In less than a week, Admiral Chester W. Nimitz boarded a plane on Guam that would take him to Pearl Harbor, then to San Francisco, where he was presented the key to the city. He held it up and remarked, "What wouldn't Yamamoto have given for this?"

In October when he was to be honored with a triumphal sail up the coast from Norfolk, Virginia, to New York City for a big parade in his honor, he refused to sail on *Missouri*.

After his victory parade through Washington, D.C., the secretary of the navy asked him what position he wanted in the Navy Department. Nimitz answered promptly that he wanted to succeed Admiral King as Chief of Naval Operations. At that point the damage MacArthur had done him became clear. Secretary Forrestal did not want him in that position. A new administration was in Washington, the old was swiftly being brushed away. Even Douglas MacArthur in faraway Japan was not where he wanted to be. Only with the promise that he would take the job for two years could Nimitz win Forrestal's consent. Less than two years had passed when in November 12, 1947, he made his final plea for a unified army, navy, and air force. The following day, Truman announced the appointment of a new Chief of Naval Operations.

For the rest of his life, Nimitz lived in San Francisco where he was in great demand as a speaker. He talked mostly of peace and the constant vigilance needed to maintain it. On February 24, 1966, he died three days short of his eighty-first birthday.

Though a memorial exists today, his memory must be of his deeds for they are the measure of his heroism. He was the hero who never fired a gun, never led a charge, never saw an enemy. Yet the enemy applied unremitting pressure on his every waking moment, while his superiors and his colleagues questioned and tried to undermine everything he did. Only his men loved him.

Consider this single statistic: When Nimitz assumed command at Pearl Harbor, he had forty-five people working at CinCPacFl headquarters. At the end of the war he had thousands as well as command of all the troops, ships, and planes in the Pacific—a total of two million one hundred thousand men.

It is doubtful that ever again will a single man command so many. God forbid that we should ever have to fight so many or so long again.

* * * * *

The Admiral Nimitz Museum and Historical Center in Fredericksburg, Texas, is dedicated to the hometown hero. The personal collection is housed on the first floor of the old Steamboat Hotel built by his grandfather.

A complete history of the war in the Pacific is housed in the same complex in the George Bush Wing. Among the many exhibits and historical information, are an eighty-foot Japanese submarine that carried torpedos into Pearl Harbor on the morning of the infamous attack and a B-25 Mitchell bomber of the type that Doolittle flew from the deck of *Enterprise* to bomb Tokyo.

The *Arizona* Memorial at Pearl Harbor is one of the most solemn sites Americans may visit.

Chester W. Nimitz is buried in the Golden Gate National Cemetery in San Francisco on the shores of the Pacific Ocean where he commanded for four of the most terrible years in his country's history.

Onward to the Twenty-First Century

As Texas steps into the new century and the new millennium, she will have to ask herself whether she needs her heroes now.

The need for a hero arises when civilization is in jeopardy. A special man of steel and sterling silver must step forward from the ranks of softer, gentler golden men who have become too civilized to fight for themselves.

Today many believe the Texas Rangers have outlived their usefulness. John Salmon Ford lived to see his last exploits frowned upon. As he valiantly brought the war to a close, Nimitz received thousands of letters cursing him and begging him not to send his men to fight. Within a week after the surrender he was relieved of command. Milton Holland and Audie Murphy could not have imagined soldiers captured on routine patrol for a peacekeeping mission receiving the Congressional Medal of Honor.

With no new lands to conquer and no implacable enemies to fight, perhaps the Lone Star State will no longer need heroes. Perhaps they will belong, like the Comanches and the *bandidos,* to the old bad days of the nineteenth and twentieth centuries.

With mixed feelings we will say good-bye. They were necessary but difficult to live with. They were some of the pillars on which we built the comfortable, safe world in which we live, but what if there are no more foundations to build?

We can rest assured that should the need arise, they will come back. In urban jungles and on suburban prairies, boys and girls are growing up reading the stories of the Texas heroes, hearing their tales told by their grandfathers and grandmothers, who knew Audie and Chester, whose own grandparents spoke of Jack and Quanah and Santos and Dick.

If the time comes again, they will be ready to step forward. They will see the need and they will come—because someone has to do it.

Bibliography

Catton, Bruce. *The American Heritage Picture History of the Civil War.* New York: American Heritage Publishing Co., Inc., 1960.

Cottrell, Steve. *Civil War in Texas and New Mexico Territory.* Gretna, Louisiana: Pelican Publishing Co., 1998.

De Leon, Arnoldo. *They Called Them Greasers.* Austin: University of Texas Press, 1983.

Driskill, Frank A. and Dede W. Casad. *Chester W. Nimitz: Admiral of the Hills.* Austin: Eakin Press, l983.

Dykes, J. C. "The Battle of Palo Duro Canyon" in *Great Western Indian Fights.* Lincoln: University of Nebraska Press, 1960.

_____. "The Second Battle of Adobe Walls" in *Great Western Indian Fights.* Lincoln: University of Nebraska Press, 1960.

Faulk, Odie B. *A Successful Failure: The Saga of Texas 1519-1810* Austin: Steck-Vaughn Company, 1965.

Fehrenbach, T. R. *Comanches: The Destruction of a People.* New York: Alfred A. Knopf, 1983.

_____. *Lone Star: A History of Texas and the Texans.* New York: The Macmillan Company, 1968.

Ford, John Salmon. *Rip Ford's Texas.* Edited by Stephen B. Oates. Austin: University of Texas Press, 1963.

Foreman, Paul. *Quanah: The Serpent Eagle.* Flagstaff, Arizona: Northland Press, 1983.

Frantz, Joe B. "The Alamo" in *Battles of Texas.* Waco: Texian Press, 1967.

Glatthaar, Joseph T. *Forged in Battle: The Civil War Alliance of Black Soldiers and White Officers.* New York: The Free Press, 1990.

Graham, Don. *No Name on the Bullet: A Biography of Audie Murphy.* New York: Viking, 1989.

Groneman, Bill. *Defense of a Legend: Crockett and the de la Pena Diary.* Plano: Republic of Texas Press, 1994.

Handbook of Texas Online. "Benavides, Santos."

_____. "Bowie Knife."

_____. "Mexican Texans in the Civil War."

_____. "Parker, Quanah."

_____. "Peta Nocona."

_____. "St. Denis, Louis Juchereau de."

_____. "St. Denis, Manuela Sanchez Navarro de."

_____. "Travis, Charles Edward."

Hinojosa, Gilberto Miguel. *A Borderlands Town in Transition: Laredo, 1755-1870*. College Station: Texas A&M University Press, 1983.

Keating, Ben. *An Illustrated History of the Texas Rangers*. New York: Rand McNally and Company, 1975.

Kelley, Dayton. "The Texas Mounted Rifles in Mexico" in *Soldiers of Texas*. Waco: Texian Press, 1973.

King, C. Richard. *Susanna Dickinson: Messenger of the Alamo*. Austin: Shoal Creek Publishers, 1976.

Lott, Arnold S. LCDR, USN (Ret.) and Robert F. Sumrall, HTC, USNR. *Pearl Harbor Attack*. Honolulu: Arizona Memorial Museum Association, 1977.

Marshall, Bruce, "Santos Benavides: 'The Confederacy on the Rio Grande'" in *Civil War* Issue XXIII, pp. 18-20, n.d.

Medal of Honor Recipients, 1863-1973. Washington: U.S. Government Printing Office, October 22, 1973.

McHenry, J. Patrick. *A Short History of Mexico*. New York: Doubleday & Co., 1962.

Morfi, Fr. Juan Agustin. *History of Texas 1673-1779*. Vol. 1. Translated from the Spanish by Carlos E. Castaneda. Albuquerque: The Quivira Society, 1935.

Morison, Samuel Eliot. *The Two-Ocean War: a Short History of the United States Navy in the Second World War*. Boston: Little, Brown, and Company, 1963.

Murphy, Audie. *To Hell and Back*. New York: Holt, Rinehart, Winston, 1949.

Phares, Ross. *Cavalier in the Wilderness: The Story of the Explorer and Trader Louis Juchereau de St. Denis*. Gretna, Louisiana: Pelican Publishing Company, 1976.

Reynolds, Clark G. *The Carrier War*. Alexandria, Virginia: Time-Life Books, 1982.

Richardson, Rupert N. "The Battle of Adobe Walls, 1874" in *Battles of Texas*. Waco: Texian Press, 1967.

Simpson, Col. Harold B. *Audie Murphy: American Soldier*. Hillsboro, Texas: The Hill Jr. College Press, 1975.

_____. "John Salmon (Rip) Ford," in *Rangers of Texas*. Waco, Texas: Texian Press, 1969.

_____. "Sabine Pass, September 8, 1863," in *Battles of Texas*. Waco, Texas: Texian Press, 1967.

Sizer, Mona D. *The King Ranch Story: Truth and Myth*. Plano: Republic of Texas Press, 1999.

Taylor, Colin, "The Plains," in *The Native Americans: The Indigenous People of North America*. London: Salamander Books, 1991.

Texas Almanac for 1857, a 1986 Facsimile Reproduction. Originally published in Galveston: Galveston News, 1856.

Thompson, Jerry Don. *Laredo, A Pictorial History*. Norfolk: Donning Company Publishers, 1986.

_____. *Vaqueros in Blue and Gray*. Austin: Presidial Press, 1976.

_____. *Warm Weather and Bad Whiskey: The 1886 Laredo Election Riot*. El Paso: Texas Western Press, 1991.

To Hell and Back. Universal-International Pictures, 1955.

Wallace, Ernest and E. Adamson Hoebel. *The Comanches: Lords of the South Plains*. Norman: University of Oklahoma Press, 1952.

Webb, Walter Prescott. *The Texas Rangers: A Century of Frontier Defense*. Austin: University of Texas Press, 1935.

Welch, Douglas Welsh. *The USA in World War 2: The Pacific Theater*. London: Bison Books Ltd., 1982.

Wilkinson, J. B. *Laredo and the Rio Grande Frontier*. Austin: Jenkins Publishing Co., 1975.

Winfrey, Dorman H. "John Coffee Hays," in *Rangers of Texas*. Waco, Texas: Texian Press, 1969.

Index

Other books from Republic of Texas Press